More Praise for *Painting the Impressionistic Landscape*:

" . . . informative, humorous, and lively. [Dustan Knight] understands the creative process and has a way of encouraging folks to develop their own style of painting. I appreciate how she inspires her students to get excited about creating."
—Kathy Tangney, professional artist, Tong Ren Master

"Dustan Knight uses her poetic language and painting expertise in guiding readers to take a fresh look at nature and create original, impressionistic watercolors and acrylics. This is far more than a how-to book, but a window into the creative mind, exploring new ways of working and seeing."
—Debbie Hagan, arts writer and critic and former editor-in-chief, *Art New England*

Dustan Knight "is a painter who combines artistic skill, knowledge, and enthusiasm with a flair for explaining the creative process in an easy and inspiring way. [She] paints from the heart, and this book will encourage every artist, from novice to experienced."
—Joni Taube, art consultant and owner, Art 3 Gallery, Manchester, New Hampshire

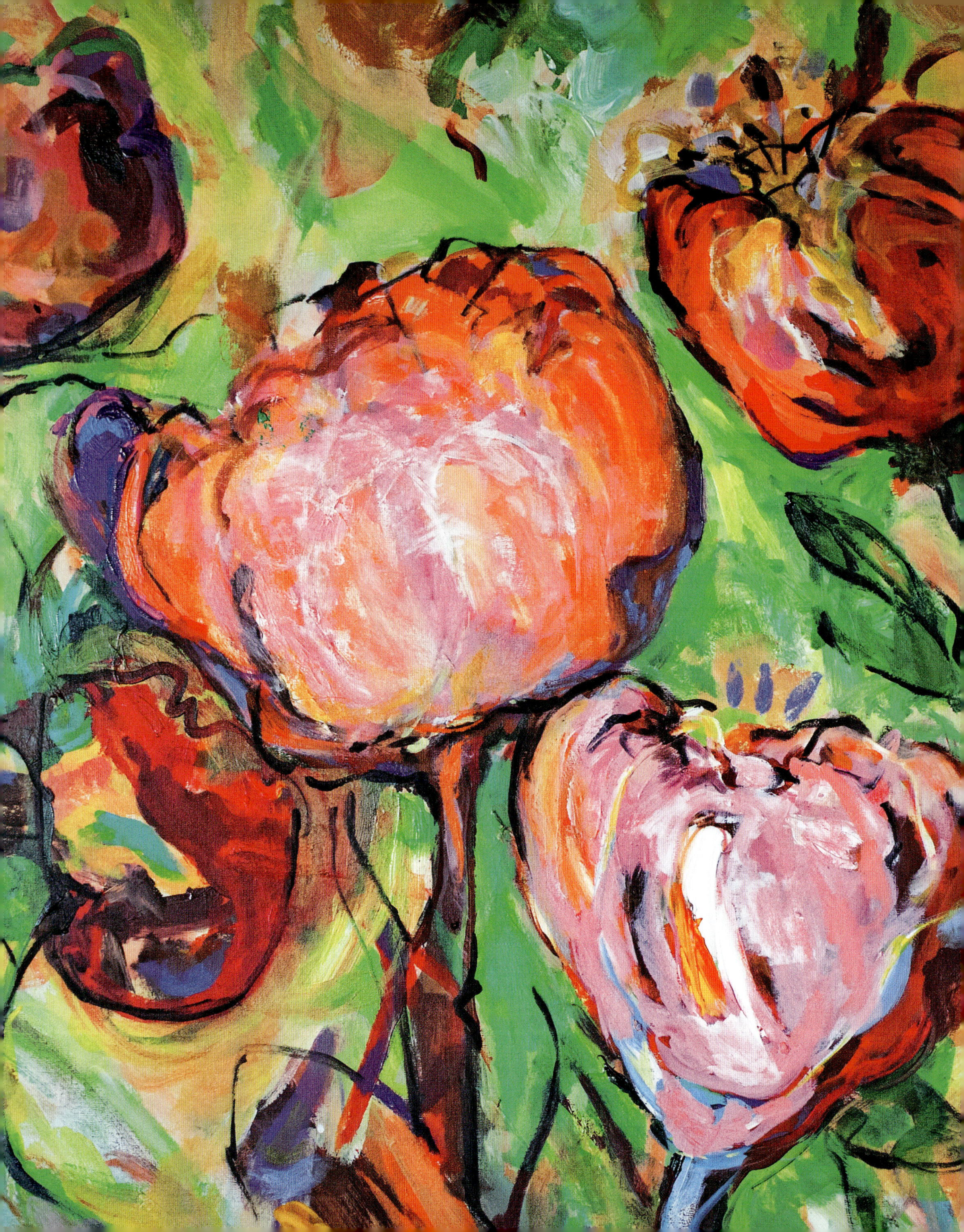

PAINTING the IMPRESSIONISTIC LANDSCAPE

Exploring Light & Color in Watercolor & Acrylic

Dustan Knight

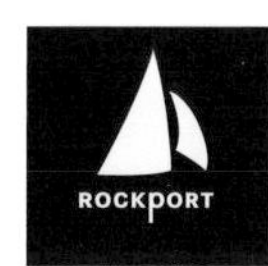

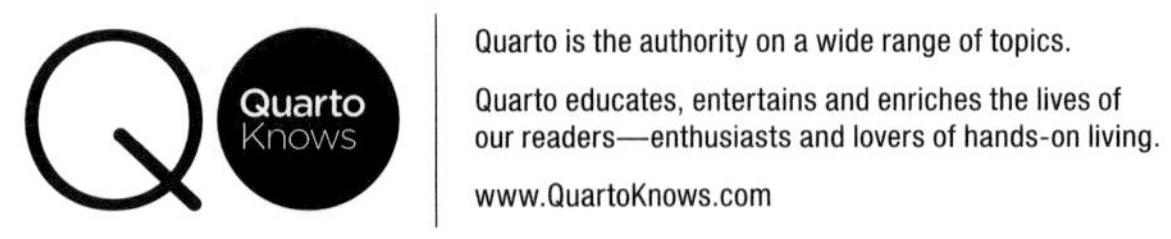

First published in the United States of America in 2017 by
Rockport Publishers, a member of
Quarto Publishing Group USA Inc.
100 Cummings Center
Suite 406-L
Beverly, Massachusetts 01915-6101
Telephone: (978) 282-9590
Fax: (978) 283-2742
QuartoKnows.com
Visit our blogs at QuartoKnows.com

10 9 8 7 6 5 4 3 2 1

ISBN: 978-1-63159-138-9

Library of Congress Cataloging-in-Publication Data
Knight, Dustan, author.
Painting the impressionistic landscape : exploring light and color in
watercolor and acrylic / Dustan Knight.
Description: Beverly, Massachusetts : Rockport Publishers, 2017.
Identifiers: LCCN 2016023513 | ISBN 9781631591389 (paperback)
Subjects: LCSH: Painting--Technique. | BISAC: ART / Subjects & Themes /
Landscapes. | ART / Techniques / Painting. | ART / Techniques / Watercolor
Painting.
Classification: LCC ND1500 .K56 2017 | DDC 751.42/2436--dc23
LC record available at https://lccn.loc.gov/2016023513

Design: Rita Sowins/Sowins Design
Cover image: Dustan Knight
Photography: Karen Hill
Printed in China

OVERLEAF: *Tango Tulips*. Acrylic. 40" x 30" (101.5 x 76 cm).

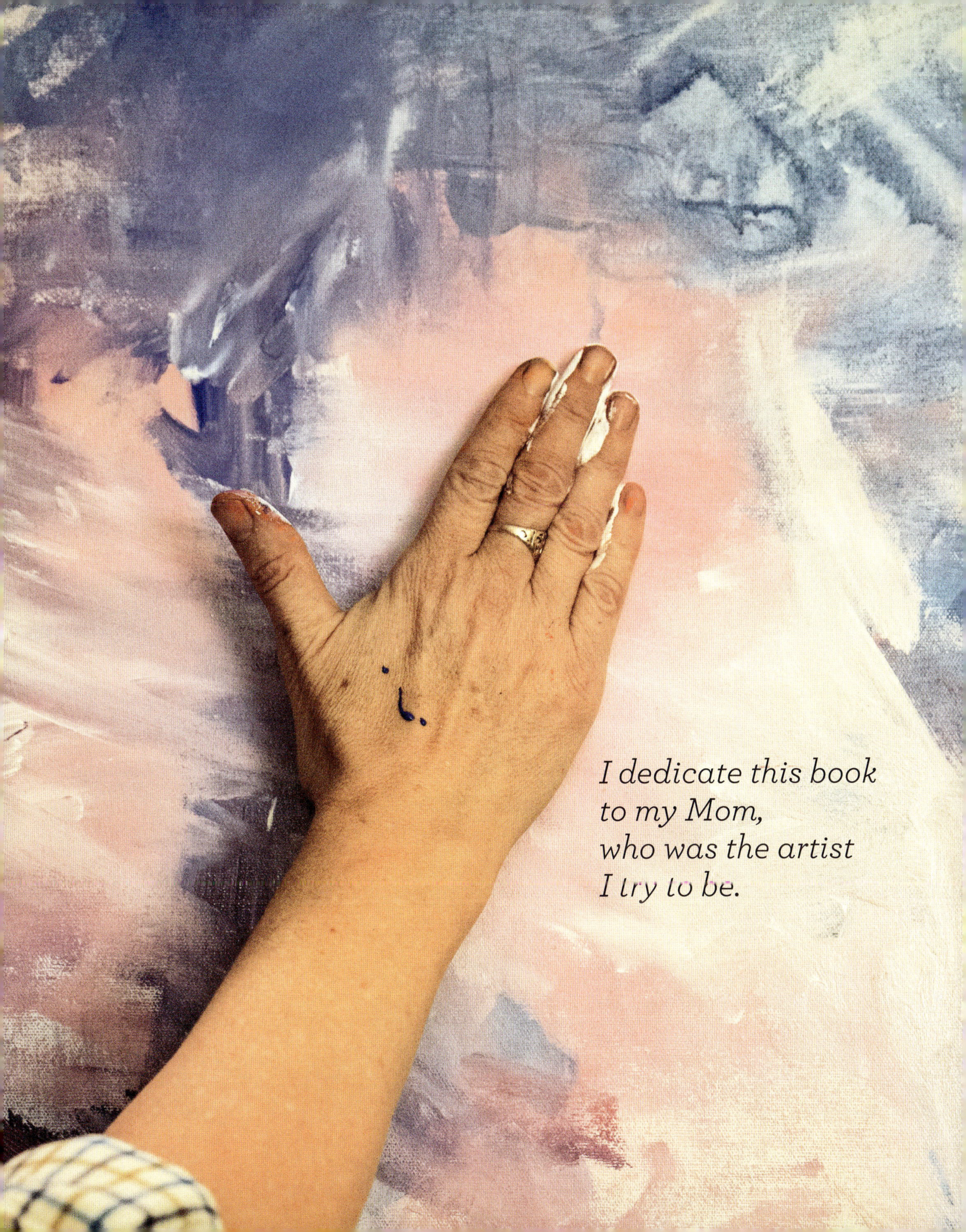

*I dedicate this book
to my Mom,
who was the artist
I try to be.*

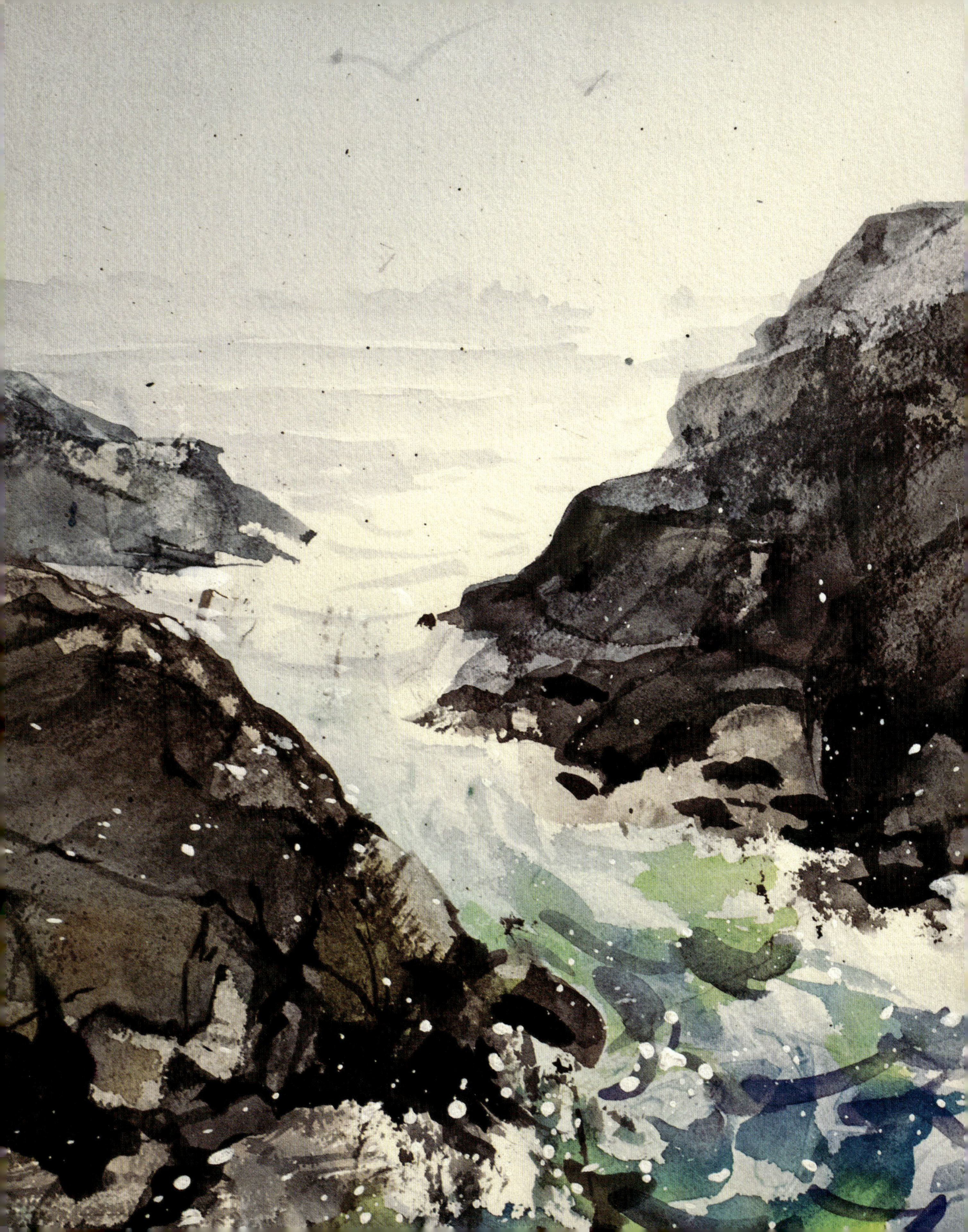

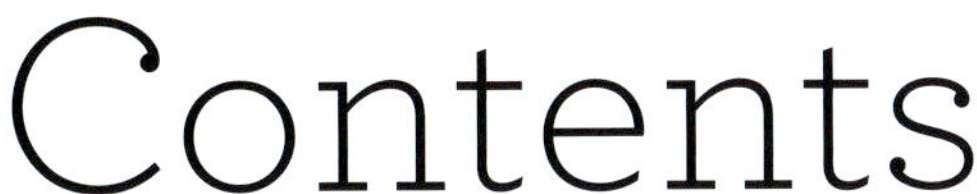

Contents

INTRODUCTION 8

Approaches and Impressions 10
Tools and Materials 14

PAINTING THE WOODS 21

Demonstration: Watercolor 24
» The Approach 24
» In the Studio 30

Special Watercolor Technique: Lifting with a Thirsty Brush 38
» How to Create the Look of Mist 38
» Gallery 42

Demonstration: Acrylic 44
» In the Studio 46

PAINTING FLOWERS FROM THE GARDEN 53

Demonstration: Watercolor 58
» The Approach 58
» In the Studio 62

Special Watercolor Technique: Plastic Wrap 74
» Creating Texture 74
» Gallery 78

Demonstration: Acrylic 82
» In the Studio 84
» Gallery 92

PAINTING THE ROCKS AND

Demonstration: Watercolor 100
» The Approach 101
» In the Studio 107

Special Watercolor Technique: Wax Resist and Scraping for Texture 118
» Capturing a Moment 120
» Gallery 121

Demonstration: Acrylic 122
» In the Studio 125
» Gallery 132

Conclusion 134
Resources 136
Acknowledgments 139
About the Artist and Photographer 140
Index 142

OPPOSITE: *Morning Chop.* Watercolor. 22" x 33" (56 x 84 cm).

Introduction

One of the best things about being an artist is having an excuse to actually stop and look around.

Seeing is a rare and luxurious activity these days. My paintings in watercolor and acrylic are inspired by the things I see and my impressions of them. When I paint I'm not attempting to replicate what's in front of me. I'm searching for subjects that I want to look at and experience deeply, for a long, focused time. I enjoy the process of translating them into my own vision of the world. I try to avoid the clichéd scene but I don't want to deprive myself of possibilities either, so I try to look deeper than the obvious. I try to experience a subject as closely and as intimately as possible.

Sometimes it's the atmospheric effects of mist through the trees that intrigues me as much as the trees themselves. Sometimes it's the riot of contrasting color in the garden more than the actual blooms that I love. Sometimes it's the sound of a wave booming under a seaweed covered ledge that makes me want to capture my impression of the sea on paper. My heightened experience of the woods, the garden, and the crashing waves involves all my senses: seeing, hearing, feeling, and even smelling. That's what I am interested in capturing in my work.

I like to think my way of working is a continuation of the way the Impressionists approached painting. I have always felt their influence, both for the beauty of their work and for their philosophy. Originally the Impressionists insisted their artwork was based solely on an analytic reaction to a scene. But ultimately it became clear that their impressions were vastly informed by their feelings, expectations, and desires—in fact, very romantic. I like that and I like being part of the continuum of painting impressionistic landscapes.

In this book I am pleased to walk you through my creative steps. I have chosen three landscape themes—woods, garden flowers, and water—inspired by the natural features of the granite New Hampshire island where I live. I will show you several approaches and various ways to think about them. Each theme is considered separately with images and step-by-step demonstrations. The demonstrations detail the progress from concept to finished painting. I hope to share my way of seeing as well as the thought process and continual problem solving that develops as I paint.

Dustan Knight

OPPOSITE: *Rebecca's Flower.* Watercolor. 36" x 36" (91.5 x 91.5 cm).

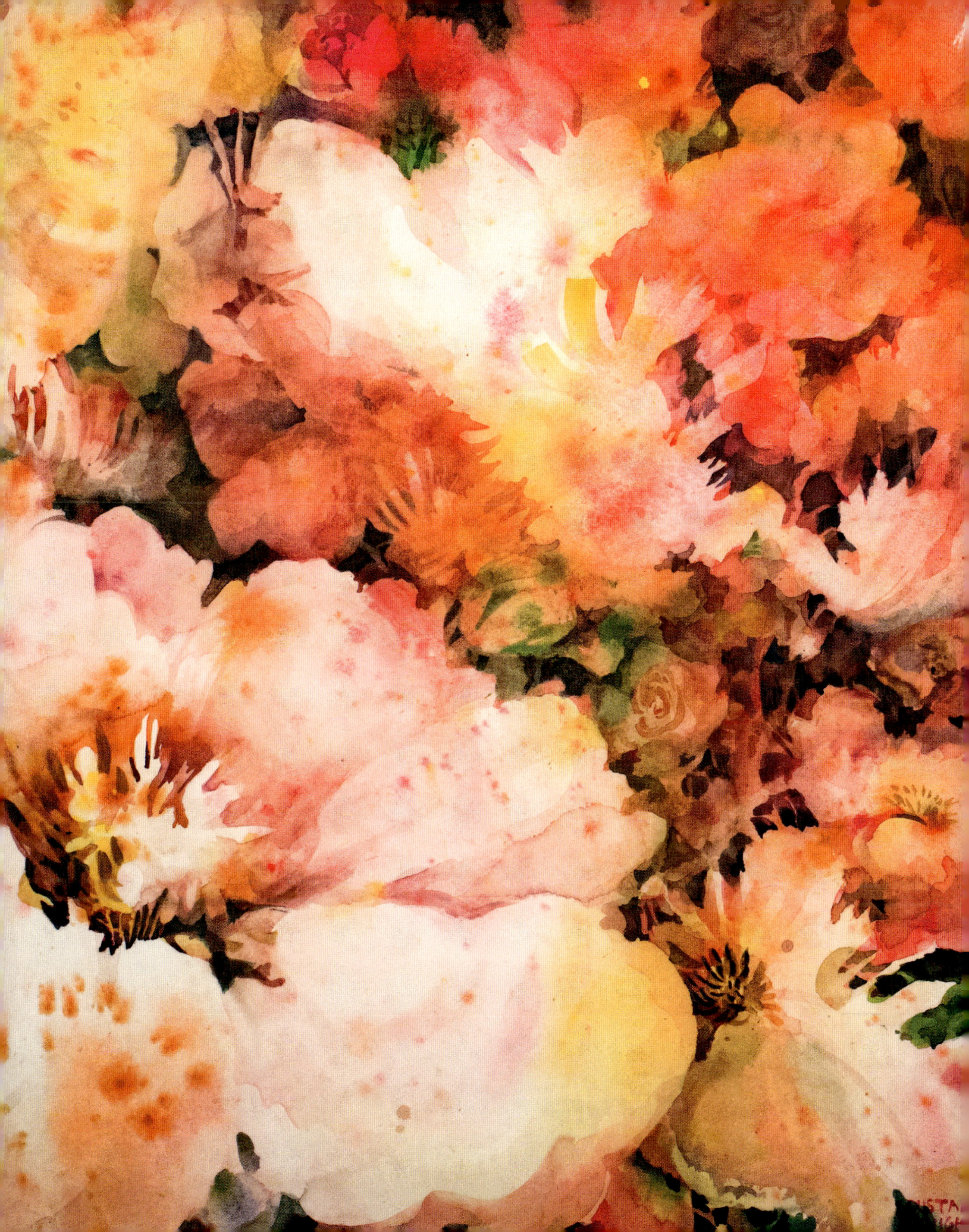

Approaches and Impressions

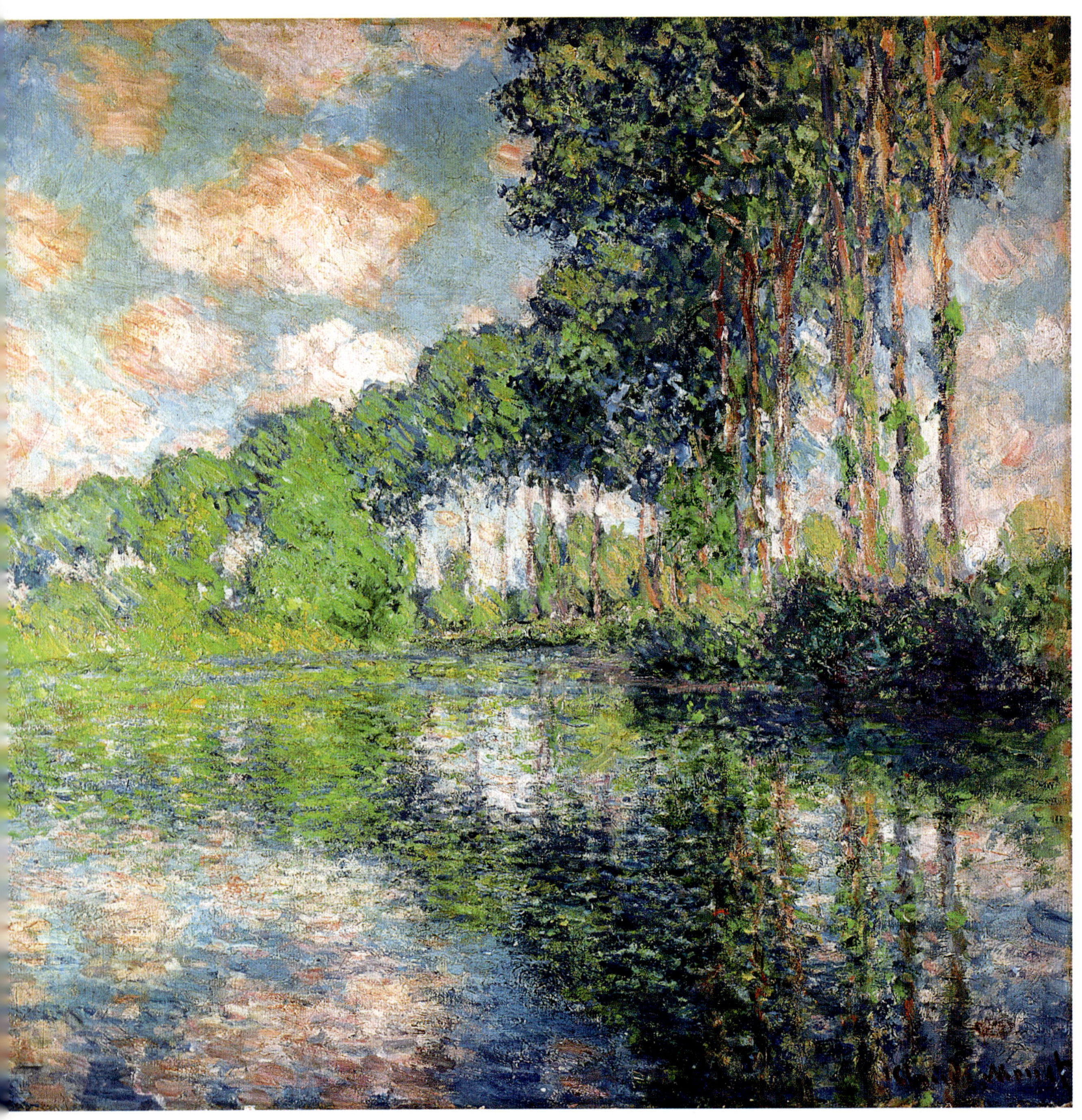

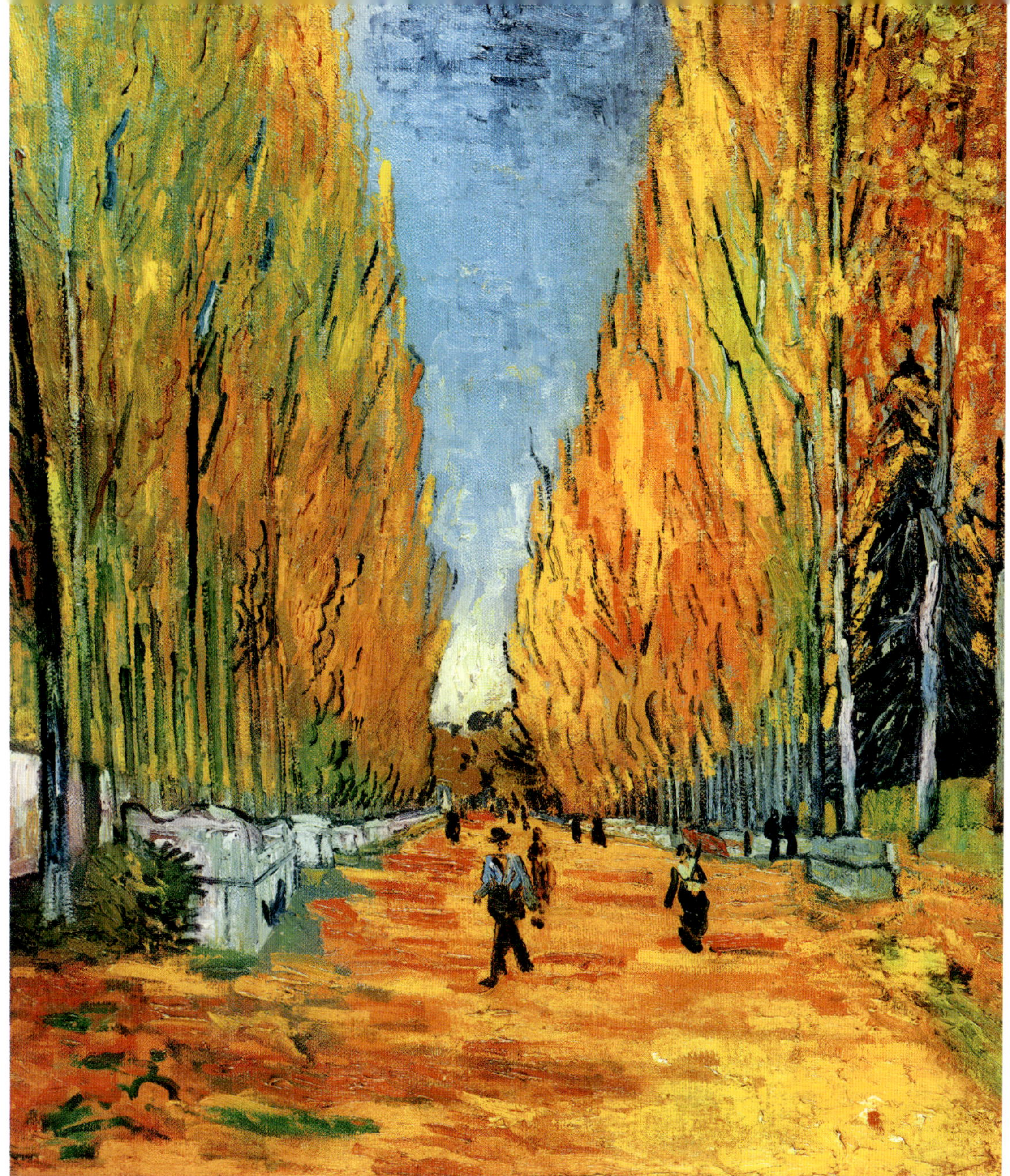

ABOVE: *L'Allée des Alyscamps*, 1888. Oil on canvas. Vincent van Gogh, Dutch, 1853–1890. Private Collection. Bridgeman Images.

OPPOSITE: *Poplars on the Epte*, c. 1891. Oil on canvas. Claude Monet, French, 1840–1926. Scottish National Gallery, Edinburgh. Bridgeman Images.

It's hard for me to imagine anyone having fun painting before Monet and Renoir. Before they tossed a sandwich into a knapsack, packed their tubes of paint, and headed outdoors to look for something to paint, art was stifling, jammed with parameters for correctness and tiresome allegories for subjects.

Thank goodness the Impressionists shucked the Royal Academy of Art and

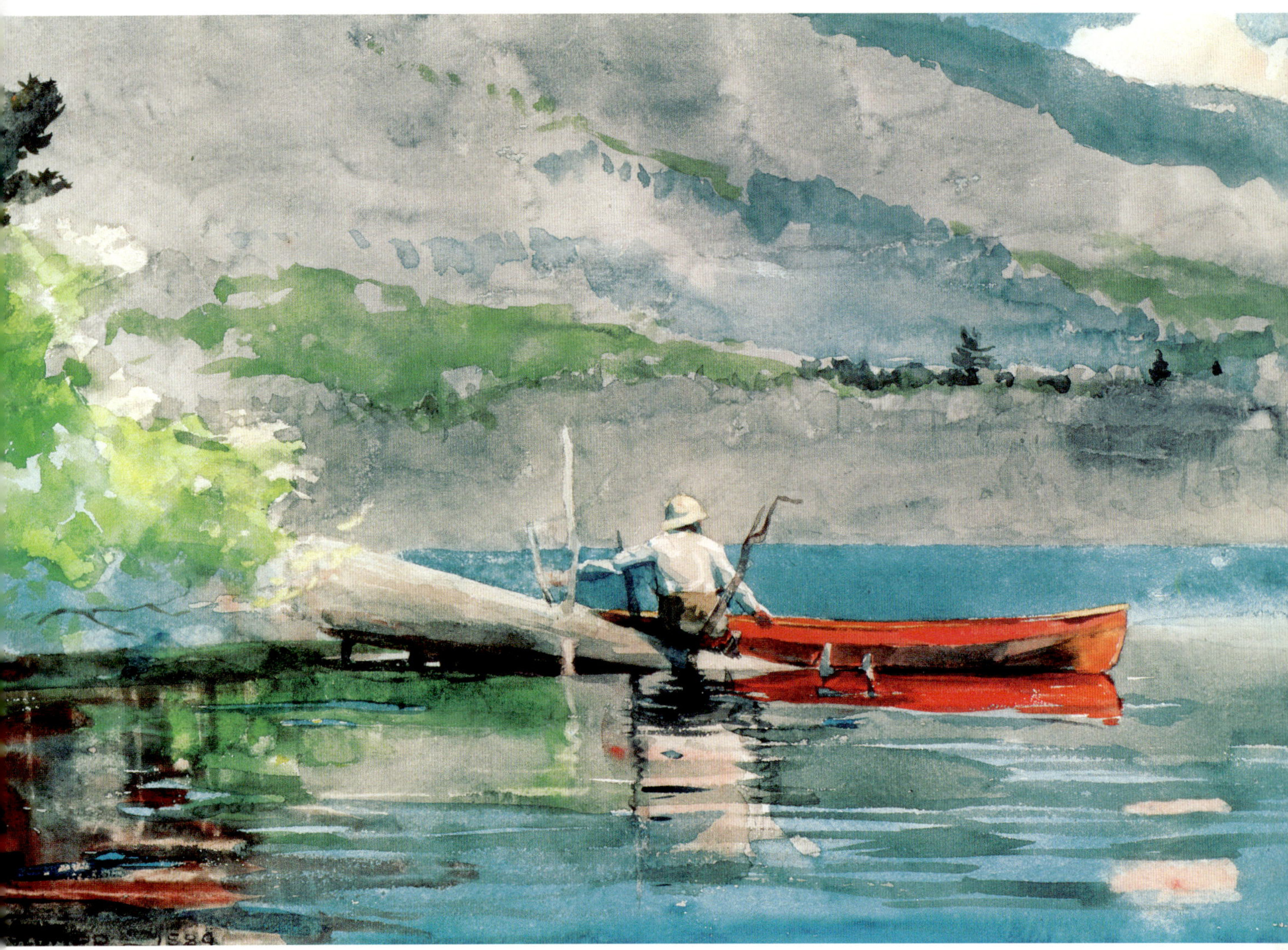

The Red Canoe, 1884. Watercolor on paper. Winslow Homer, American, 1836–1910. Private Collection. Bridgeman Images.

depended on their own eyes to see and their own inner vision to express what they saw. That's what I respond to in their landscapes and this is a book about what I've learned from that relationship—my own impressionistic approach to teaching and painting landscapes in watercolor and acrylic.

One of the highlights of teaching, for me, was to take my students on a field trip to the works-on-paper archives at the Museum of Fine Arts in Boston. The curator would arrange watercolors on low easels for the class to discuss. Being able to see how Sargent scraped white into a shadow with a pen knife or where Homer dragged a wax candle across his paper as a resist made me feel as though I was sitting on the grass beside them, watching them paint.

Sargent and Homer painted in a broad, loose style with bouncing color and visible brushwork capturing the feeling of light. They picked up the color in one area and used it in another as a detail. They seemed to work from bigger to smaller, looser to more detailed, light to dark, and sometimes back to light again. Childe Hassam painted about 10 miles (16 km) off the shore from my own studio in New Hampshire, and I can tell by looking at his paintings that the air is similar and the breeze smells the same. The connection is still there. The conversation continues.

Duck Island, Isles of Shoals, 1906. Watercolor on paper. Childe Hassam, American, 1859–1935. Private Collection. David Findlay Jr. Fine Art, NYC. Bridgeman Images.

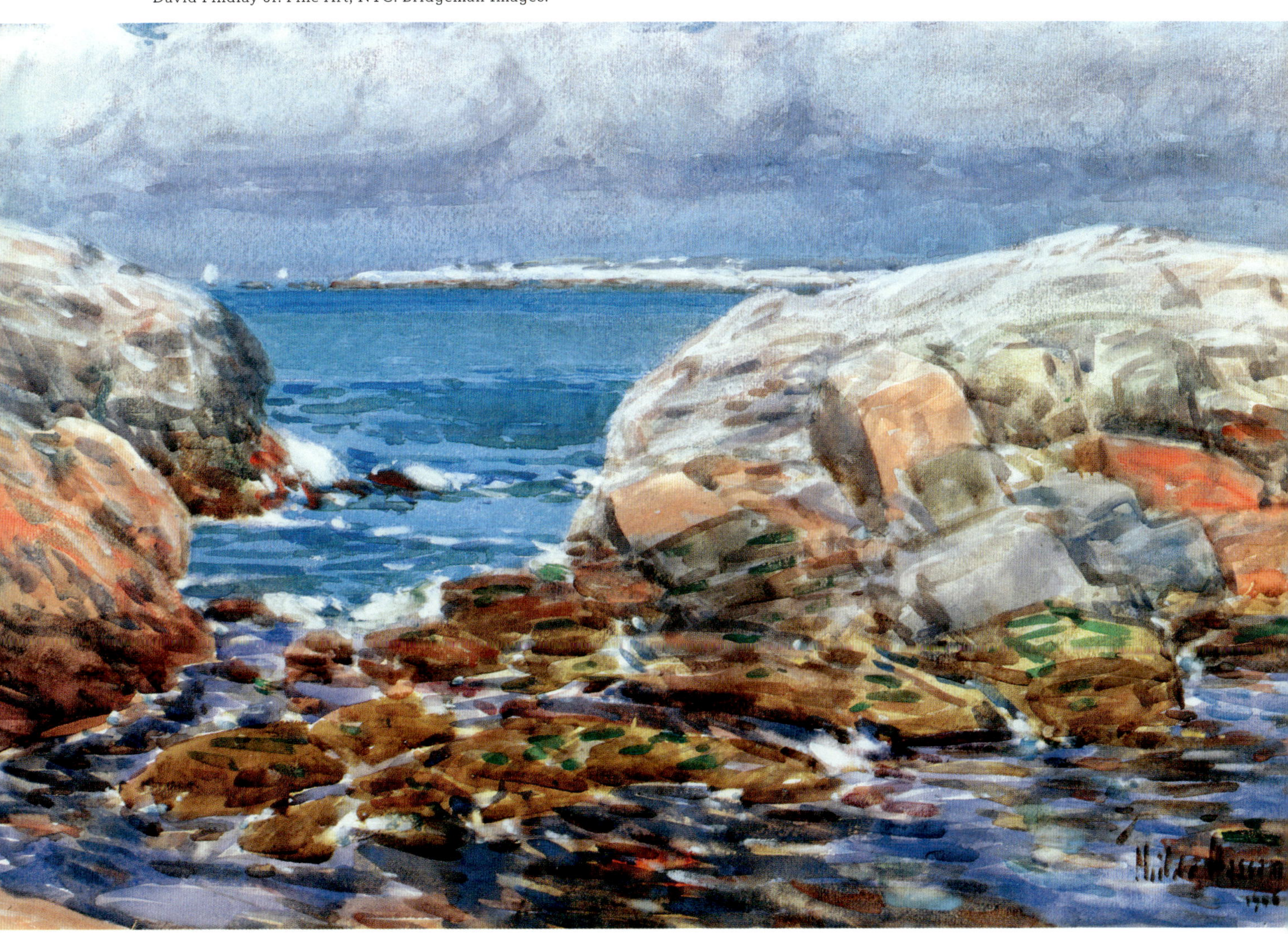

Tools and Materials

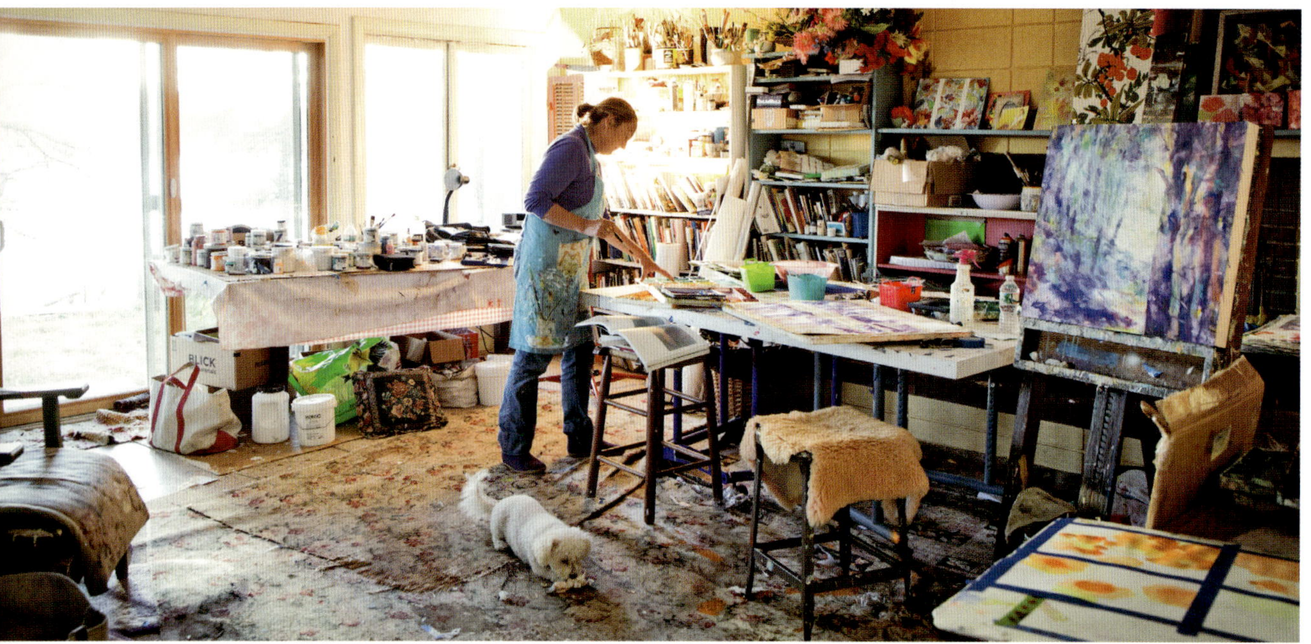

Creative moments in the studio

Paper, canvas, paint, brushes: your art materials are truly a matter of your personal choice. Choose wisely because stocking your studio or outdoor painting kit can get expensive. I've outlined my personal choices here, as well as a few suggestions for saving money.

Watercolor Paper

Watercolor paper comes in various thicknesses or pounds—the higher the number, or poundage, the thicker and more substantial the paper. I recommend using at least a 140 lb (300 g/m^2) paper, which will hold up to being soaked with water, scratched, and reworked. At the upper range, 300 lb (640 g/m^2) paper is expensive and so heavy it's almost rigid. At the other end, 90 lb (185 g/m^2) paper buckles as soon as you drop water on it, making painting with it frustrating. I suggest staying away from it.

You can buy watercolor paper in large sheets, rolls, and blocks. Blocks are pads that are glued around the edges and are particularly useful for outdoor painting. The glued edges hold the paper taut when it's wet, so that it dries flat. Once your painting is dry, you use a box cutter or craft knife to cut around the glued edge to remove the sheet from the block.

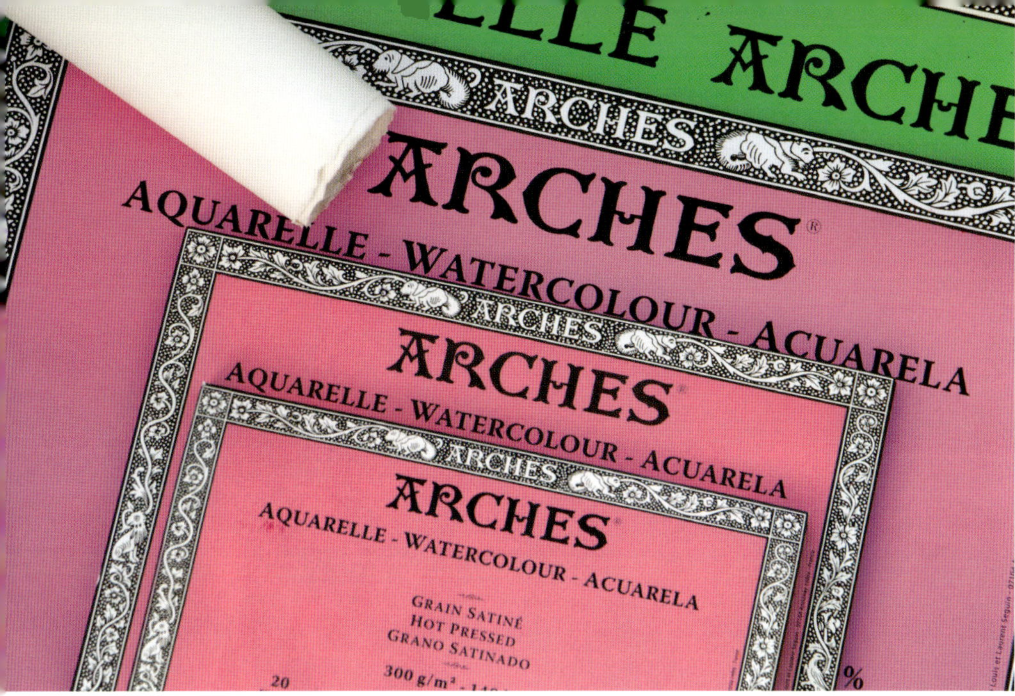

My first choice for watercolor paper is Arches bright white, in 140 lb (300 g/m²) weight or heavier. There are several sizes of blocks. You'll want to take at least two with you when you work outdoors so that you can shift from one to the other while allowing your paintings to dry.

You can easily fold and tear large, individual sheets of watercolor paper to your desired dimensions. Good quality paper tears beautifully and leaves a lovely edge. Use masking tape to attach the edges of a loose sheet of paper to a sturdy support board before you start painting or applying water. Leave the tape in place until the paper dries to prevent it from buckling.

There are three paper-surface types: Hot press has a smooth surface. Cold press has a medium-textured surface. Rough has a highly-textured, bumpy surface. The surface is important because it determines the look of your watercolor washes. On smooth paper, the water and color flow freely, allowing lots of unexpected things to happen. A rough surface catches color and water unevenly, often creating a dry-brush effect. Cold press is a good paper for beginners. As you become more advanced, hot-press papers and the newer synthetic papers are a lot of fun to try.

Canvas for Acrylic

If you're just starting in acrylic, I suggest purchasing pre-stretched, prepared canvas in the size that works best for you. You might also try hardwood or particle-board panels like those made by Ampersand. I don't recommend canvas covered cardboard because it warps easily.

Further along, you'll have time to learn about stretching canvas and preparing the surface with gesso. But even in choosing pre-stretched canvas, you'll want to be aware of the surface quality. Cotton duck canvas has a rough surface. More expensive linen canvas has a smoother surface that is lovely; painting on it is like working on paper. But for the money, especially for larger canvases, cotton duck is just fine.

I like to buy canvases with stretchers that are at least 2" (5 cm) deep. They stand out on the wall when hung, and if I paint the edges, I don't need to frame the painting.

Brushes

There are three basic styles of brushes: flats, rounds, and wash brushes. Flats carry the most pigment. They are best for filling larger areas, though we usually let the water do the work in watercolor paintings.

Rounds are the best for drawing strokes. There are all sorts of tip types: long, thin riggers; big, chubby Goliaths; filberts; and fans. For watercolor, a slightly chubby round holds water well, and a fine tip allows you to control where you make contact with the paper.

Watercolorists use a wide-wash brush to get a lot of water on the paper quickly. This can be important because as soon as the paper begins to dry, the surface can get streaky: A flat-wash brush allows the water and pigment to blend across large areas.

For acrylic, synthetic sables are the best for shoveling up paint and putting it on canvas where you want it. Acrylic painters often use fine-tipped watercolor brushes for detailed work.

Ultimately, for watercolor and acrylic, you'll want rounds and flats in various sizes. Those who work with acrylics will also benefit from having wider, flat brushes to transfer larger and thinner amounts of paint to the canvas. The size of brush you use will depend on the size of your paper or canvas. The smaller and more detailed the painting, the smaller the brush. Your choice of brush size will also depend on your preference for the size of your brush marks in a painting. I usually work with larger brushes so the brushstrokes are looser.

Because acrylic paint has some heft to it, your brushes need to be a little stiffer than watercolor brushes, though not as stiff as oil brushes. Avoid pig bristle. In fact, for anyone starting out in watercolor or acrylic, I would recommend buying one of the wonderful sets with synthetic brushes in various sizes. These are available in an affordable range and will get you used to working with round and flat brushes.

Of course, if you are game for it, there are many fancy, niche brushes to try, but remember, a brush is only as good as its handler. The best and the most expensive watercolor brushes are the Kolinsky sables. I have a few of these, but because I work spontaneously and often with various mediums at the same time, I prefer working with medium-priced brushes that I can be rougher with. Whatever the quality of your brushes, take good care of them. Never leave them standing in water, and always clean them before putting them away.

OPPOSITE: A well-loved ½" (1 cm) flat brush.

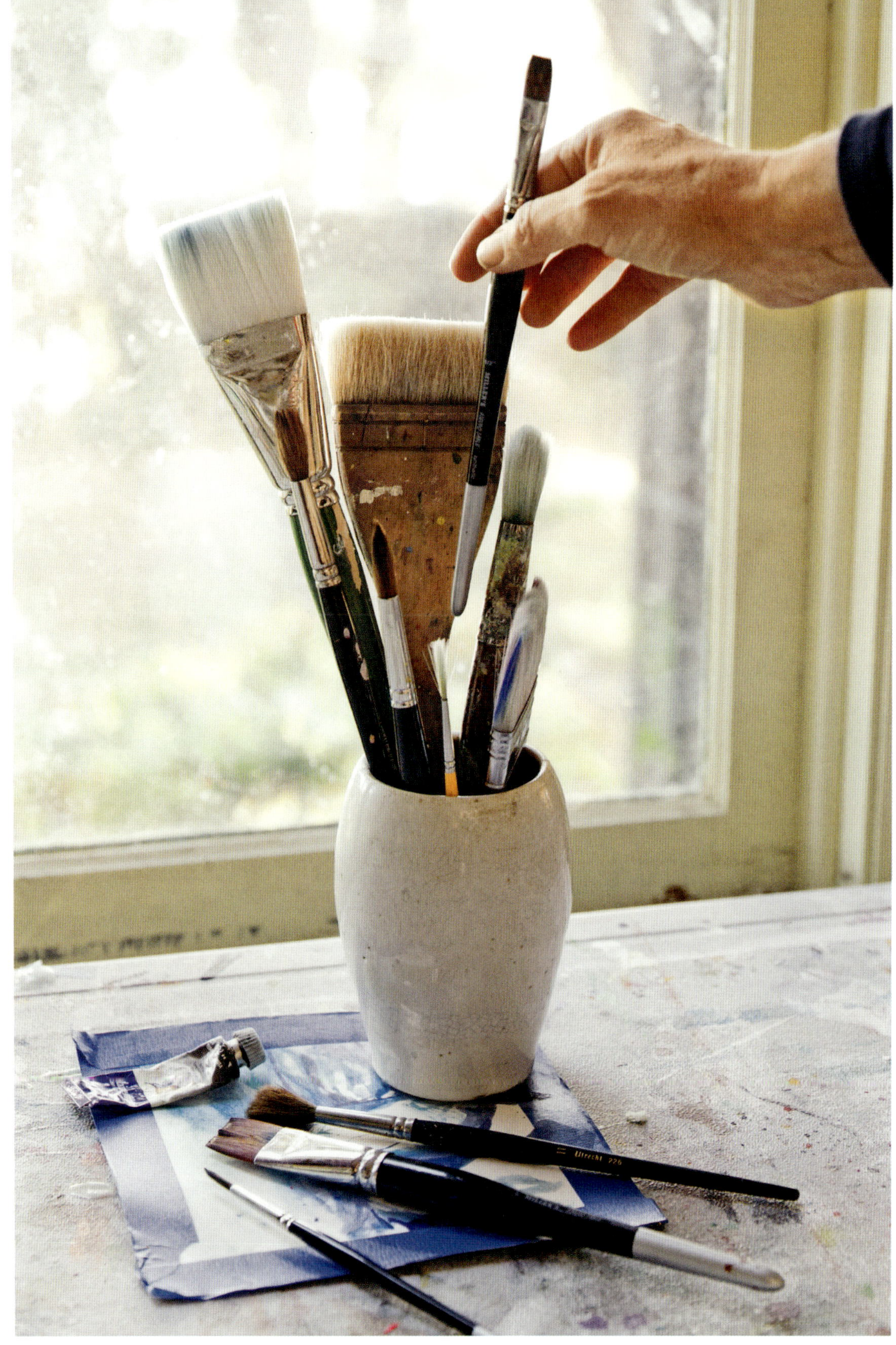
Utrecht 226

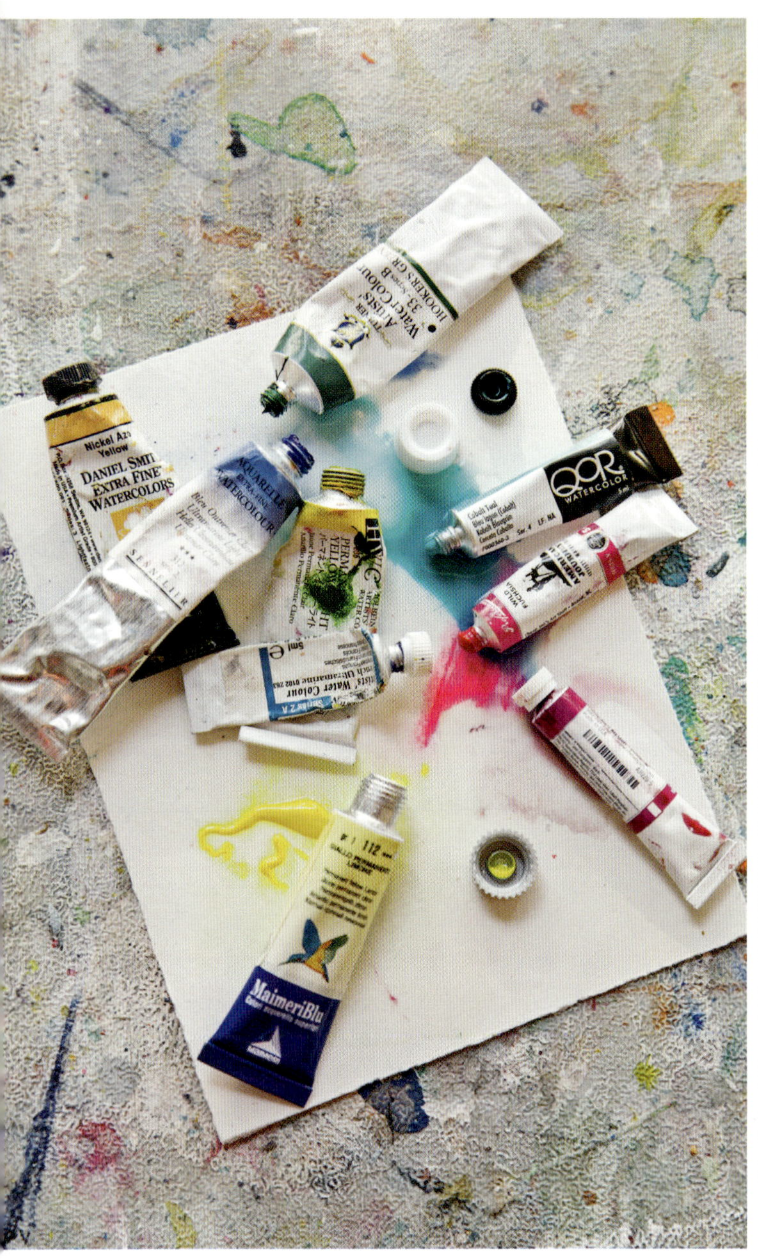

I love trying new brands and colors of watercolor paint as long as they are professional grade. My regulars include Sennelier, Winsor & Newton, Graham, Daniel Smith, Holbein, Maimeri, Turner, and Cheap Joe's American Journey.

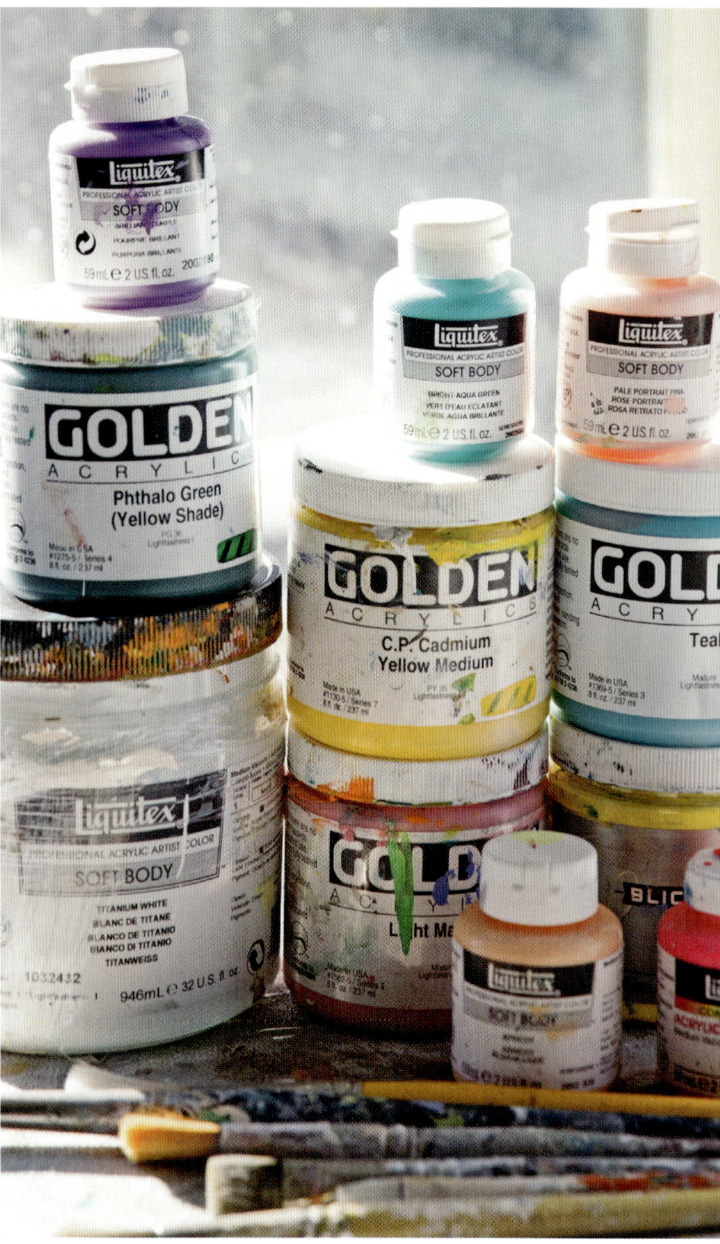

For acrylics, I stick with Golden and Liquitex paints. Their densities range from heavy body (like paste) and more fluid (like cream) that are fun to try. Both brands also have a wide range of additive mediums.

Paint

The cost of paint is directly related to the quality of the color. Paint is made up of color (pigment), medium (water soluble for watercolor, latex for acrylic), and small amounts of driers.

Bargain paints have weaker colors. Professional grades have brighter, more intense colors created by using more pure pigment and less medium. I usually suggest that my students buy fewer colors of better grade paint rather than lots of cheaper tubes. Watercolor paints, in general, cost more than acrylics because they use more pigment and less medium.

Some of the best paint brands have student-grade lines, such as Cotman Watercolors by Winsor & Newton. I encourage you to visit the big online art supply stores when you are shopping for paint. These sources can really help you to keep your costs down. (See resources on page 136.)

Choosing Colors

Start with the three primaries: red, yellow, and blue. Then gradually add to these by sampling some of the variations. Cadmium red is a warm, yellowish red. Scarlet or alizarin crimson is a bluer, blood red. Cadmium yellow light is like sunlight in a tube. Lemon yellow is a more transparent, greener yellow. Ultramarine blue has a touch of purple. Cerulean blue is considered a warmer blue. Cobalt blue is a beautiful china blue.

For watercolor, I do not recommend using black or white. They can be very sneaky, turning your beautiful colors opaque and gray.

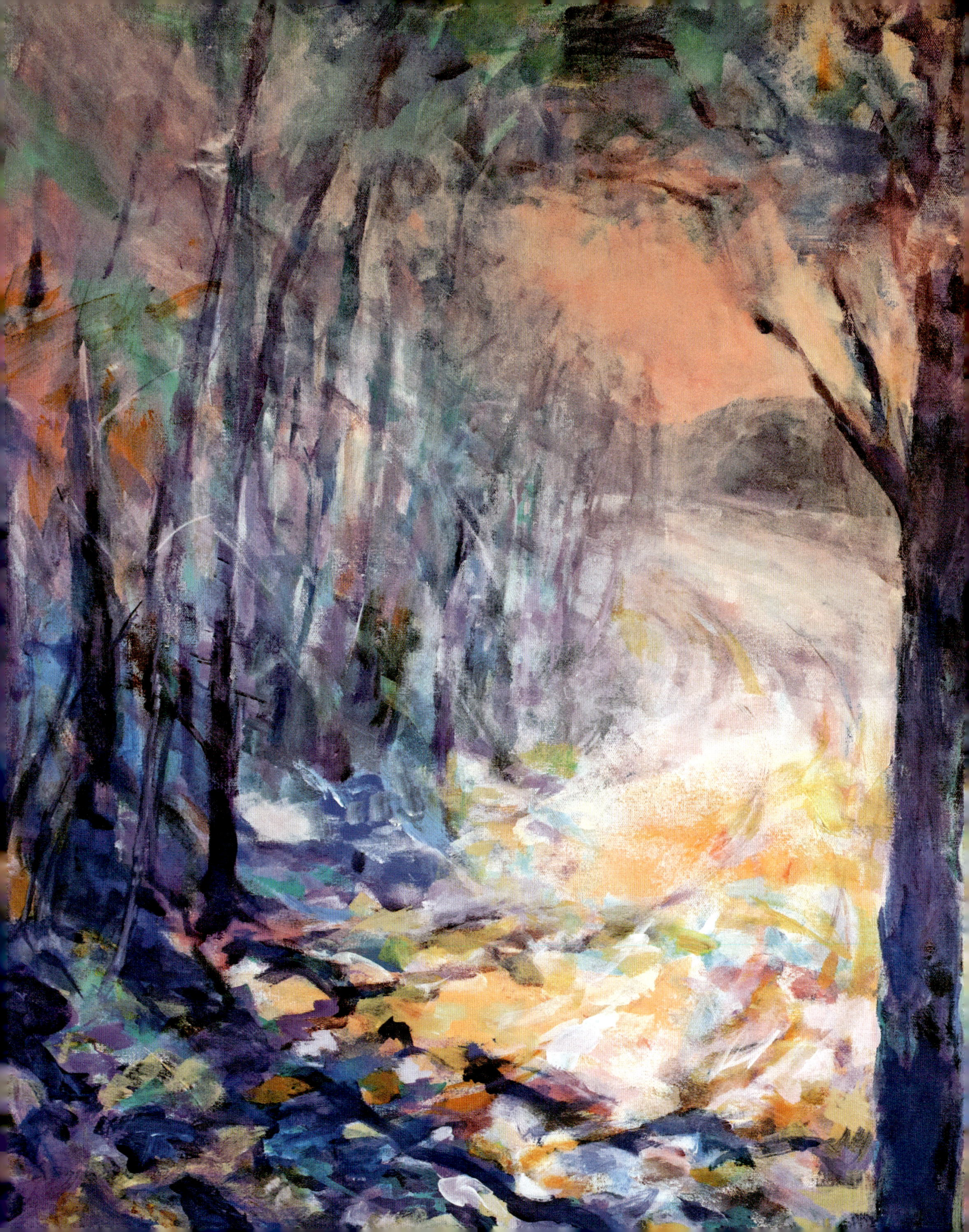

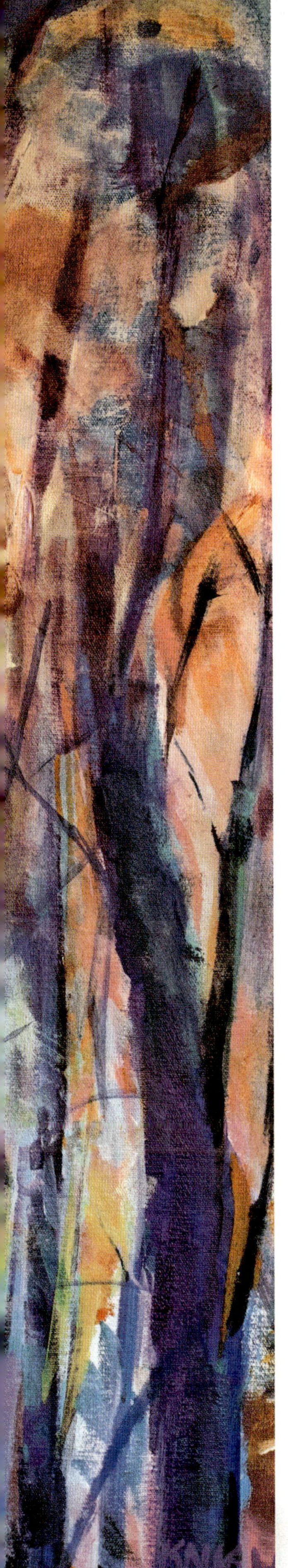

PAINTING THE WOODS

I FINISH MOST OF MY PAINTINGS IN THE STUDIO, but I start them outdoors. This is a personal choice that works well for me. I am not a renderer of what's in front of me. I don't feel the need to match colors or chase changing shadows. I like to get a deep impression of a subject or scene and then turn away from it so I can do a new version based on my memory and what I felt, as much as what I saw.

I enjoy the physical distance created by returning to the studio to develop the image. It's a process, often leading to a finished watercolor on paper and then to an acrylic on canvas with many sketches in between. By freeing myself from the actual location and going to my studio I can work on the aspects of the scene I really like, such as the softness of light falling through the trees, or the transparent delicacy of a flower petal. As soft as an impressionistic painting may appear, there's structure behind it, and steps to getting there.

The woods are among my favorite subjects. I spend a lot of time wandering through them looking at things. I particularly enjoy early mornings. Light seems to have more personality in the morning than at any other time of day. The presence of light slanting through the trees can be almost mystical in the way it unites ephemeral and solid nature.

Mornings are wonderful opportunities to notice how light streaks across a flat stone, intensifying the blue lichen and bedazzling raindrops on the edge of a leaf. When you begin seeing light and noticing the effect it has on everything, then your way is open to noticing what usually goes unnoticed.

I work in New Castle, an island on the New Hampshire coast. Most of the trees here are pines: straight, smooth-skinned white pine and crooked, scaly-barked pitch pine, with an occasional fir or hemlock, and remnants of the original hardwood forests of oak and maple.

Woodland Road. Acrylic. 36" x 36" (91.5 x 91.5 cm). The woody hillside rising up and the light in the center offer a soft passage through the painting. Notice the overglazing of thinned white paint.

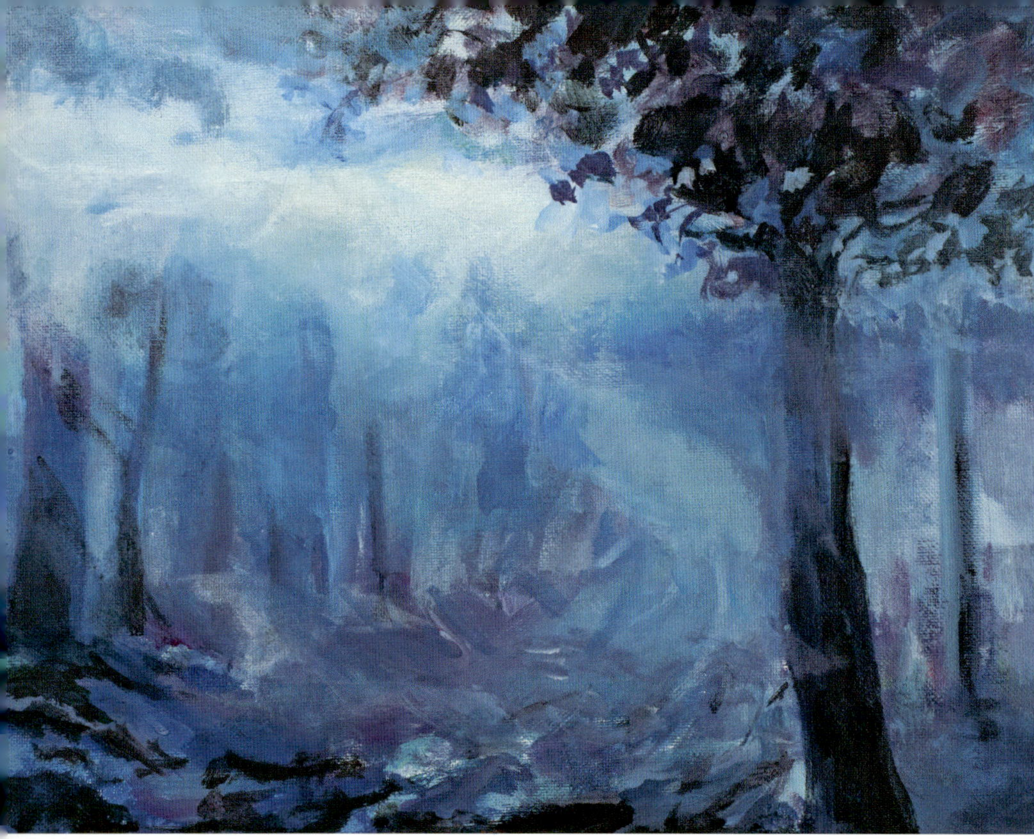

Ocean Fog Along the Road. Acrylic on canvas. 10" x 14" (25.5 x 35.5 cm). This was a fast painting, playing with the drama created by the fog through the trees.

I think what continues to attract me to the woods is that I can move through the trees with the island's promise of sea and sky just beyond them. I love the feeling of the architectural shapes arching up around me like a cathedral. Colored light filters through the foliage like light through a church window. Breezes shake the leaves, making the light flit about.

Mornings invite me to step out and open myself to experience the magic of a fresh day. Maybe the ground is covered by fog that, having thickened in the cool shadows of night, is quickly disappearing in the morning light. Or maybe the fog is from the ocean, socked in and settling down like a gray blanket. Sometimes there is snow, sometimes drifting autumn leaves. The woods may be familiar but they're never the same.

When I set out to look around, thinking about my next painting, I take a lot of phone snaps. Here is the thing, once I've taken the pictures, I don't rely on them very much. I keep them as reminders of what attracted me: how magical the light looked on a lichen-covered branch or how it outlined the texture of moss against granite. I don't paint from them. Painting from a photo lacks the excitement of seeing. The snapshot is my reminder of the scene, but it's not *the* scene. When I paint, I want to create from the experience of what excited me about what I saw in nature, and the impression of what I see in my mind.

OPPOSITE: *Berry Brook.* Watercolor. 20" x 16" (51 cm x 40.5 cm). Green light filtering through the trees colors the mossy rocks and the water in the brook.

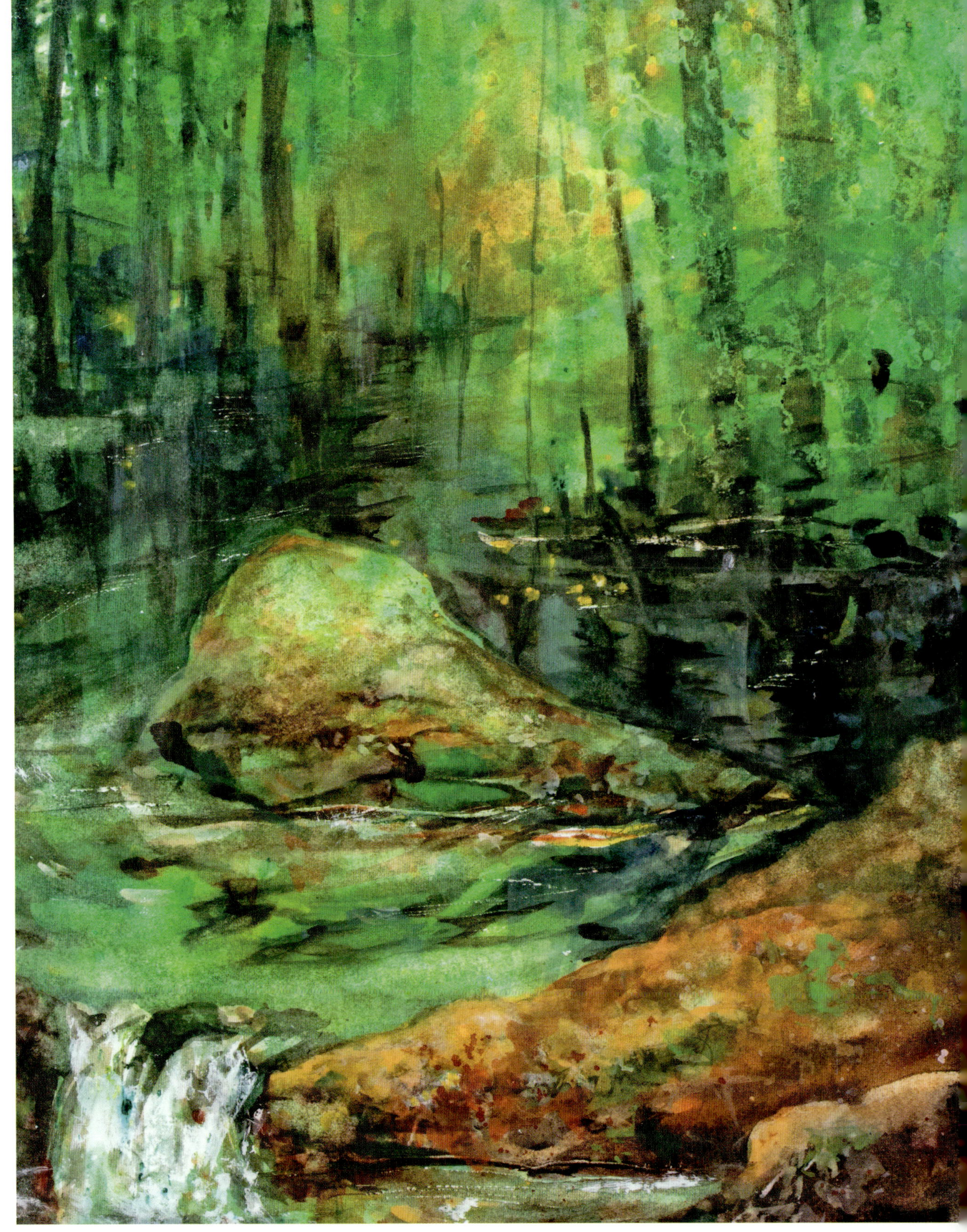

Demonstration: Painting the Woods in Watercolor

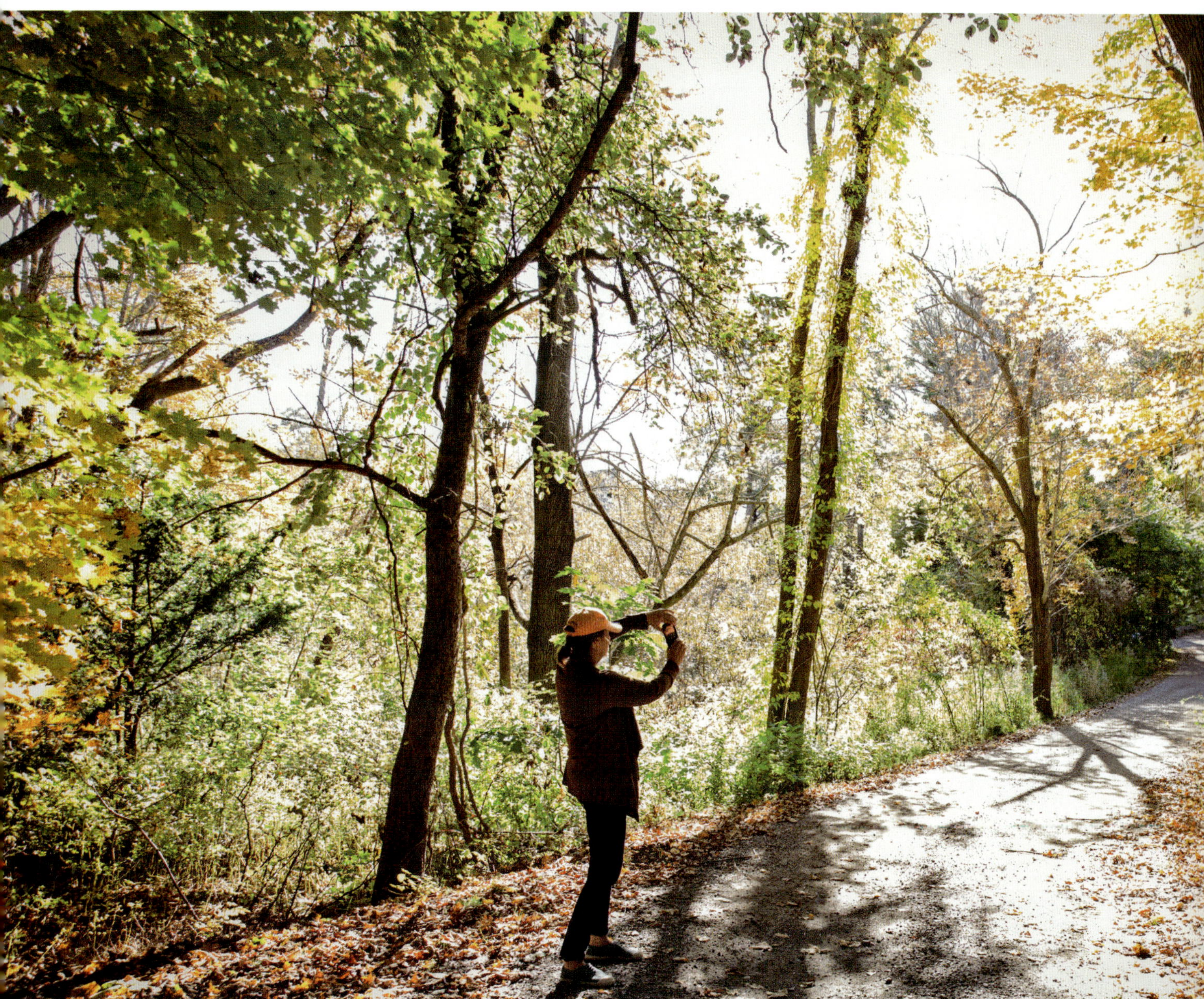

Finding inspiration

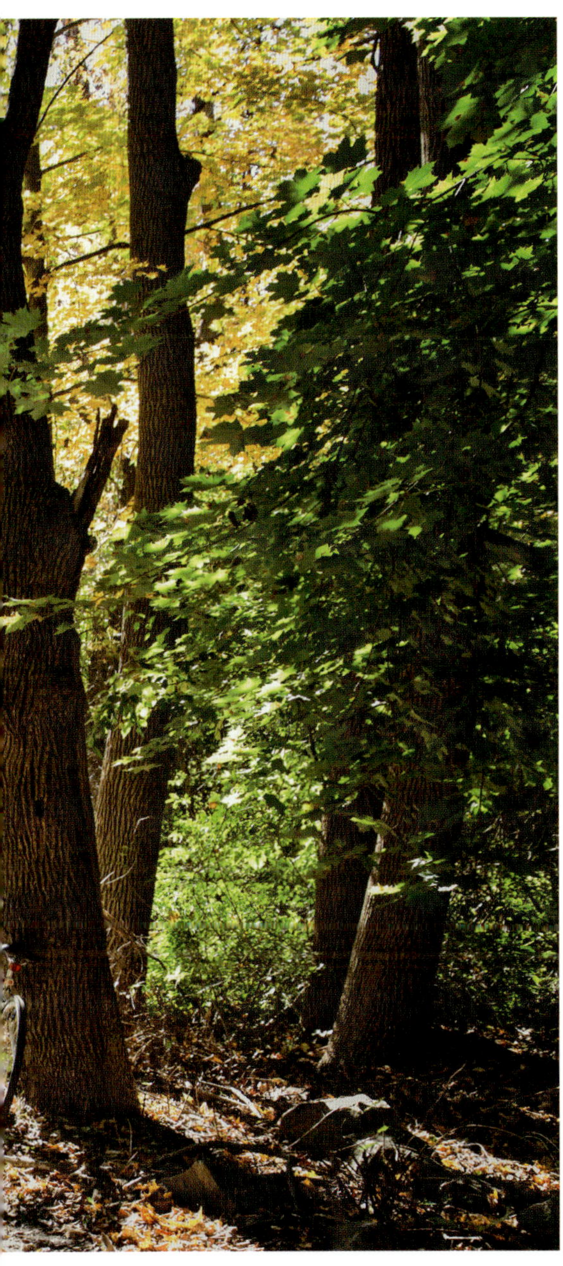

The Approach

Choosing a place you're deeply familiar with as a subject can make painting both easier and more complicated. The physical reality of the place is apt to be layered in memories of things you've experienced, good and bad. The challenge is to try to see your familiar surroundings as if you've never been there before.

There's a narrow dirt road that cuts across the center of this island. When I was young, it was an overgrown footpath where the boys would dare each other to bike at night and teenagers would go to do teenager things. Now the road has been leveled and widened and there are more houses on it. But it's still a dirt road and it still has a picturesque mystery. This summer I've been walking my dog there in the early morning. Something keeps drawing me back, so I decide it's a good subject for a watercolor demonstration.

PHOTOGRAPHY

Step 1. I begin, as I do every painting, with phone snaps. Every time I click the shutter I'm making a decision about what I see. When I realize I've taken ten photos of sunlight falling in patterns across the road and the silhouette of an old pitch pine tree, I know there is something going on there for me. The light is inviting. Perhaps there's a story unfolding, with the dirt road disappearing into the darkness of the woods. Where will it take me?

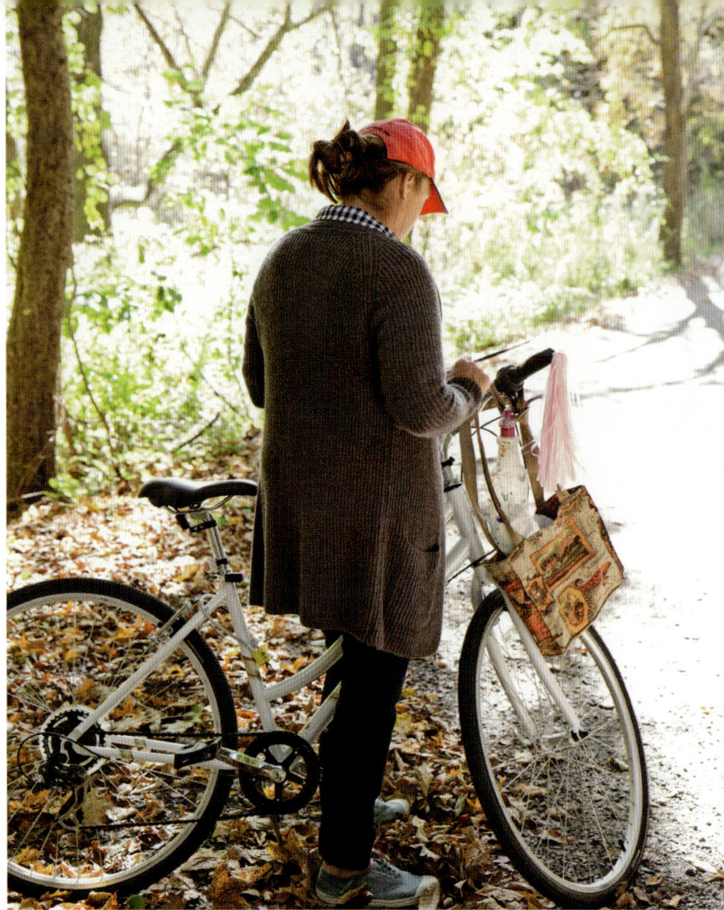

LEFT: Back on my bike
OPPOSITE: Sketching my impressions

PENCIL SKETCH THE EXPERIENCE

Step 2. The next day I bike back at the same early hour. Here's my first test. Does the spot still capture my interest? Is the magic I felt yesterday still there? If it's gone, I look for other locations.

To really engage with a painting, I have to know I've made the right choice and put any other choices out of my mind. This helps me keep a clear impression of what I want to do in my mind.

This step is not just about sketching; it's about taking notes of what drew me to the spot. I always bring along a small spiral-bound sketchbook, pencils, and an eraser, so that I can jot down notes—and not just about what I see. I write down whatever I notice: what attracts or repels me, what the scene reminds me of, what I smell, what I hear, what the sun feels like on my neck, whether I'm hungry, whether I can smell the trees. I try to write down enough details so that I can re-create those impressions in my mind when I get back to the studio.

I also make quick pencil sketches of the views I liked when I was photographing, and when I do, I notice more details. Drawing demands more attention. Even with quick sketches I notice the way the shadows lengthen and pool across the road, the way that colors lurk and change in the foliage. When I sketch I'm not trying to replicate the scene, I'm trying to capture my experience of the road. In many ways these early stages of "seeing" my painting before it's begun are my favorite moments of being an artist.

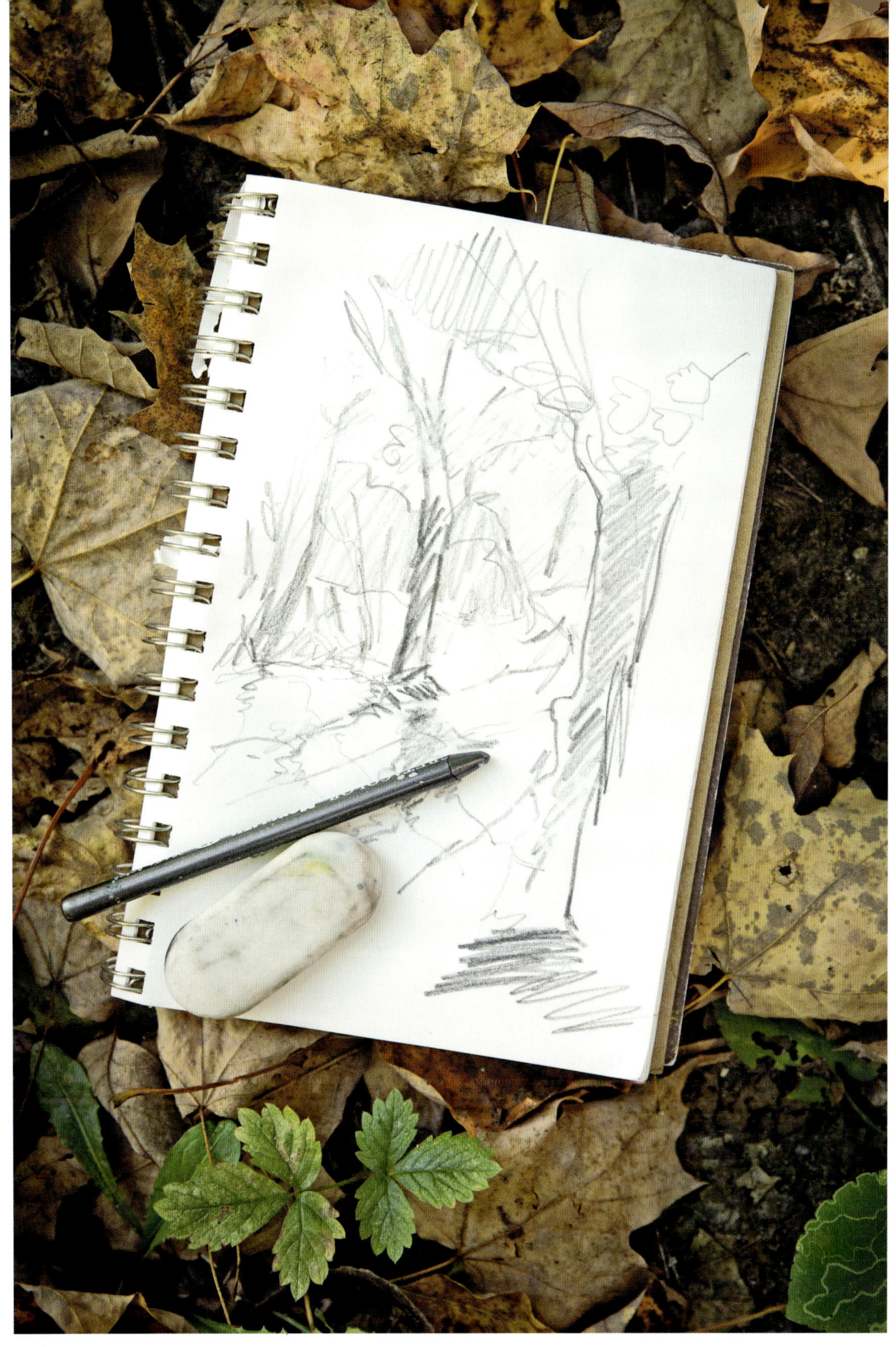

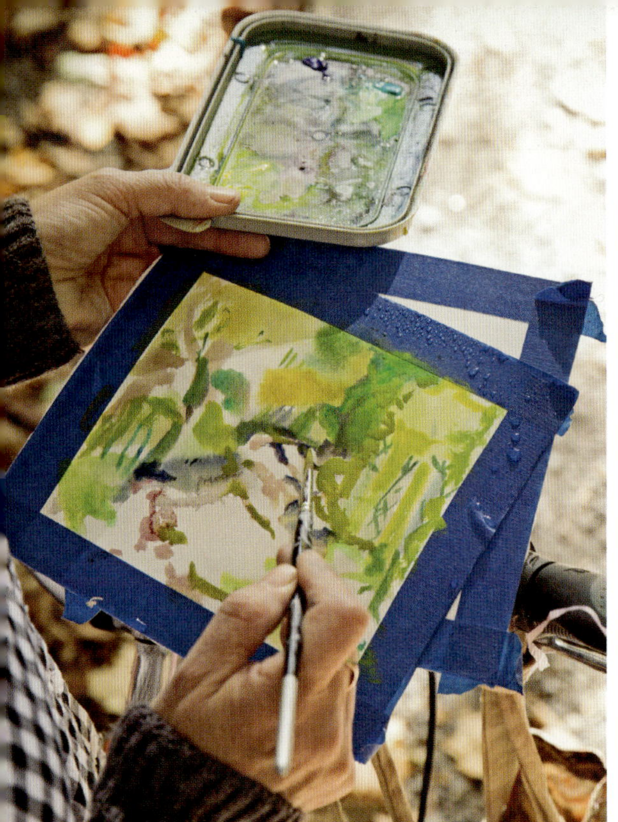

Balancing my outdoor watercolor kit in one hand while I sketch

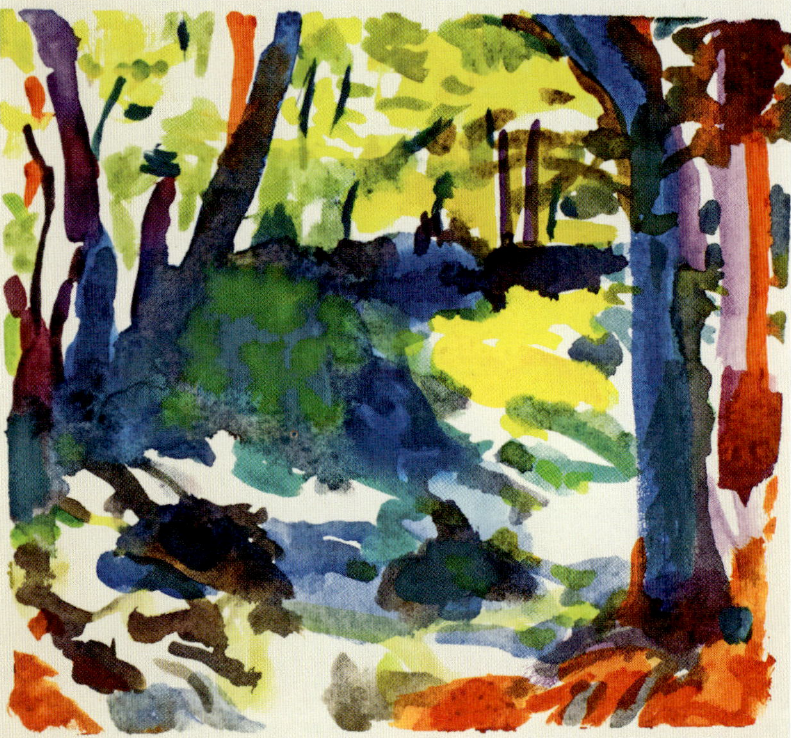

ABOVE & OPPOSITE: Woods and dirt road color sketches

WATERCOLOR SKETCHES

Step 3. Next I bring out my tiny outdoor painting kit—this is the minimum I need to sketch an on-site watercolor. I can carry everything in a small carpet bag on my bike. I have a pencil, a flat plastic lid with some dabs of dried paint on it—red, yellow, and blue—a ¼" (6 mm) flat, synthetic sable brush, a spray bottle filled with water, and a stack of 6" x 6" (15 x 15 cm) watercolor scrap paper, or a watercolor block.

There's a freedom in working with such an abbreviated palette. As I begin my sketches, I'm not trying to match colors with nature; instead, I'm approximating color families and values. As I look at the scene in front of me, I'm thinking about the main shapes, but also the transitions at their edges: what makes them stand out or blur together.

Step 4. My quick watercolor sketches of the view record only my impressions—no details. I try different combinations of color to find out which capture the light and shadows the way I want to remember them when I go back to the studio. I may use greens and golds or try for a quieter mood with cool purples. As the sun comes out, I use strong, bright, exciting colors. All three sketches express different impressions of the same location at different moments. Though the colors differ in the sketches, similarities begin to appear: the weight of the trees framing the road, the way the shadows fall at an angle. Without really thinking about it, the painting I want to do is evolving in my mind. I'm ready to take the sketches to my studio and get to work.

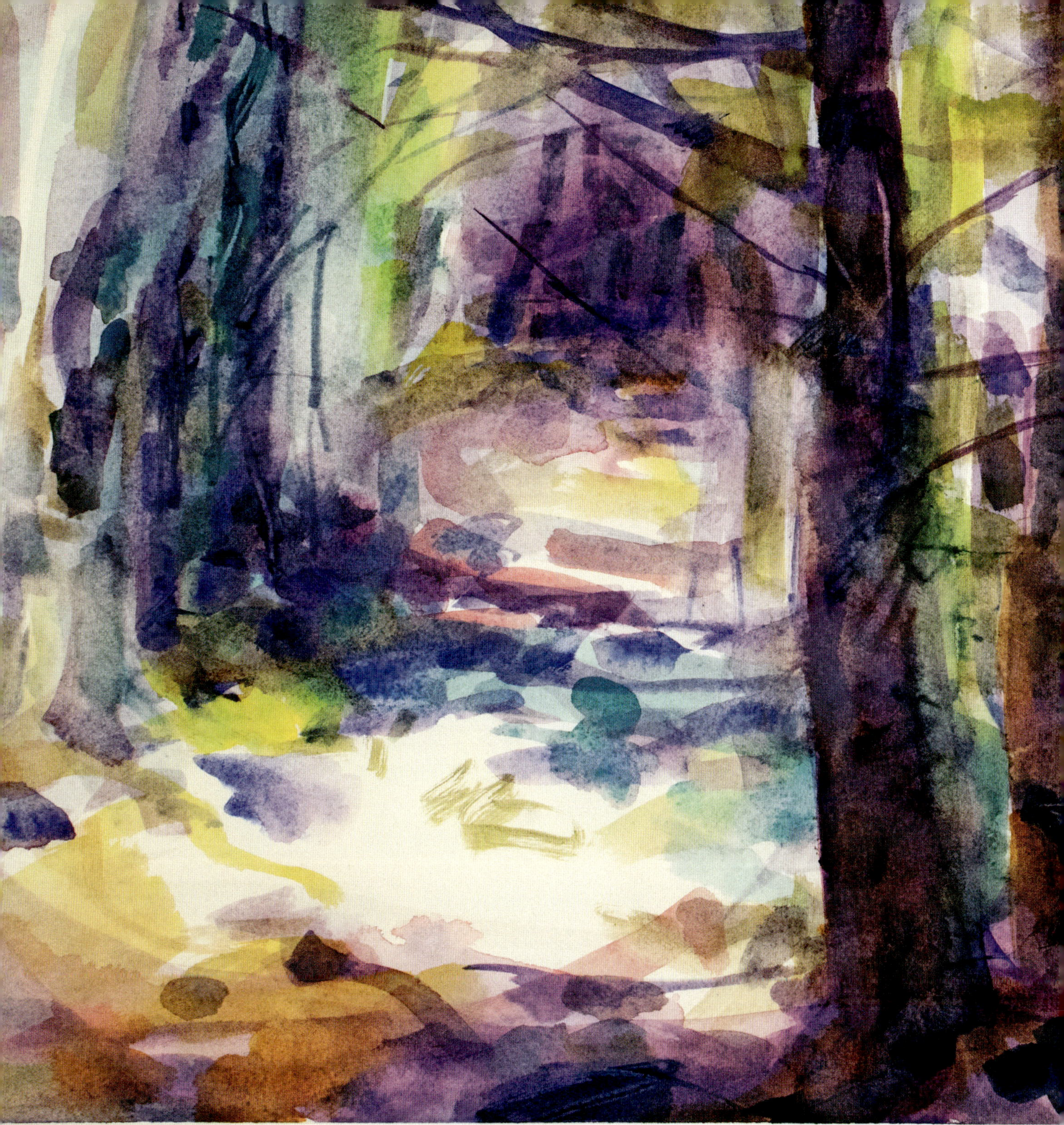

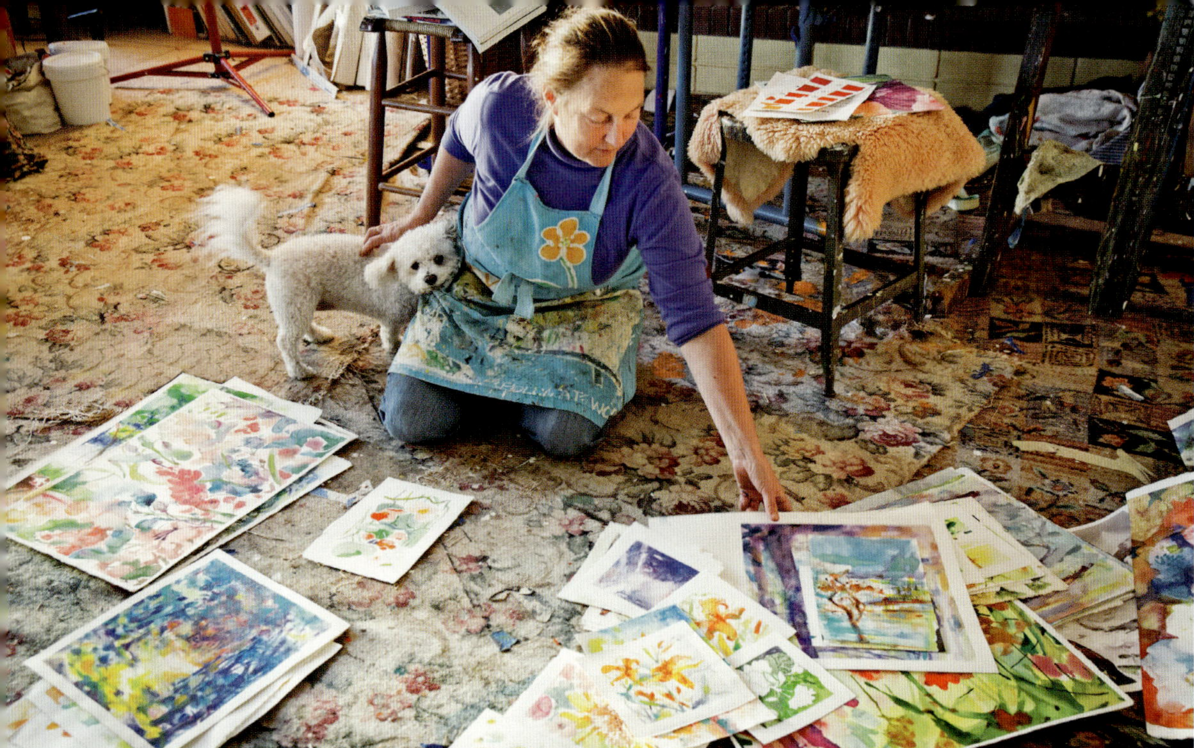

Lilly helps me look at sketches.

In the Studio: Research, Dialogue, and Visualizing

In my studio, my relationship with the on-site experience changes. First of all, there's a shift from responding directly to the situation in front of me to working in a more deliberate, thoughtful fashion. But another important change is that this is where I become more critical of my work.

Sketching on site, I work quickly and don't stop to evaluate the quality of my work: I'm only trying to capture my impression of the scene on paper. In the studio, I slow down and make critical decisions. It's a necessary transition—the trick is preventing the deliberateness of thinking from suffocating the immediacy of the fresh impression.

I put on a Sarah Vaughan CD and sit down to look through my sketches and photographs and reread my sketchbook notes. I pull out some art books by artists who've explored the same ideas I am interested in and flip through images that seem to have some relevance to what I'm beginning to develop in my mind. For instance, I might find Wolf Kahn's landscapes and Monet's garden pond images important in that moment. I'm not thinking about copying what they do, or expecting their approach to provide solutions for me, not at all. For me, looking at other artists' work when I'm getting ready to paint is like a conversation. It doesn't matter how many centuries have gone by since they were working. There's still a give and take and an exchange of ideas when I look at their work and think about mine. It can be very energizing.

I look through my on-site sketches again and begin to design the watercolor in my mind. I like the way the trees in the foreground of my sketches frame the road as it winds away. I like the way the road curves invitingly and disappears mysteriously.

I want the design to be simple, clear, and strong. It's the choices I make about color, value, and contrasts that will make the painting special. The Impressionists often painted the most unassuming subjects—a field, an orchard, the woods—but their compositions are not accidental.

I begin a fresh series of sketches to work out my plan for my painting: design, value, and color.

I want to begin easily, without concern about process, or materials, or finishing a great work of art. Sometimes I am unstoppable, but usually I waver between caution and laziness, exuberance and fuzziness. So I start small.

Tape a grid of smallish squares or rectangles on a large sheet of Arches 140 lb (300 g/m^2) bright white hot press paper using artist tape, which is available in art supply shops. I do this because it lets me try my ideas in sequence. I like to see the sequence of the stages all together and the similarity of size and format. It's a kind of story board of the painting to be. The tape visually separates the panels clearly and creates clean edges when I take it off at the end.

Dividing a large sheet of paper into small frames

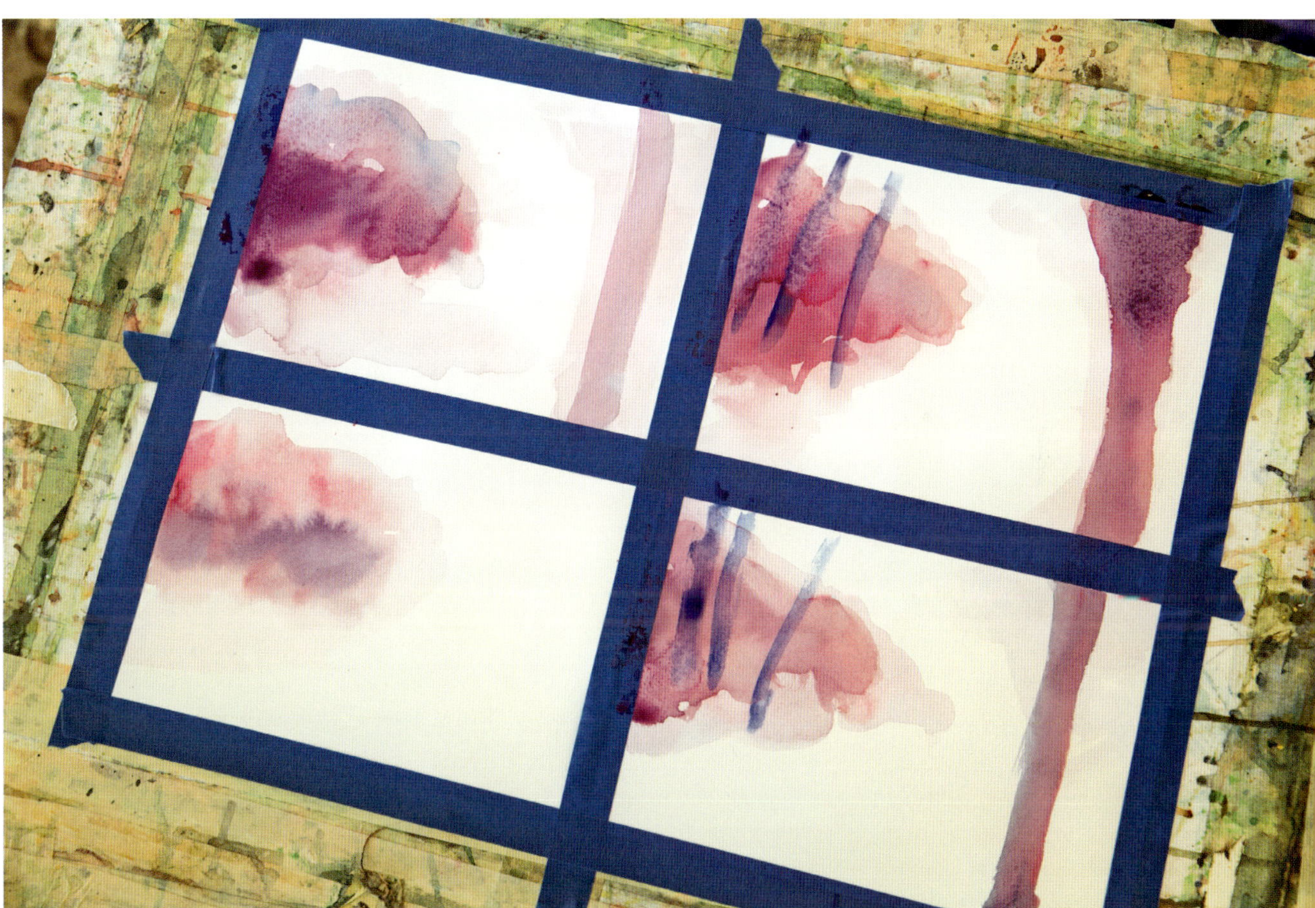

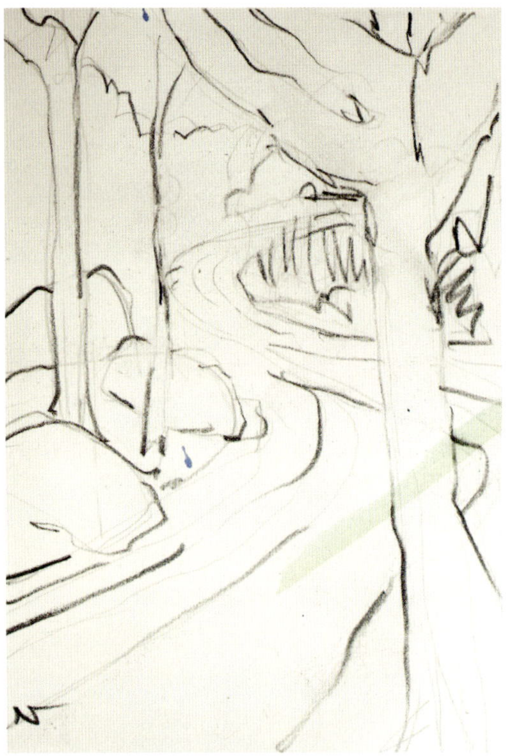

STEP 1. The first step toward the studio watercolor is creating a design I like in pencil.

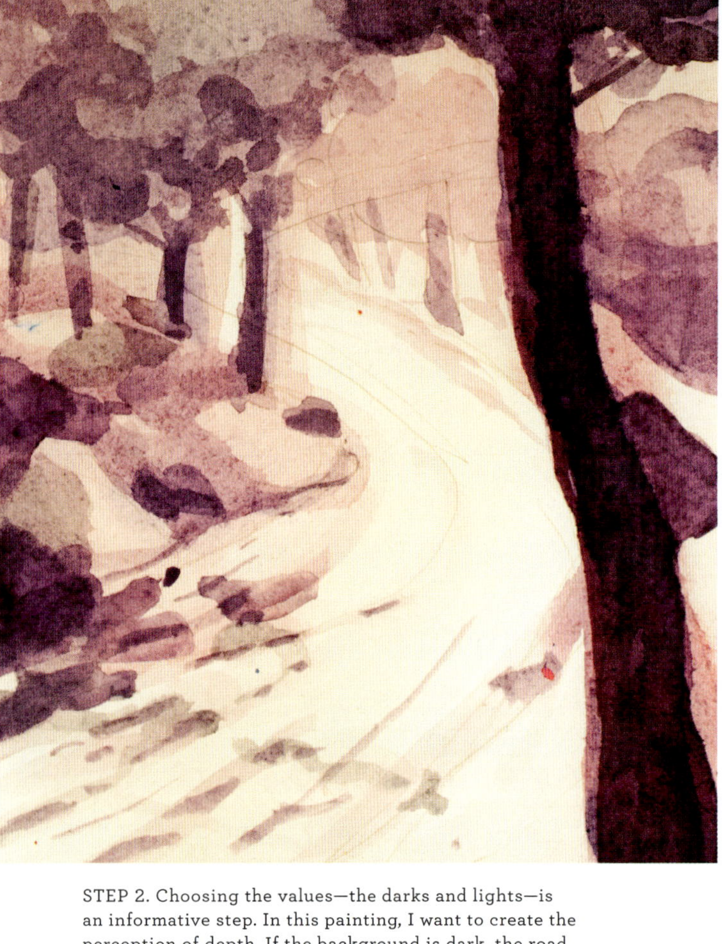

STEP 2. Choosing the values—the darks and lights—is an informative step. In this painting, I want to create the perception of depth. If the background is dark, the road will look like a tunnel into the darkness. If the foreground is dark, the background will become more atmospheric.

Step 1. Design. I begin with a design sketch in pencil on paper. This is where I work out the vertical and horizontal proportions. I'll try several designs using light pencil marks, simplifying the shapes until I find the most balanced, attractive composition.

Step 2. Value. The value sketch can be in pencil to shade in the design sketch, establishing lights and darks. Values are the sequential range from white to black that you see in a black and white photograph. I often darken the shapes along the edge of a painting and use lighter values in the center. This establishes a center of interest and pulls the viewer into a light-filled place.

In my second sketch I choose a single color, purple, to work out where the darkest and lightest areas of the painting will be. Then I begin to build and fit in the middle values.

One universal truth about looking at paintings—all paintings—is that your eye is attracted first to the areas of highest contrast. It's like the start of a story. Think about that when you start a painting—where do you want the viewer's eye to focus first? I decide to focus the high contrast in my painting at center front, where the dark shadows of the trees cross the pale dirt road and lead you in.

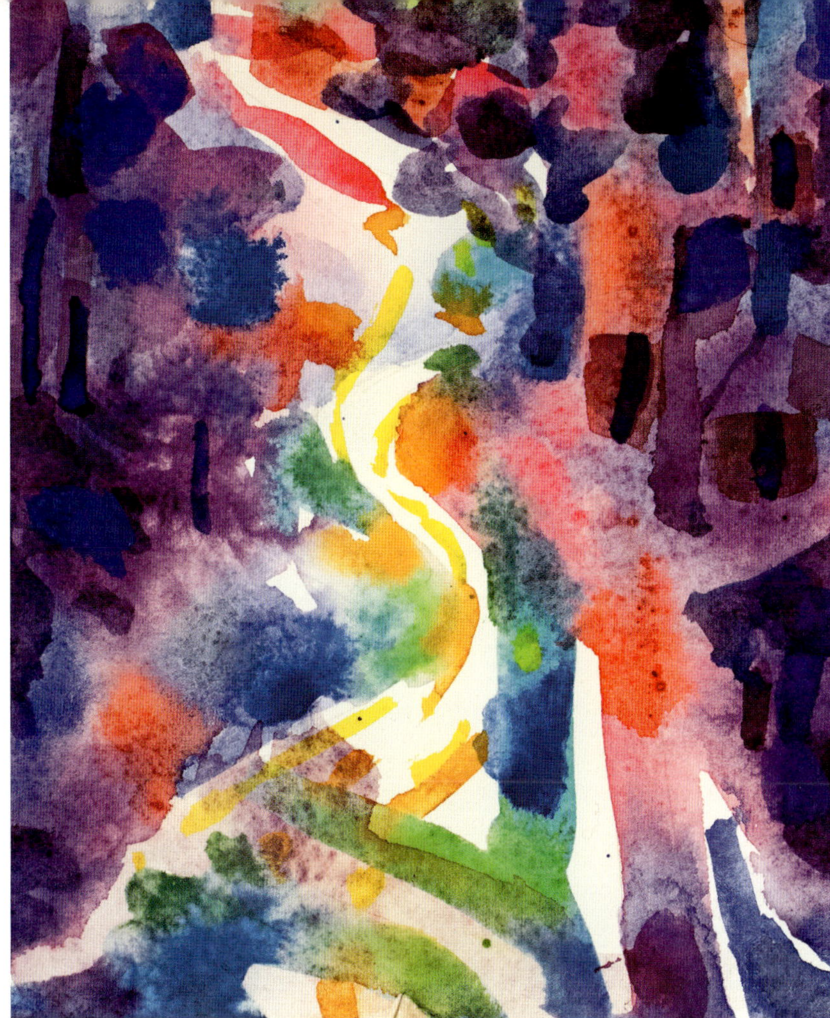

STEP 3. Choosing a color scheme is personal. For me it helps express my feelings about the scene such as the jostling warms and cools of this location.

Step 3. Color. Now that I have a good design and feel for the values, I work out my color scheme. Inspired by the Monet paintings I've been looking at, I decide to use predominately blues, purples, and red. I want the painting to feel like New England—a cool, shady woods with a warm, sunny road. My dominant woodsy color will be a combination of French ultramarine blue and pink-red quinacridone red. For the road through the center, I will add yellow, warm green, and turquoise.

In many ways, the most difficult part of creating the painting—making all the decisions in the studio—is now done. Now I can move ahead with my watercolor painting.

CHOOSING COLORS

A note about choosing colors–for any painting that you do. Your approach to color is a lifelong pursuit. For me what works best is to choose a dominant color. I think of it as the grandmother color. Then I support it by surrounding it with analogous colors, like a family at a dining table. My choice of a dominant color depends on the impression I want to express. Were the woods moist? Did the garden glow in the sunlight? Was the water icy cold?

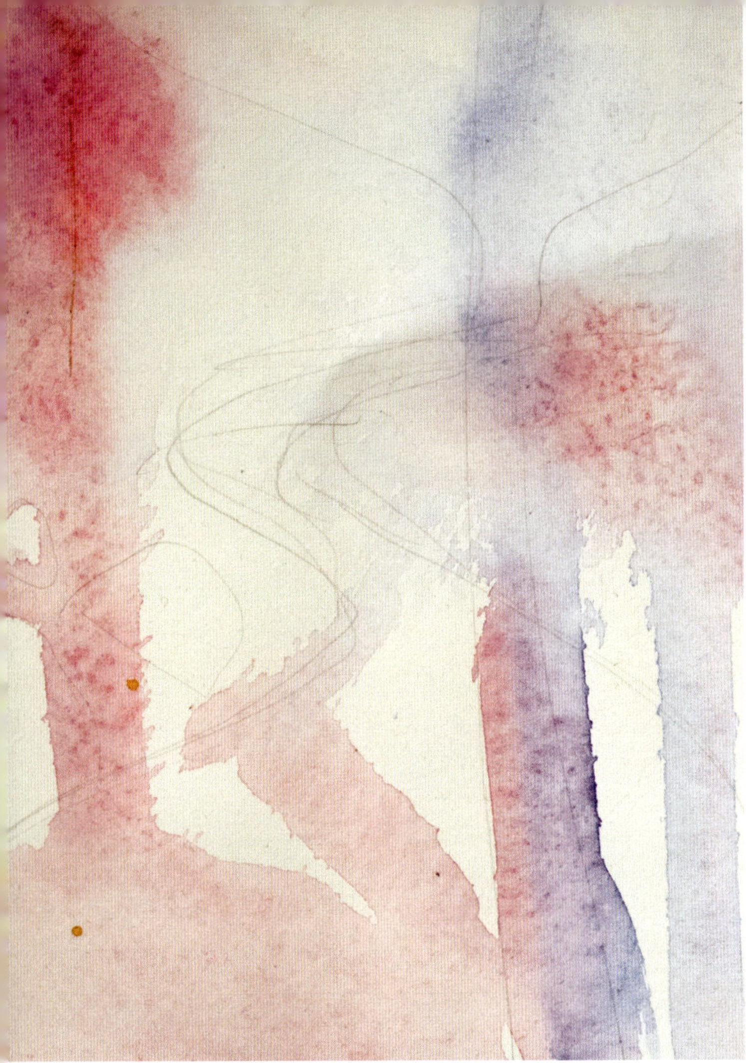

STEP 4. I do a watery first wash of the painting with a big wash brush, ghosting in the main shapes. I like the idea of light pinks shining among the darker trees.

Step 4. I tape the edges of a large piece of watercolor paper to a board and divide the paper into smaller squares and rectangles with tape. Working on several small paintings at once allows me to try out variations on my basic idea. With light pencil marks, I sketch the design.

Using a 2" (5 cm) flat brush, I paint the first wash of lightly tinted color to establish the size and placement of the major shapes. My earlier value sketch tells me where the whitest areas will be.

When the first wash has dried, I go back in and paint the tree. Leaving the road as bare, white paper, I stroke rich cobalt blues into the right foreground tree trunk with a #10 round brush. This tree is an important part of the design because it places the viewer just outside the scene by its position between us and the road. It also gives the road a bit of mystery.

Step 5. I use my big wash brush to paint the tree shadows across the road. The angled shadows were important to me during the early stages of sketching. They have become a critical part of the painting, offering a diagonal shape through the center, with flickering lights and darks to attract the eye.

Step 6. I lay in washes of transparent colors to create dark, rich tones. Placing pure colors beside and on top of one another makes the trees look denser and the dirt road more interesting. I use a thirsty brush technique (see pages 38 to 41) to lift damp color out from between the trees, and I smudge the surface to look like mist.

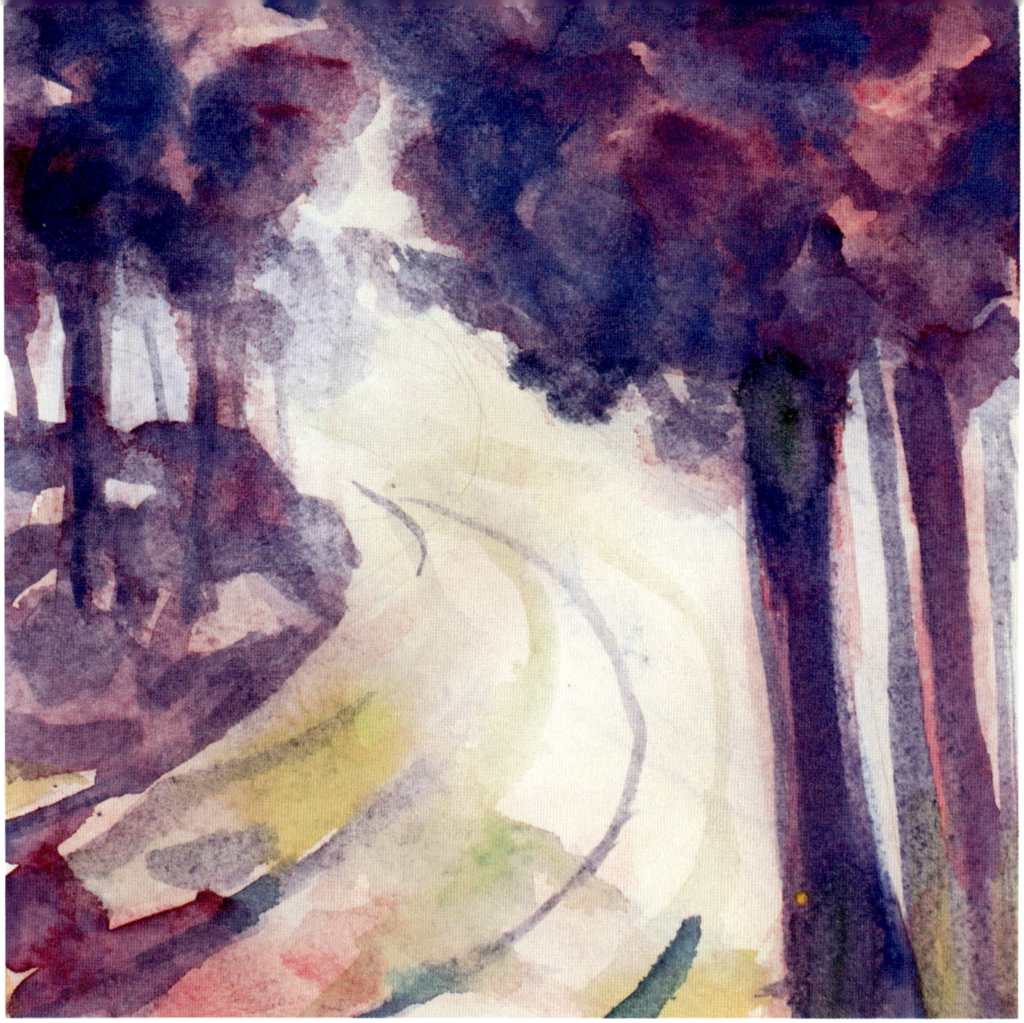

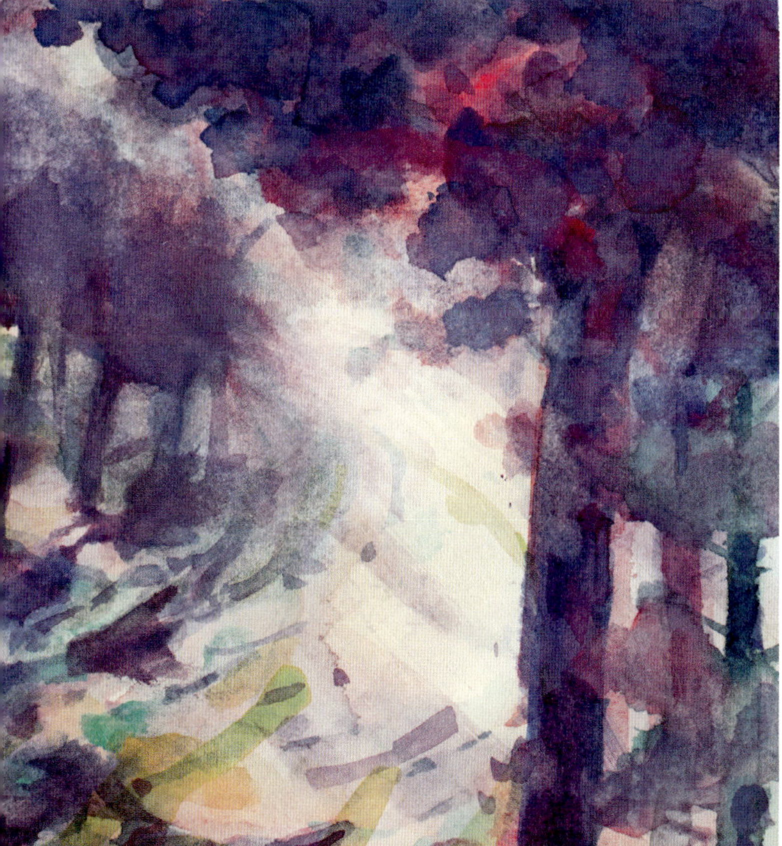

ABOVE:
STEP 5. I build up layers of color, allowing each to dry before applying the next. As I add color and detail, I work using larger to smaller brushes and painting larger to smaller areas.

LEFT:
STEP 6. I add layers of color to build up dark, rich tones. I use the thirsty brush technique to lift color out.

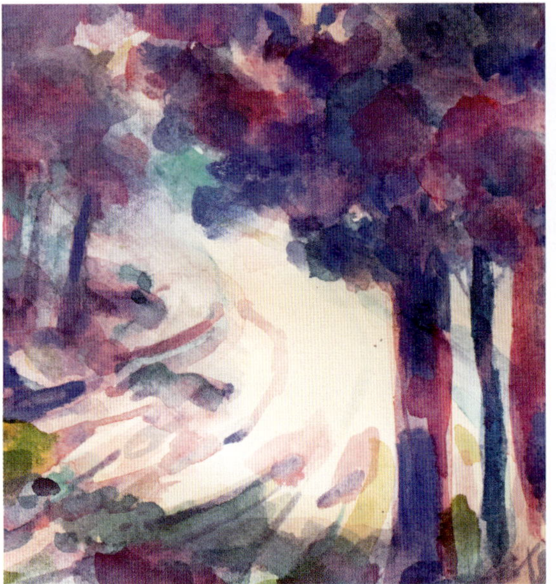

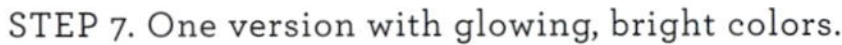

STEP 7. One version with glowing, bright colors.

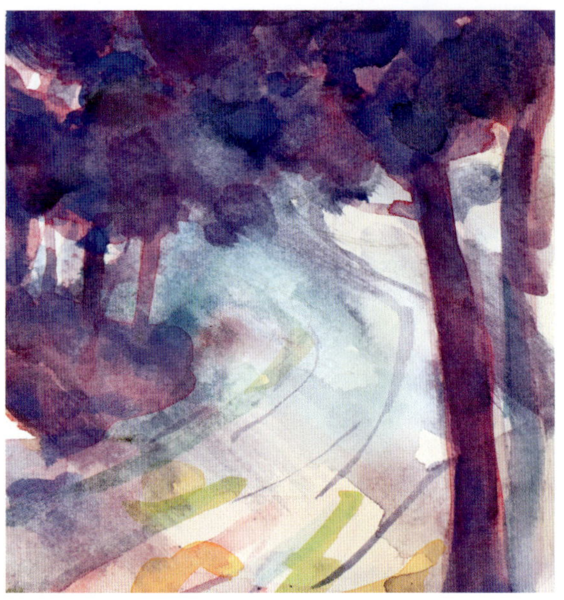

STEP 7. Another version stays soft and loose through the center.

Step 7. Now I explore variations on my idea by adding violets and saturated purples to one painting, creating a glowing, bounced-light effect that adds vibrancy to the woods. To another, I purposefully leave the center misty and mysterious. Finally, I add a range of cool blues and sweep pale greens across the dirt road. The shadows appear cool, wet, and heavy, and the light glows clear and fragile across the painting's center.

Step 8. After deciding which of the variations I like best, I can either complete my color work by adding the final contrasts and details, or put it aside and start fresh, knowing exactly where I'm going as I begin a larger exhibition painting. (Ultimately, I decide to finish up the cooler purple version by adding small, dark branches and smudging and softening the areas of light on the road.)

These important considerations require me to step outside the creative interior of my thoughts and plan this painting's future home. Do I want to exhibit it? Do I have the perfect place for it in my own home? Sometimes I'm so involved in the painting that I brush these thoughts away and plunge ahead. Ultimately, though, if you exhibit and expect to sell your work, these are practical concerns you'll need to think about. Creating an exhibition piece takes time, planning, and energy.

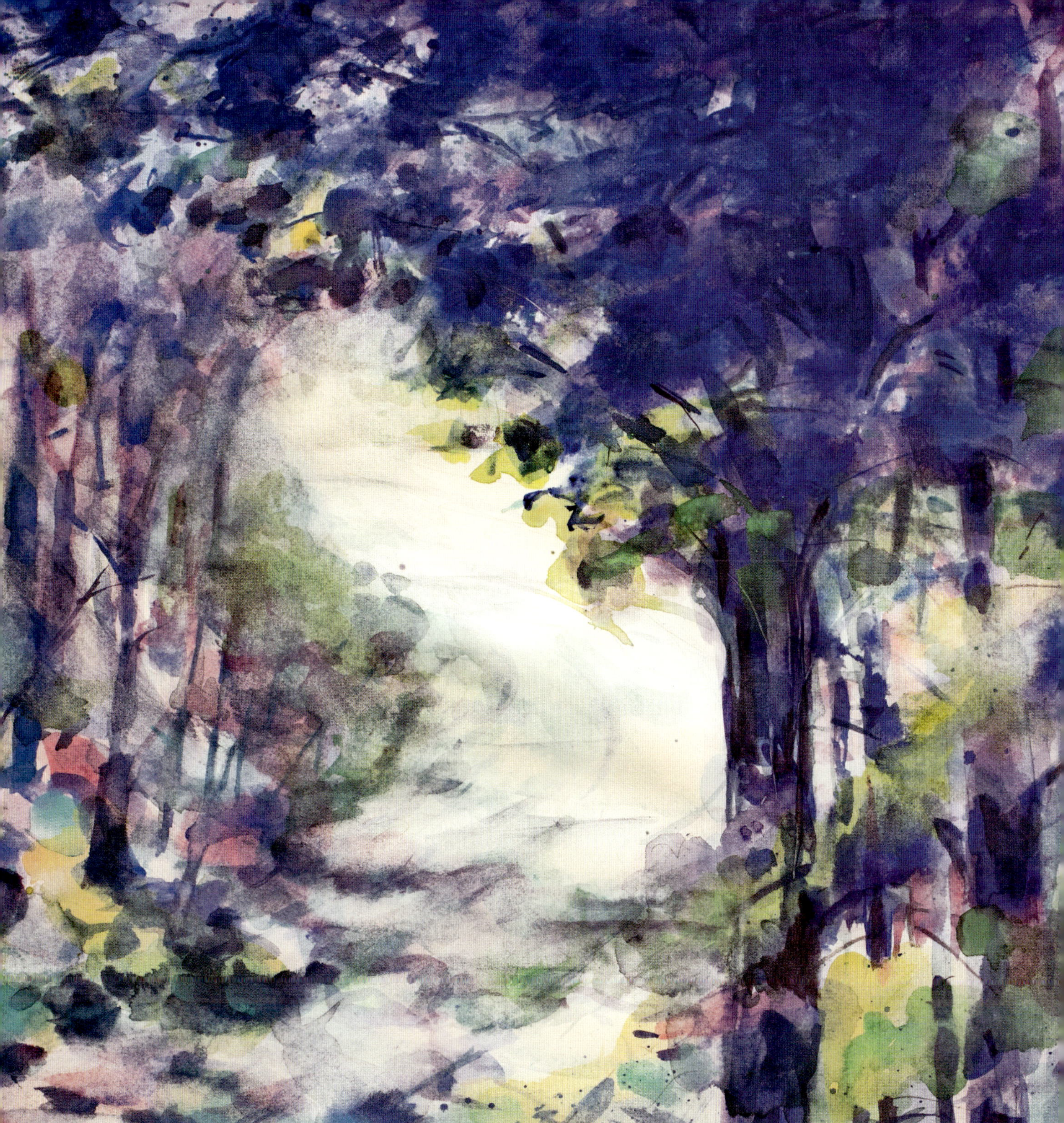

STEP 8. *Morning Woods*. Watercolor. 20" x 20" (51 x 51 cm). The finished painting successfully captures my impression of a cool summer morning, after I add final details.

Special Watercolor Technique: Lifting with a Thirsty Brush

How to Create the Look of Mist

The "thirsty brush" technique allows you to lift paint off of your watercolor painting. You might want to do this to create the effect of mist moving through woods, or perhaps an area of blinding sunlight in a garden.

Step 1. The most important tools for the thirsty brush technique are clean water and a clean brush. Choose a round medium size brush, such as a #8 or #10.

I'll demonstrate this technique on a view much like the watercolor I just completed, using a similar palette: cobalt and ultramarine blue, quinacridone red, cobalt violet, and dioxide purple. I tape sheets of watercolor paper onto a support board and set up my paper as a grid of four, so that I can test the technique several different ways.

These blues and reds I've chosen are staining pigments that will not lift completely from the paper. That's what I want. (If I wanted to lift them off completely, I would use lifting watercolor medium, which you can purchase at art supply stores or online. Alternatively, I'd start out with Yupo synthetic paper instead of Arches. Yupo does not absorb color and wipes cleanly back to white.)

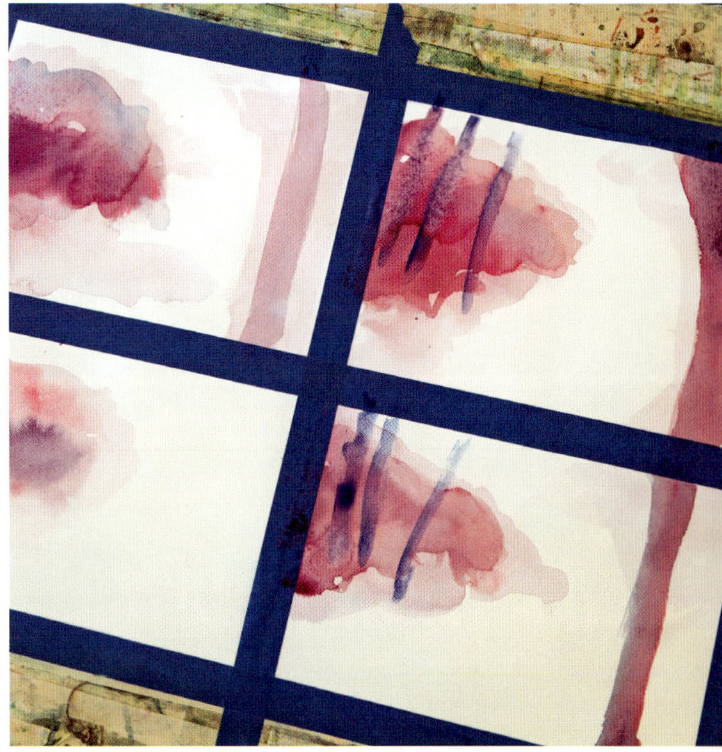

STEP 1. I divide my paper into a grid of four with tape so I can test this technique several different ways using blue, violet, and red staining pigments.

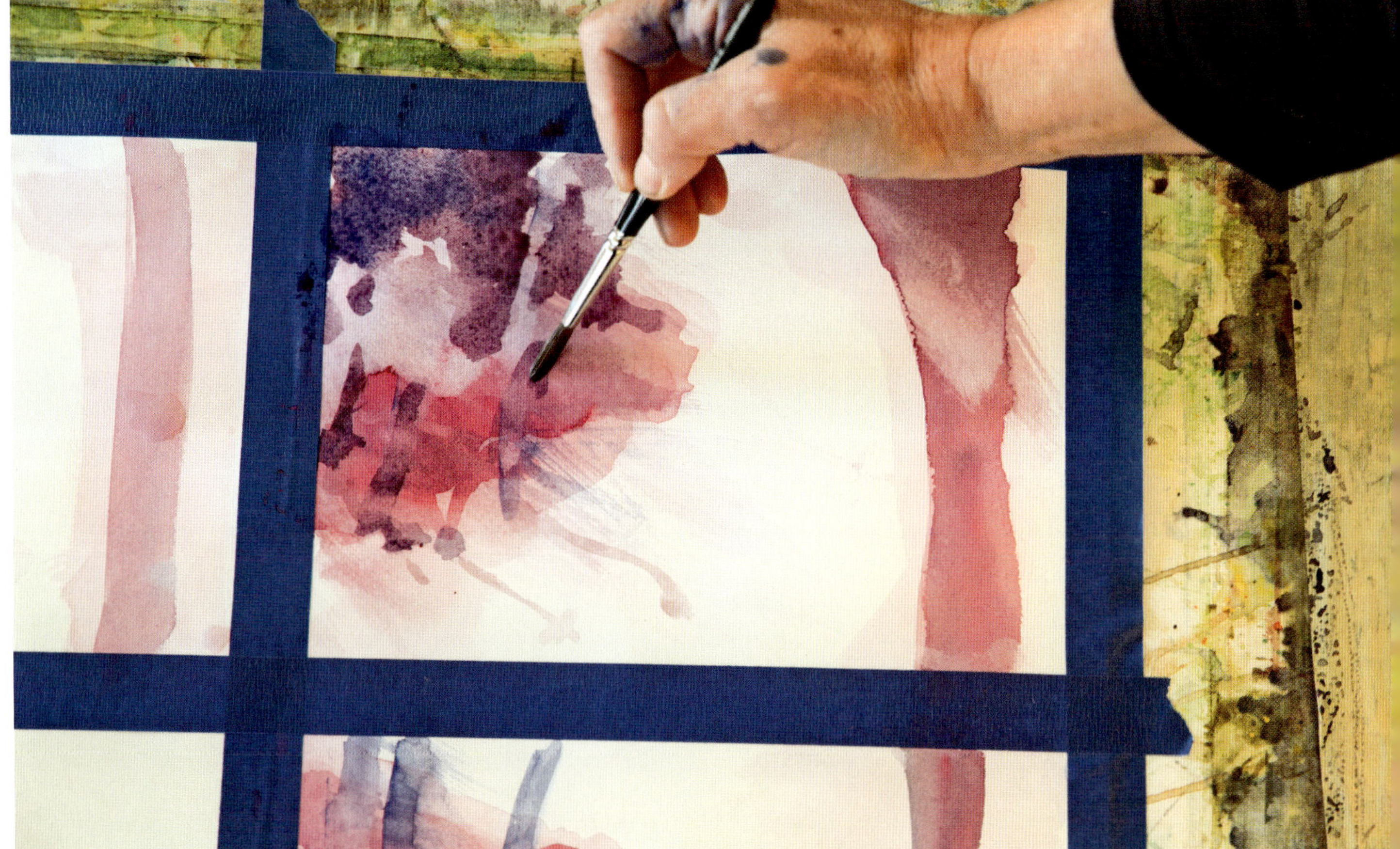

STEP 2. I drop color into clear, wet areas and then drag and spread colors with my brush.

Step 2. I make a thin puddle of clean water on the paper where I want to create the wooded area and the tall tree. I drop wet violet paint into the puddle and watch it spread. As it begins to dry, I drop in wet purple and let it spread on top of the violet.

This is where dividing the paper into grids comes into play. It takes practice to get the feeling of how wet the paint and paper should be to achieve the effects that you want in watercolor. One attempt may be too runny, another too uneven, a third just perfect. Approach the technique with an open mind and see what happens.

Step 3. As I get ready to use the thirsty brush technique, I want the paper to be just damp. You can judge how wet the paper is by gently laying the back of your hand on the paper surface. If the paper is cool against your hand, it's damp.

I stroke on the darker blue tree trunks. Now I want to lift off some of the color so it looks like mist is filtering through the woods.

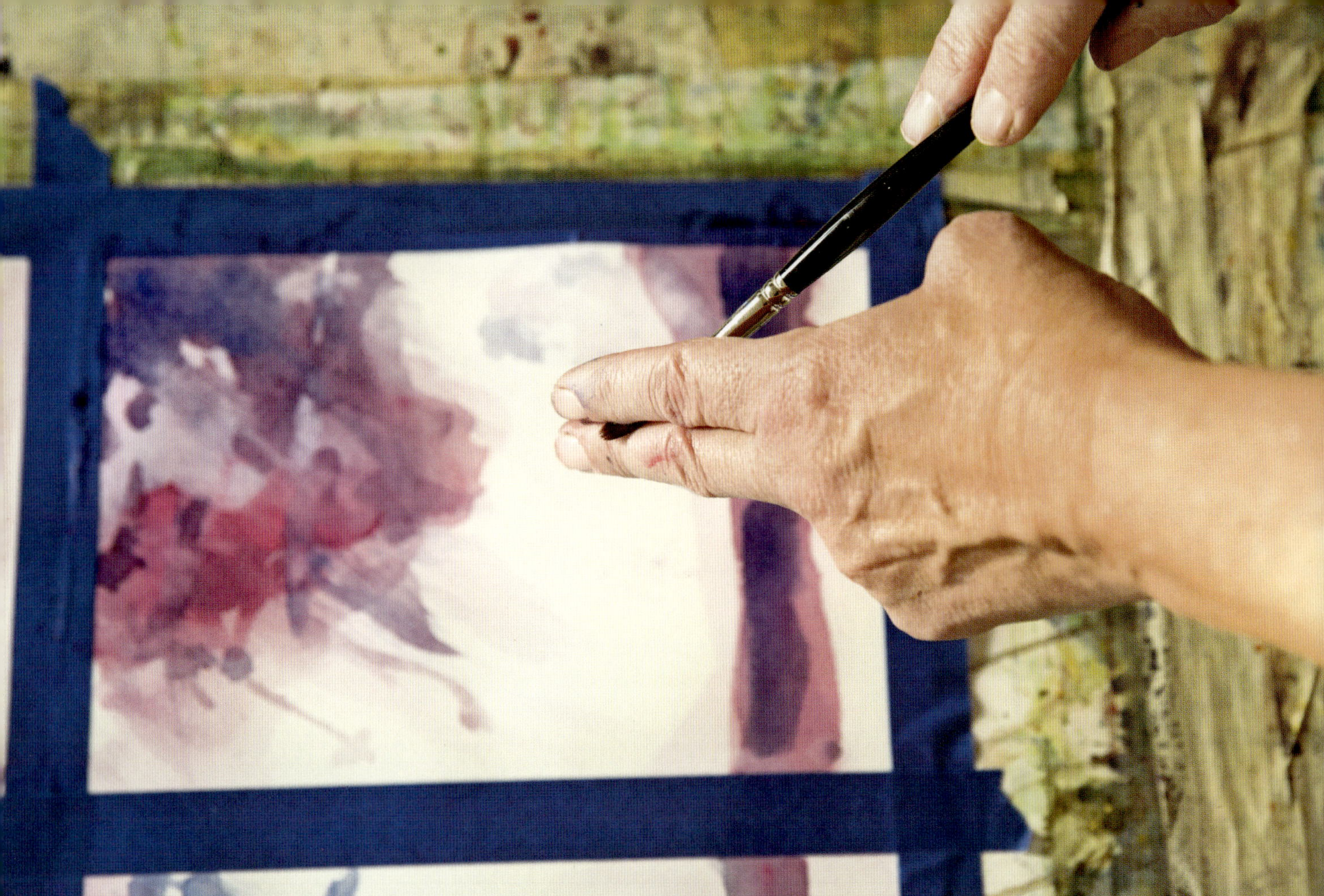

STEP 4. Squeeze the brush between your fingers to get rid of excess water. The brush is now "thirsty."

Step 4. While the tree trunks are still wet, I clean a brush with water, and then gently squeeze out the moisture by running the bristles between my fingers. The brush is now "thirsty." I can brush it across newly painted areas and it will lift up the wet paint. I can re-wet a dry area, let the paint color loosen for a moment or two, and use the thirsty brush to lift up the color. The trick is to wipe the lifted pigment off your thirsty brush between each stroke, otherwise you just smudge lifted paint back onto the painting.

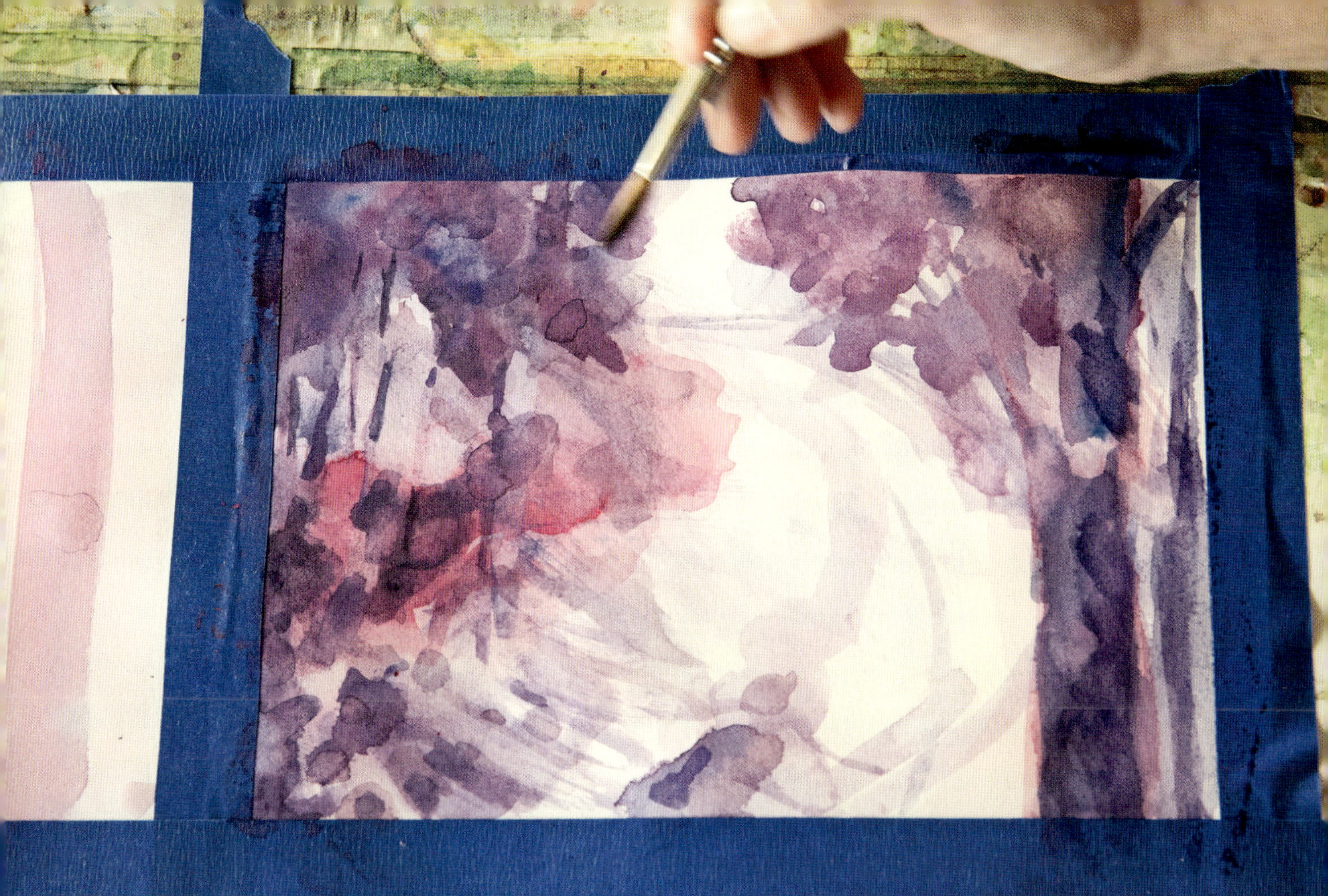

STEP 5. After lifting the wet color with the thirsty brush, I can go back and add details.

Step 5. Once the diffused color is dry and I've lifted the areas of pigment to create the impression I desire, I can go back and add darker details. To reinforce the feeling of mist, I keep the foreground richer in color, detail, and shadow.

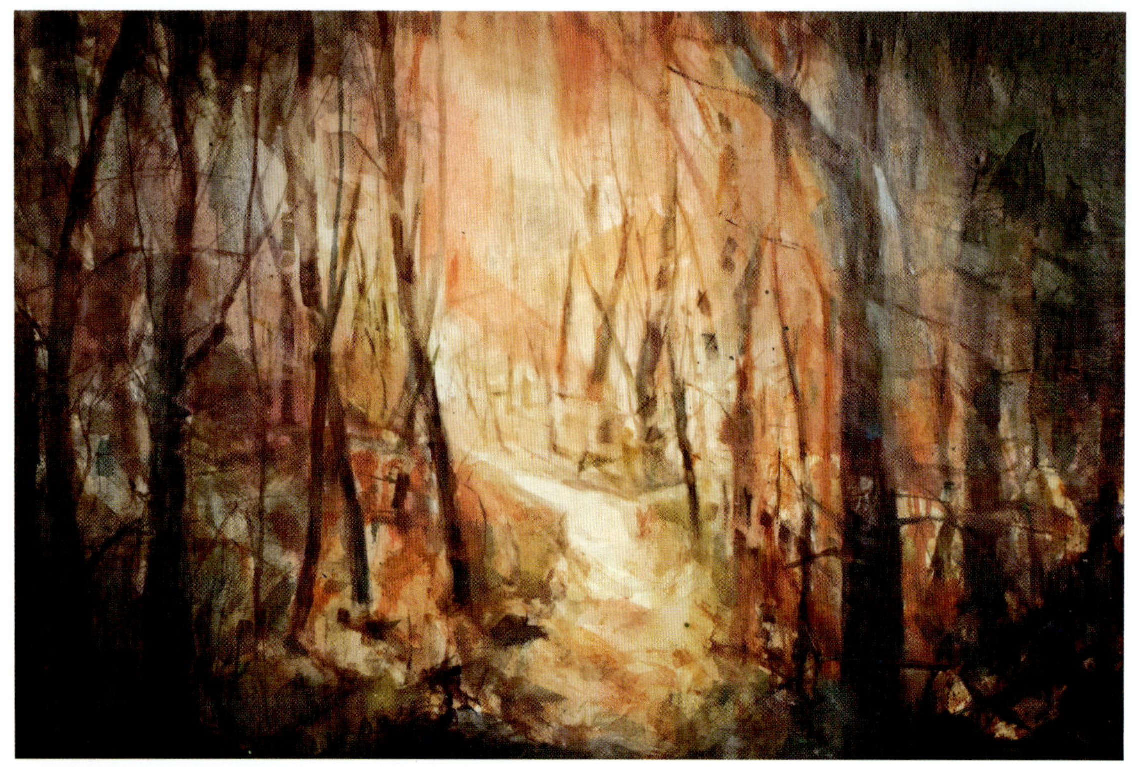

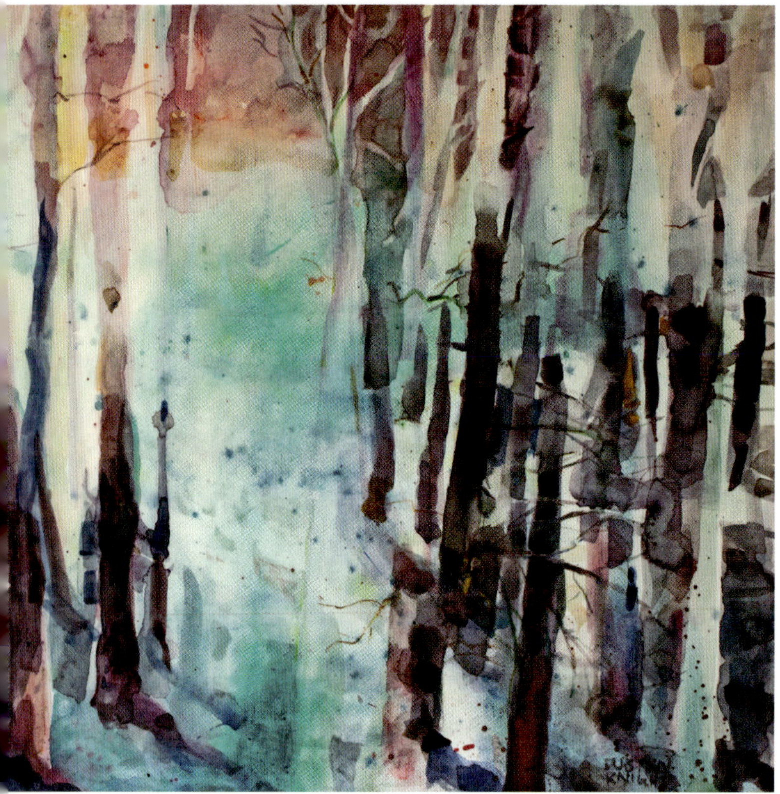

Gallery

I love painting watercolors of the woods—there are so many variations. Here are a few of my favorites.

ABOVE: *Early Spring Morning*. Watercolor. 20" x 30" (51 x 76 cm).

LEFT: *Snowy Woods*. Watercolor. 24" x 24" (61 x 61 cm).

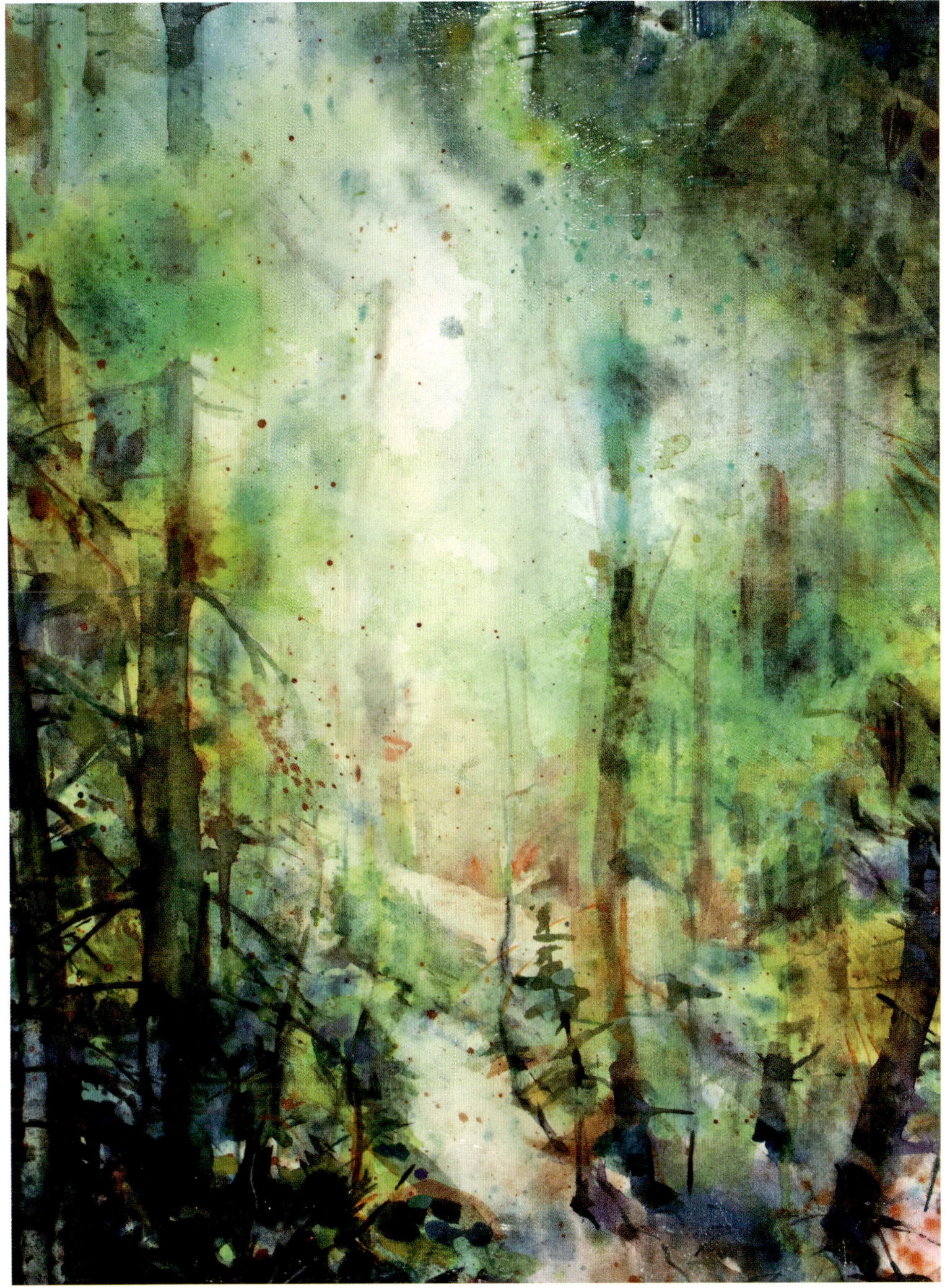

ABOVE: *Island Trail*. Watercolor. 40" x 30" (101.5 x 76 cm).

Demonstration: Painting the Woods in Acrylic

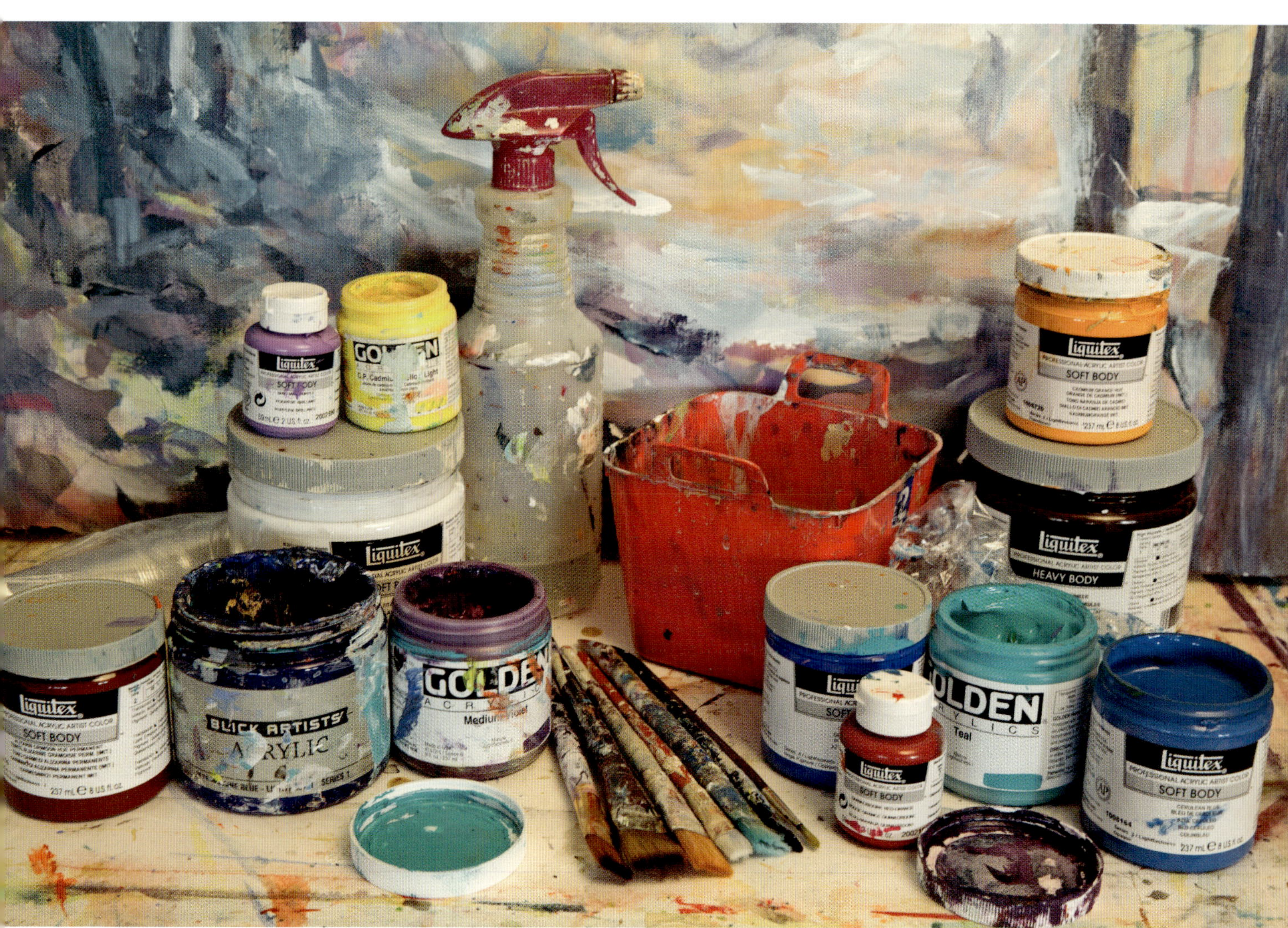

Switching from Watercolor to Acrylic

When an image looks great in watercolor, I often want to see what it will look like in acrylic on canvas. I enjoy working with acrylic. Compared to watercolor, acrylic is easygoing and lazy. The paint lands where you put it and stays there. It has great versatility, going smoothly from thin to thick and impasto. I remind myself that it dries quickly and is unmovable once it dries. When you paint with acrylic, be vigilant about keeping your brushes from drying and hardening.

My technique for using acrylic involves a physical building up of color in a process similar to the way the French Impressionists used their oil paints. Textural paint on canvas has a lot of visual weight, and can create a painting with more physical presence than a watercolor. The size of the canvas, too, of course, will contribute to its impact.

GETTING READY

For this painting, with the road disappearing into misty woods, I want the canvas large enough so that you can feel it pull you into the painting.

I make changes to my studio when I move from watercolor to acrylic. I clean and put away my sable brushes and take out my synthetic acrylic brushes. I round up my extra palettes and paper toweling and place my jars of paint within easy reach.

I like the colors I used in my misty woods watercolor and choose similar pigments: ultramarine and cobalt for some rich purply blues. Cerulean and phthalo (phthalocyanine) blue for some greener blues, though I want to keep this painting on the purple side. I have alizarin crimson, which is similar to quinacridone red, to mix a range of purples. I also have white, cadmium yellow light, and burnt umber, a deep, rich brown.

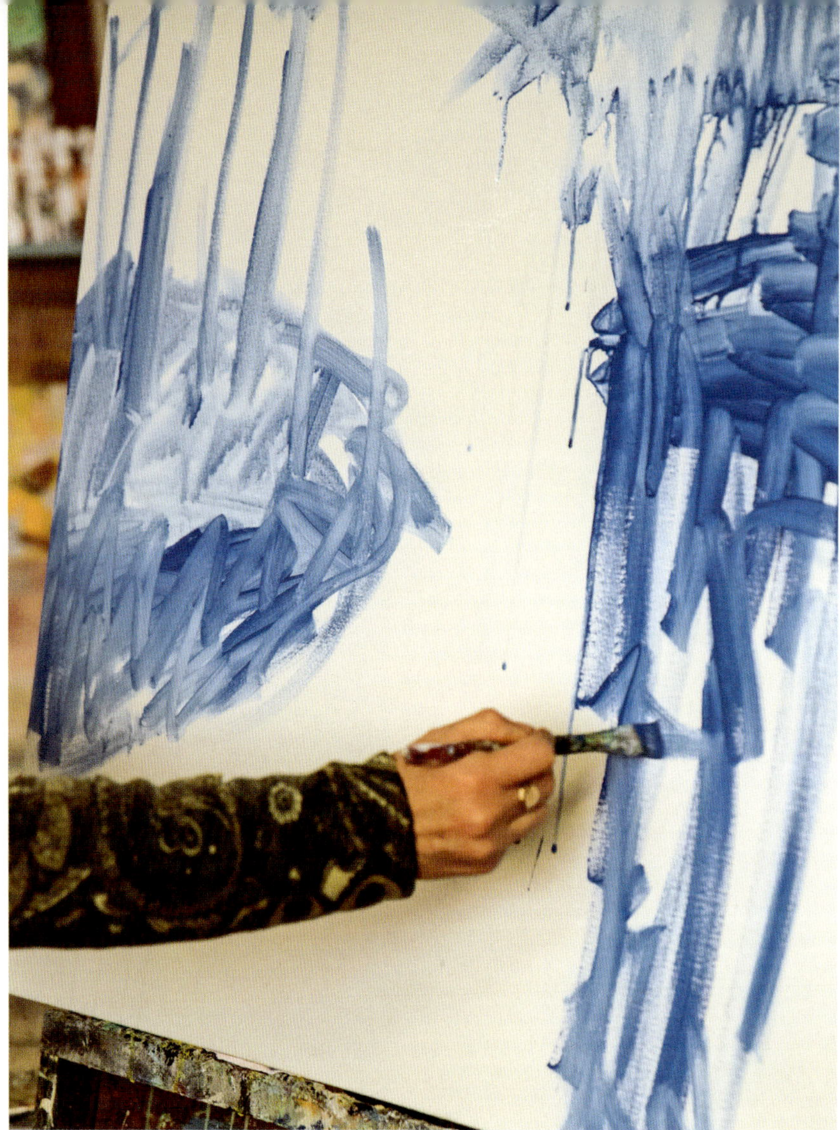

STEP 1: I use a bold blue to begin placing design elements.

In the Studio

Step 1. I start with a prepared canvas and begin much as I did with the watercolor, except that I do my sketching directly with paint, rather than starting with pencil. I use a single 1" (2.5 cm) flat brush or a #12 round, and a single color to rough in my dominant shapes and dark areas, leaving the curve of the road untouched for the moment.

With acrylic, I can work from darkest colors to the lightest, which is different than painting with watercolors. It's a more logical progression. I build up layers of color over the entire canvas. As the painting develops, I pause frequently, put the brush down, and reassess the painting.

Acrylic has great flexibility and I can easily make adjustments to the painting as I go along by just painting over areas I'm unhappy with. I want this painting to feel magical and misty, so I will keep the surface smooth and creamy.

Step 2. Once my loose, painted drawing is dry, I add more color to the trees and background. I can be pretty free at this point, experimenting with color. I look back at the sketches I did for the watercolor to get a feel for light versus dark comparisons and to see which color variations I like the most.

A loose, sketchy application of rich color adds to the impressionistic feeling.

I want to create the sense of light coming through the trees, the way it does in the morning when the mist is rising. I mix up some light pink and blend it into the canvas with my hand, almost as a color stain.

STEP 2: I add pink light coming through the trees.

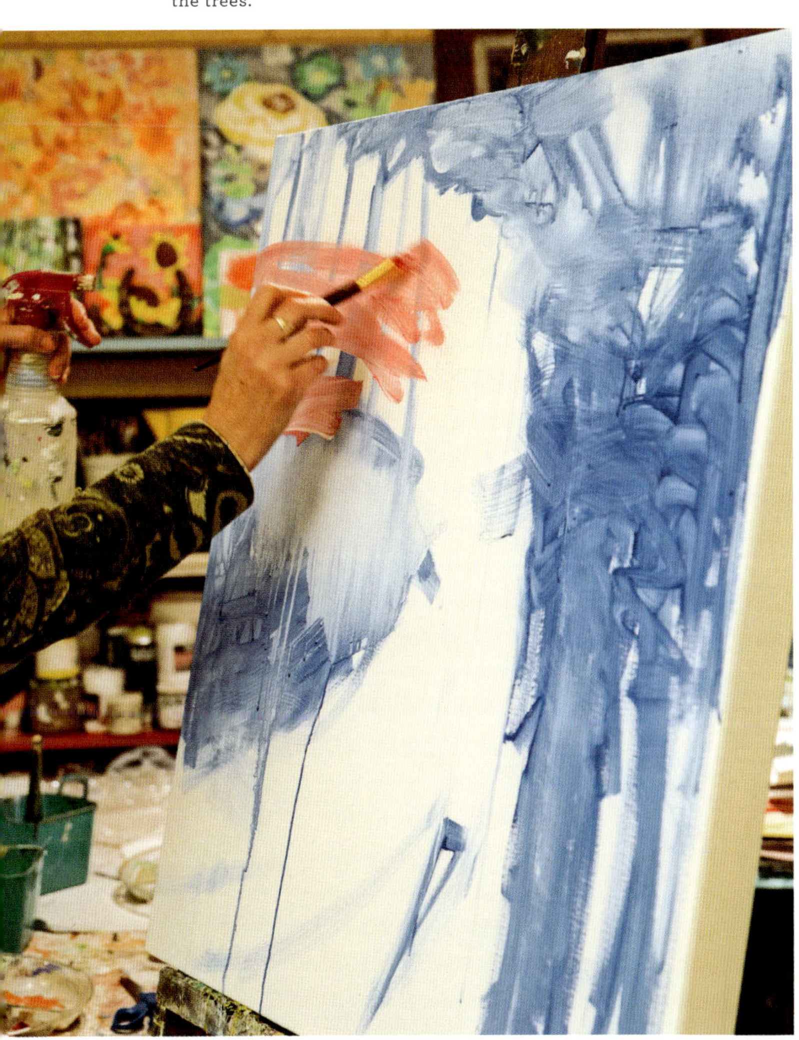

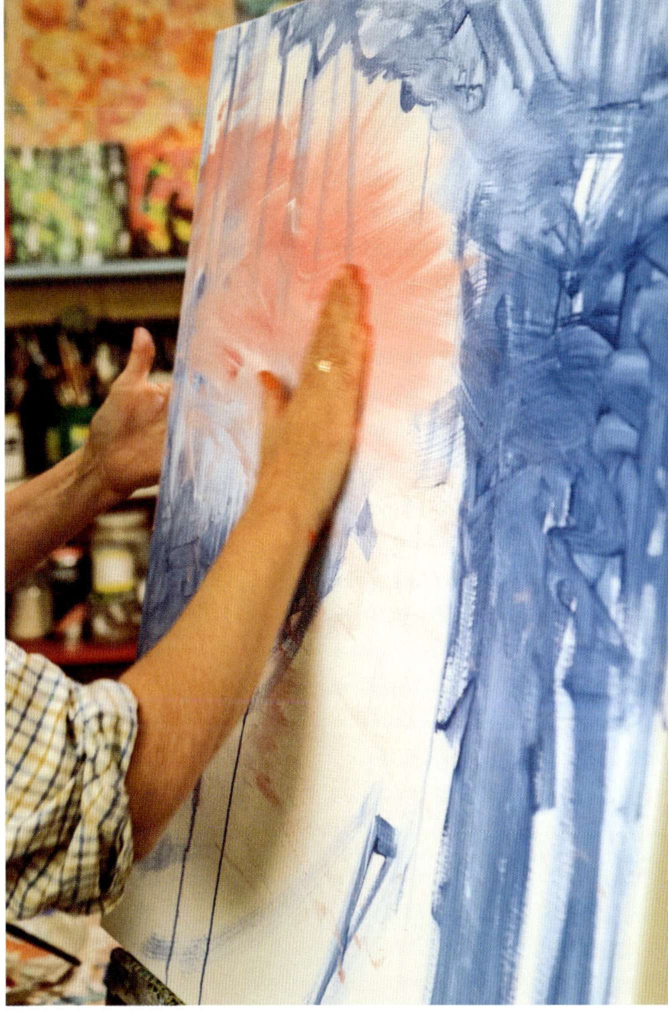

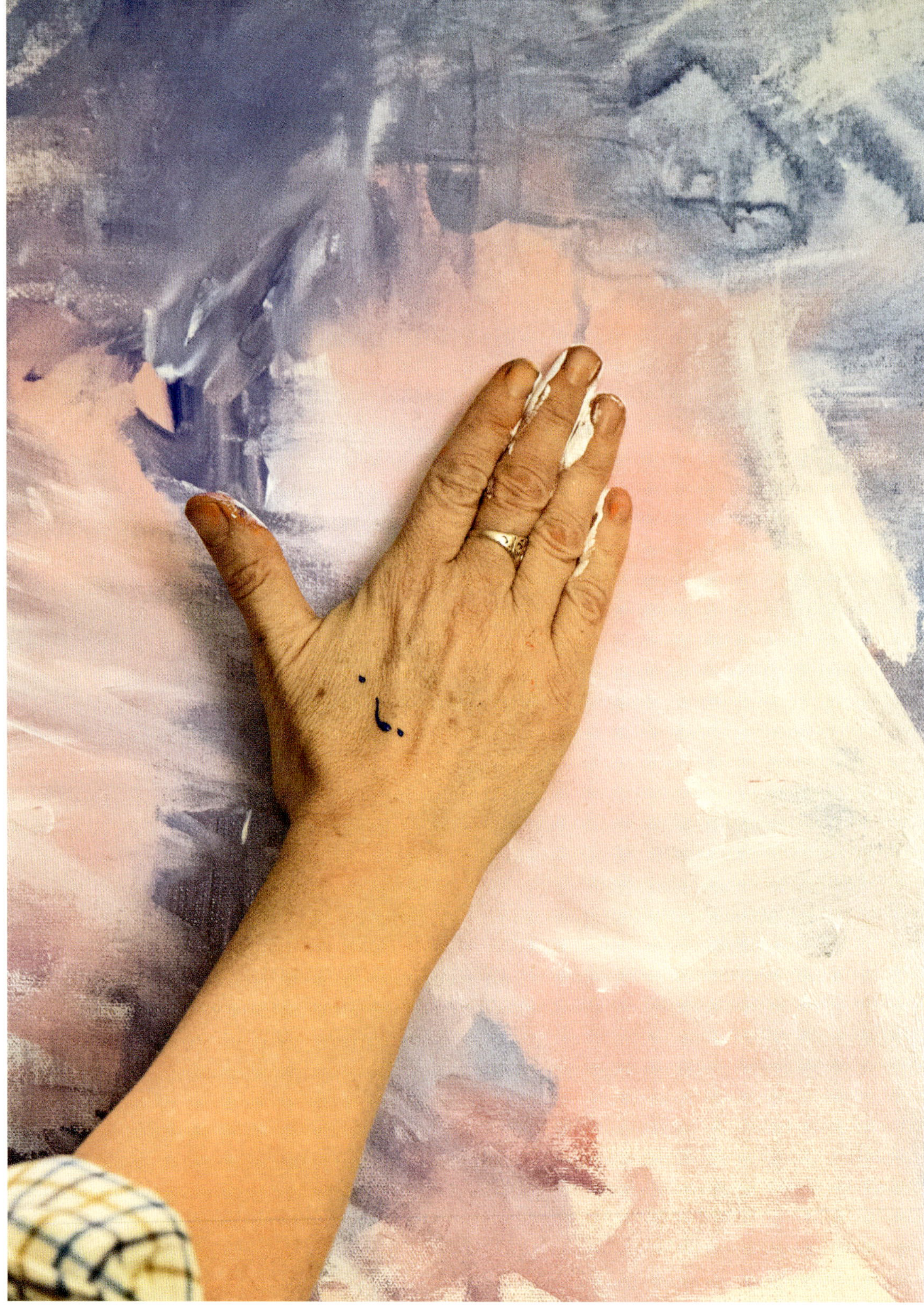

STEP 3. I use both my brush and my hands to blend paint into soft mist.

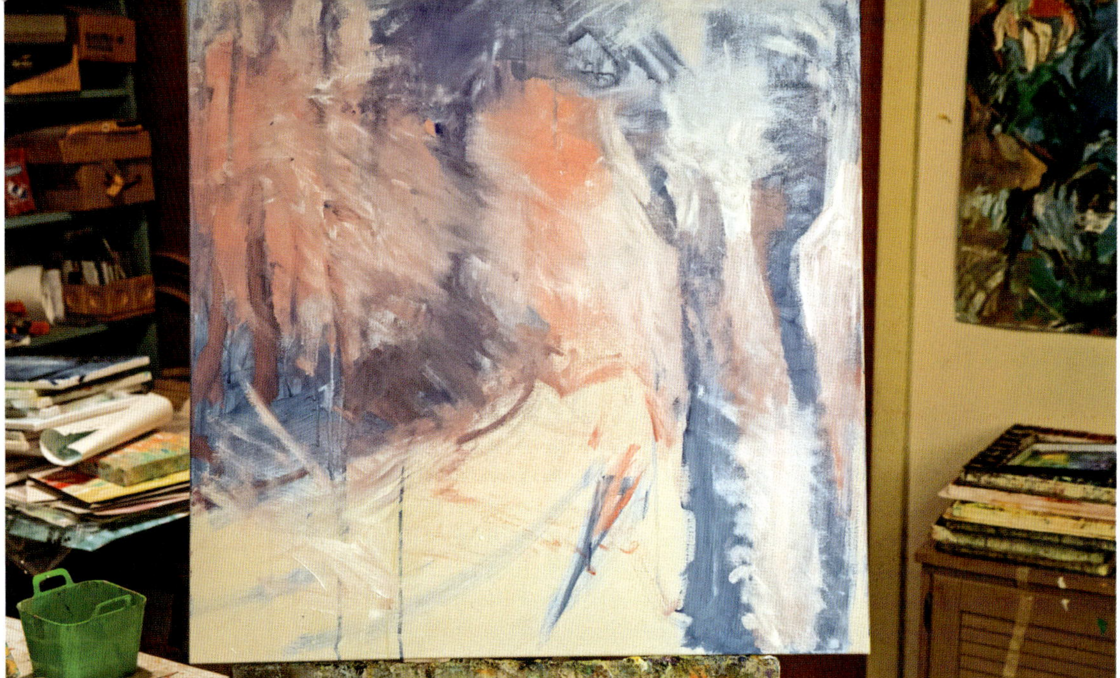

STEP 4. I step back to assess my painting. The white mist covers the entire painting and dims the foreground and the tree trunks to the right.

Step 3. And now the mist. Once the pink light has dried, I invite the mist to sift in from the left side of the image. I visualize it as being lighter in the far back of the space, darker and richer closer to the front. I add the white paint in layers, applying it first with a brush, and then blending it with my hand so that it becomes soft and wispy. The layers become whiter and more opaque as they cover each other. I remember clearly the caress of the damp sea fog against my face and how the moisture made the pages of my sketchbook stick together.

USING YOUR HANDS

Using my hand as a mark maker is a spontaneous pleasure. Artists have been using their fingers and coat sleeves to move paint around for ages. Oil paint has some unpleasant chemical attributes, which discourages this practice, but acrylic, being latex, washes easily off your hands with mild soap. Using my hands, I can cover large areas quickly with a thin coat of paint. I can give the paint the feeling of movement, and I can blend it smoothly into the canvas with no brushstrokes.

Step 4. Acrylic paint allows me to cover an area with mist and then pull out the tree trunk and then cover it again. I step back to look and I'm pleased with what is happening on the canvas. The mist gives the impression of moving and swirling the way it does when it blows in from the sea, blotting out a tree shape here and then thinning to reveal a branch over there. The purply blues create a feeling of mystery in the painting, but there is golden light coming through. Nothing is static. The composition is simple but it's alive.

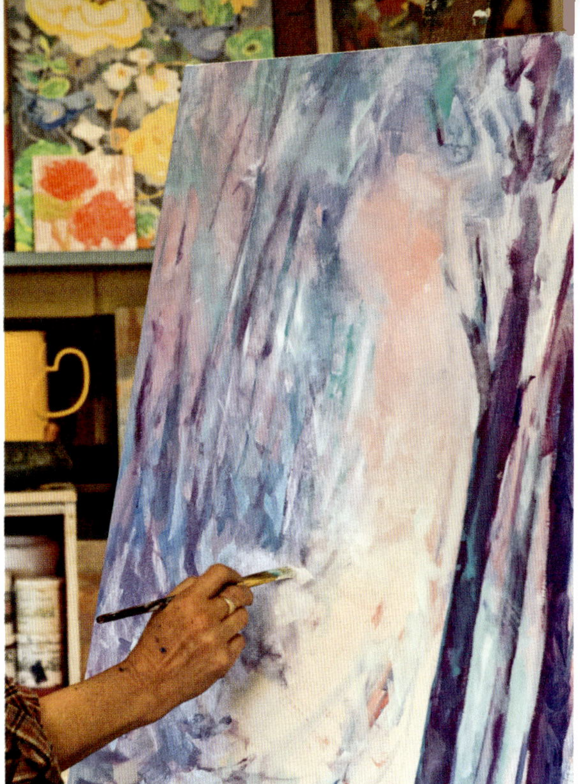

STEP 5. The mist recedes and the trees re-emerge as I add visual interest to the trunks and branches.

Step 5. I decide the trees need more detail in the bark, but wisps of mist can still streak across them. They will be darker and crisper the closer they are to the viewer. I build up the leaves of the front tree so that it appears three dimensional. To do that, I make the leaves in front the darkest, then lighter as the road curves away.

Step 6. The progression of this demonstration gives a clear idea of the wonderful flexibility of the acrylic medium. I love the way I can try different patterns of brushwork, vary lights and darks, and combine colors. All of these things are very helpful when I go to add dappled sunlight to the dirt road. As the painting progresses, I put down some pale cadmium yellows to add color to the white of the road. I decide to shift the light and lightly wisp on some darker cobalt blue and then move the light onto the shadow by layering on a delicate rose pink. I like that when I change my mind there are traces of the previous paint or brushwork visible. This works really well to suggest the filtering light.

The acrylic layers are softly brushed across each other so that I can see the layers underneath. I can try different colors and then lessen their intensity with the additional layers. The process allows me to create the feeling I get when I walk through the sun-dappled road—soft shifting bits of light and color falling around me.

Step 7. When I near the end of a painting, I love to sit in the chair in my studio and just look at it. I don't force anything I just sit and look. Often the painting will start "talking" to me and I will see areas that I need to adjust. When the painting settles down and has nothing more to say, it's finished. Allowing your painting to talk to you is an important part of the process.

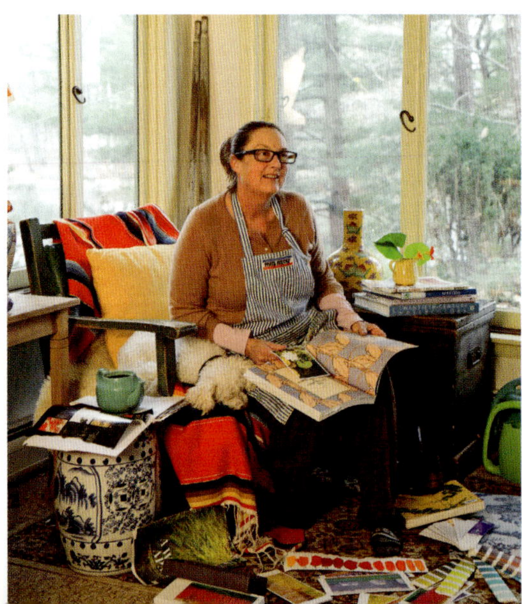

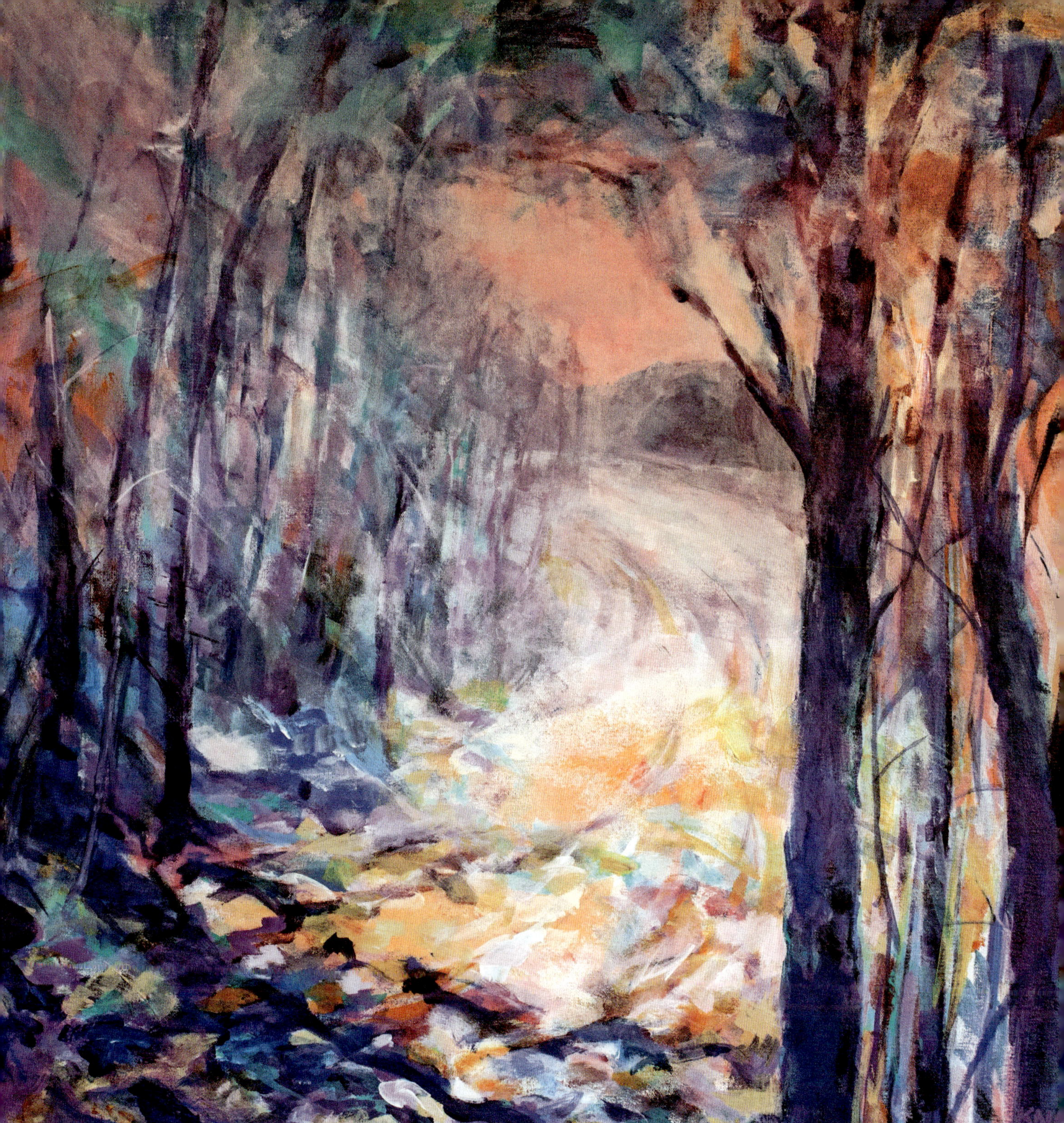

Woodland Road. Acrylic. 36" x 36" (91.5 x 91.5 cm).

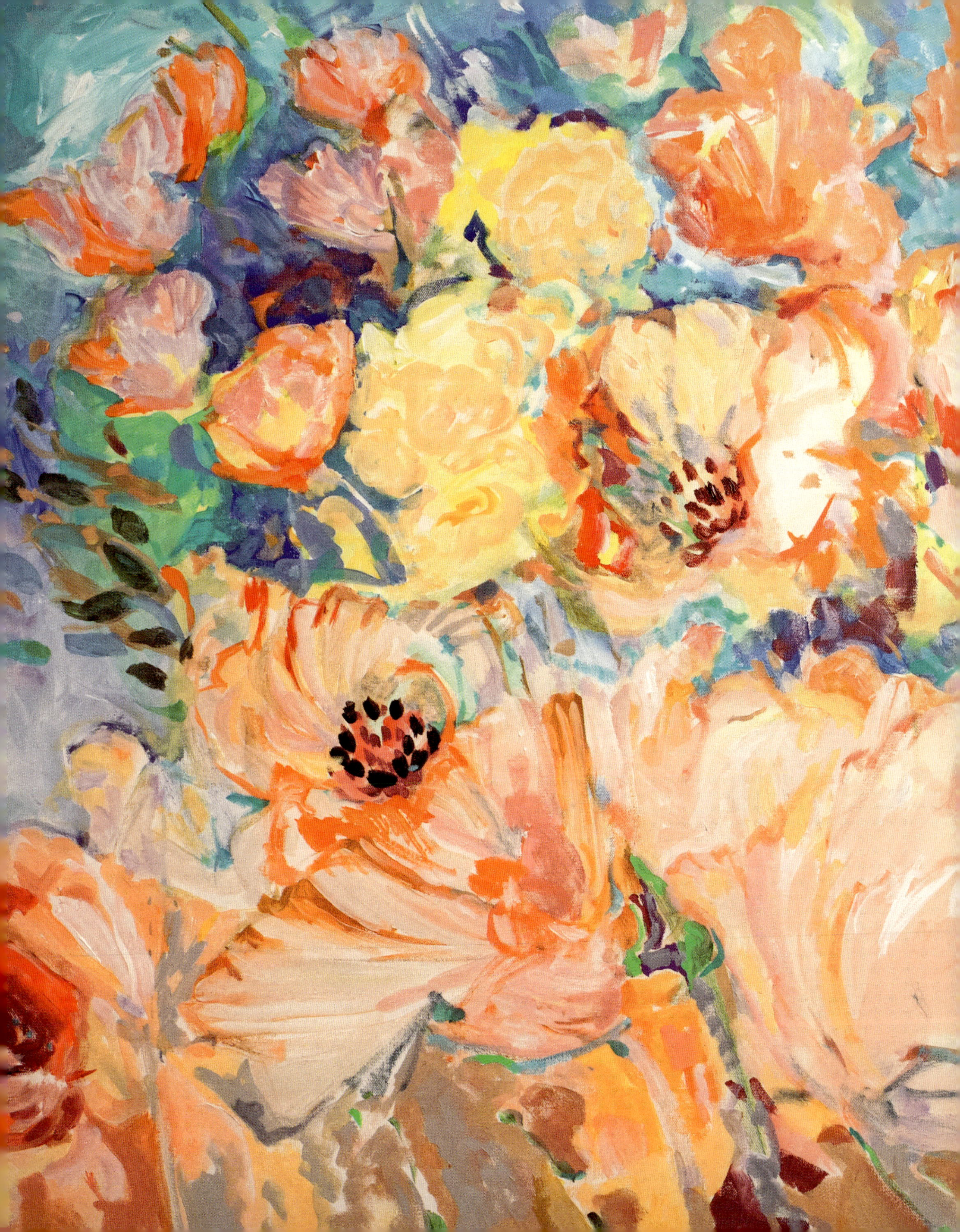

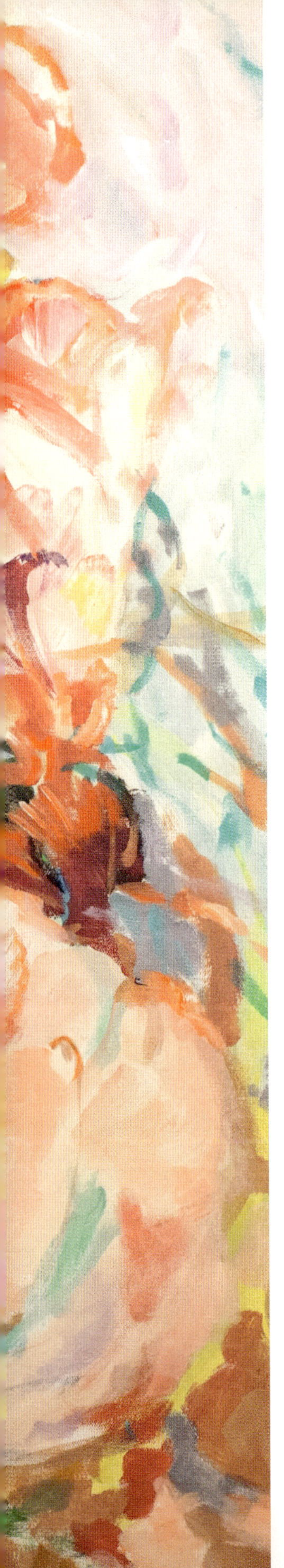

PAINTING FLOWERS FROM THE GARDEN

WHO DOESN'T LOVE FLOWERS? Despite my training in New York City art schools in the 1980s where the emphasis was decidedly not floral, I love to paint flowers. I love their color, their patterns, their structure, their textures, and their design potential. I love their variations of shapes, edge qualities, and their fleeting ever-changingness. It's reassuring to remind myself that flower painting is one of the great art traditions. The Impressionists share in that tradition.

While some artists consider flowers as unimportant and decorative, the Impressionists celebrated the very nature of flowers. Van Gogh, Monet, Pissarro, and Renoir painted fields of them—poppies, irises, dahlias, and sunflowers—as bright living color, nodding and bending under the sun. They painted orchards in bloom and single flowering sprigs. They brought armloads of flowers indoors, piled them in vases—irises, lilacs, roses, and tulips—and painted portraits of them, over and over again.

The Impressionists didn't assign symbolic meanings to flowers. They didn't try to make their paintings scientifically correct. They painted their impressions, capturing the fragility, the color, the crooked stems, and fading leaves of flowers. In doing so, they somehow caught the essence and even the scent of flowers and made them real. The public has never gotten tired of looking at Impressionist flower paintings. For many, in fact, flowers are the first thing that comes to mind when the word "Impressionism" is mentioned.

Dancing Garden. Acrylic. 36" x 36" (91.5 x 91.5 cm).

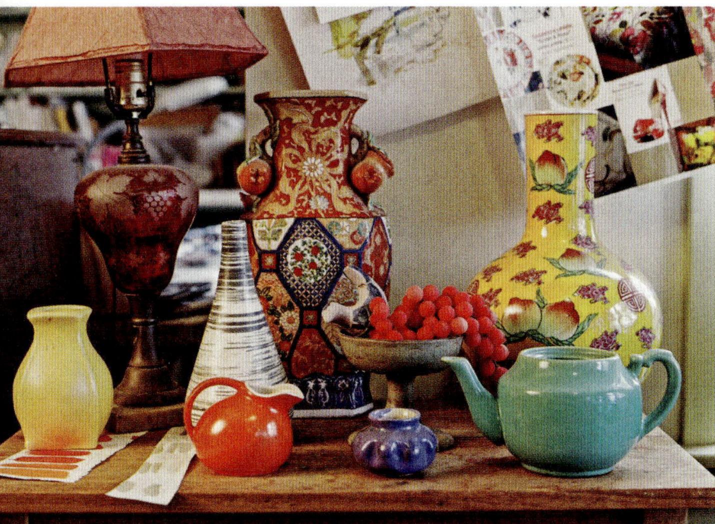

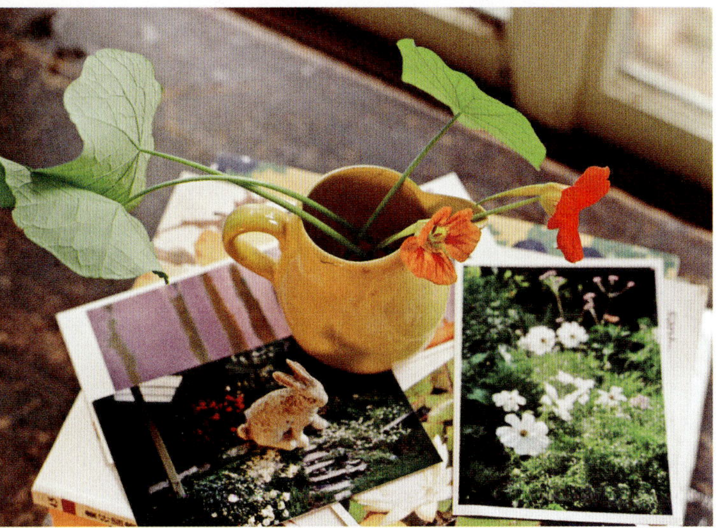

ABOVE: Floral inspiration in the studio

BELOW: Nasturtiums from my garden in my favorite yellow pitcher

My inspiration for painting flowers is all around me in the studio, on vintage fabrics, on postcards, on porcelain vases, and old tea cups. But of course my greatest inspiration is my own garden. It makes me glad when I read how Monet was intimately involved in every detail of his garden. I share his passion.

My garden is a lot like my paintings. It's wild and tangled and creeps stealthily across the bit of what's left of my lawn. Nasturtiums are a particular favorite because they have such a desire to grow, and their stems are so interesting and unexpected.

As a gardener, I continually edit. I move things if they look unhappy, I pull things out if I don't like them, and I add a new plant when a friend gives me one or I happen by a garden store. This is exactly the way I paint, always in flux. Always changing.

Every flower has its own character and personality. Some are refined with excellent posture like the iris with its ruffled evening-wear edges. Some, like daisies are casual and exude a feeling of confidence. Nasturtiums are more like teenagers—unpredictable in their size and growth direction. My whimsical interpretations of flowers make painting them more fun. I like the idea of capturing the essence of flowers—what I love about them when I see them blooming. Perhaps it's their color, or the way they nod in the breeze that attracts me.

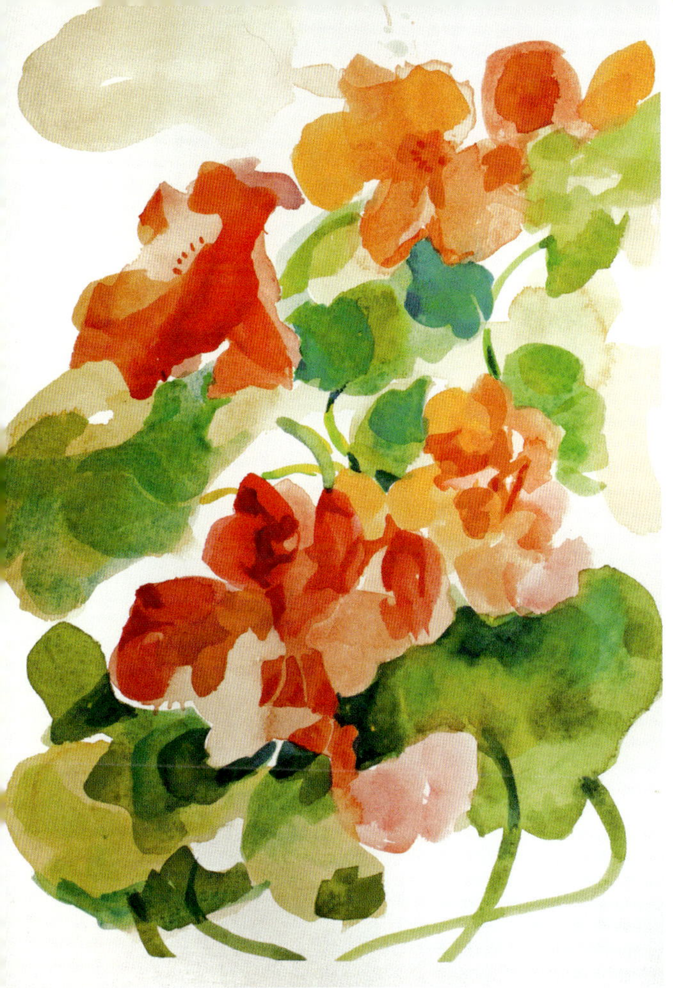

Nasturtium Impression. Watercolor. 14" x 10" (35.5 x 25.5 cm).

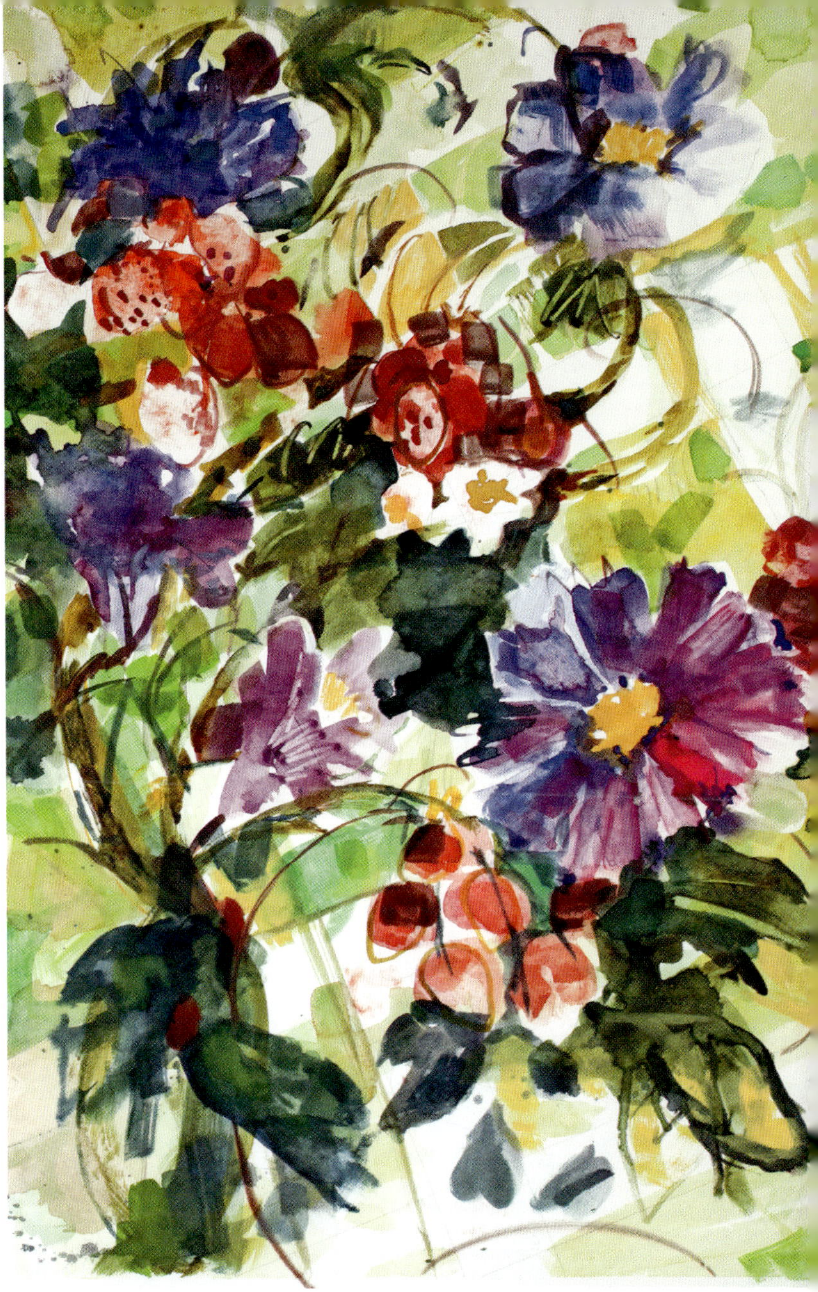

On the Trellis. Watercolor. 22" x 10" (56 x 25.5 cm).

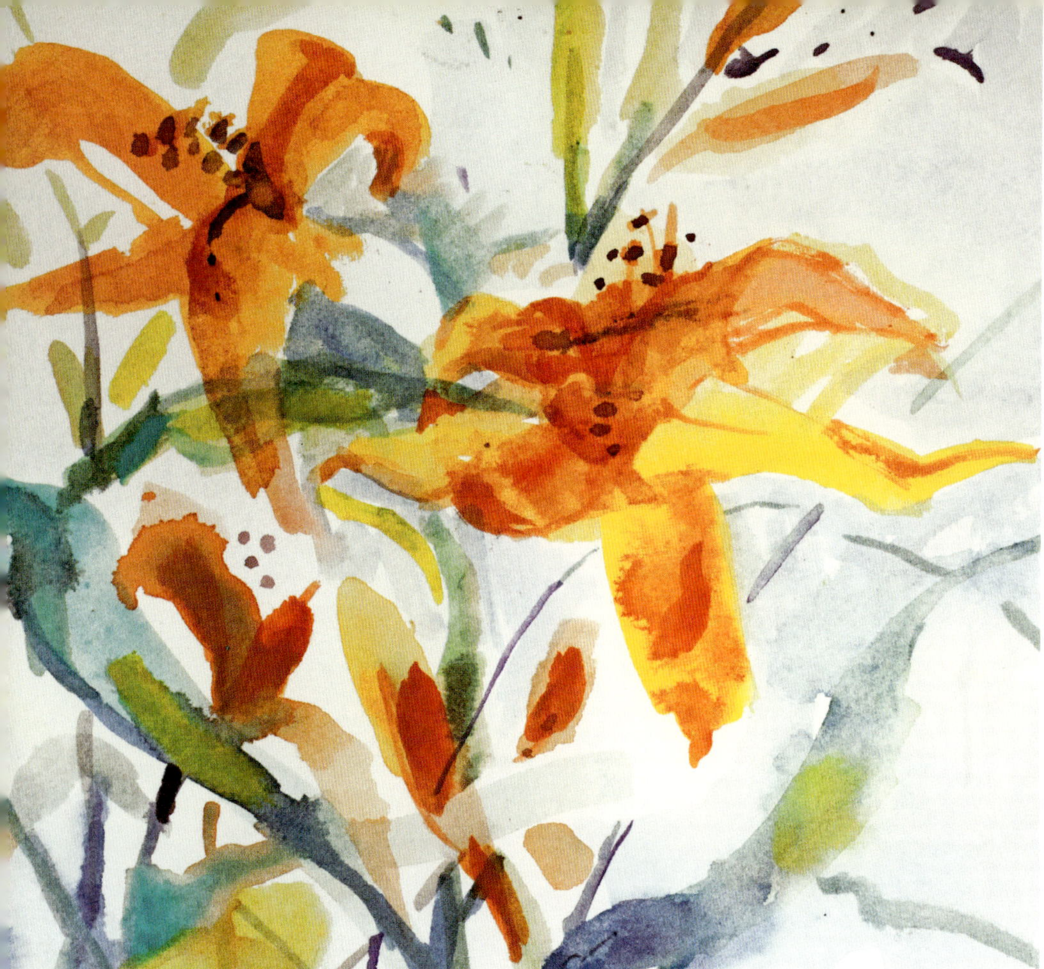

ABOVE: *Day Lilies*. Watercolor. 12" x 10" (30.5 x 25.5 cm).
OPPOSITE: *Joyful Garden*. Watercolor. 30" x 20" (76 x 51 cm).

I think of flowers as falling into three basic shapes: the circle, the cup, and the clump. The circle silhouette can be dynamically shaped with deep cuts and irregular edges like the field daisy and sunflower, or folded in on itself like a rose. The cup silhouette is the tulip, magnolia, and lily, with a smooth bottom and an articulated top edge. The clump is the lilac, the hydrangea, the goldenrod, or lavender.

Simplifying the flower shapes in my mind prevents me from being sucked into a botanical daze when I go to paint them. It allows me to focus on creating a design with the flowers in a painting, rather than focusing on their details.

Foliage is another wonderful design element. I try to use foliage that is a different shape than the blossom and I try to use it repetitively so the flower stands out, just as it does in my garden.

Along with design, good color is the foundation to a great flower painting. I use colors to share my emotional impressions. To create excitement, I surround hotter reds and yellow with cooler, darker greens and blues. Sometimes I choose a quieter, softer feeling using a dominant color like golden yellow or pale blue and the whole picture glows.

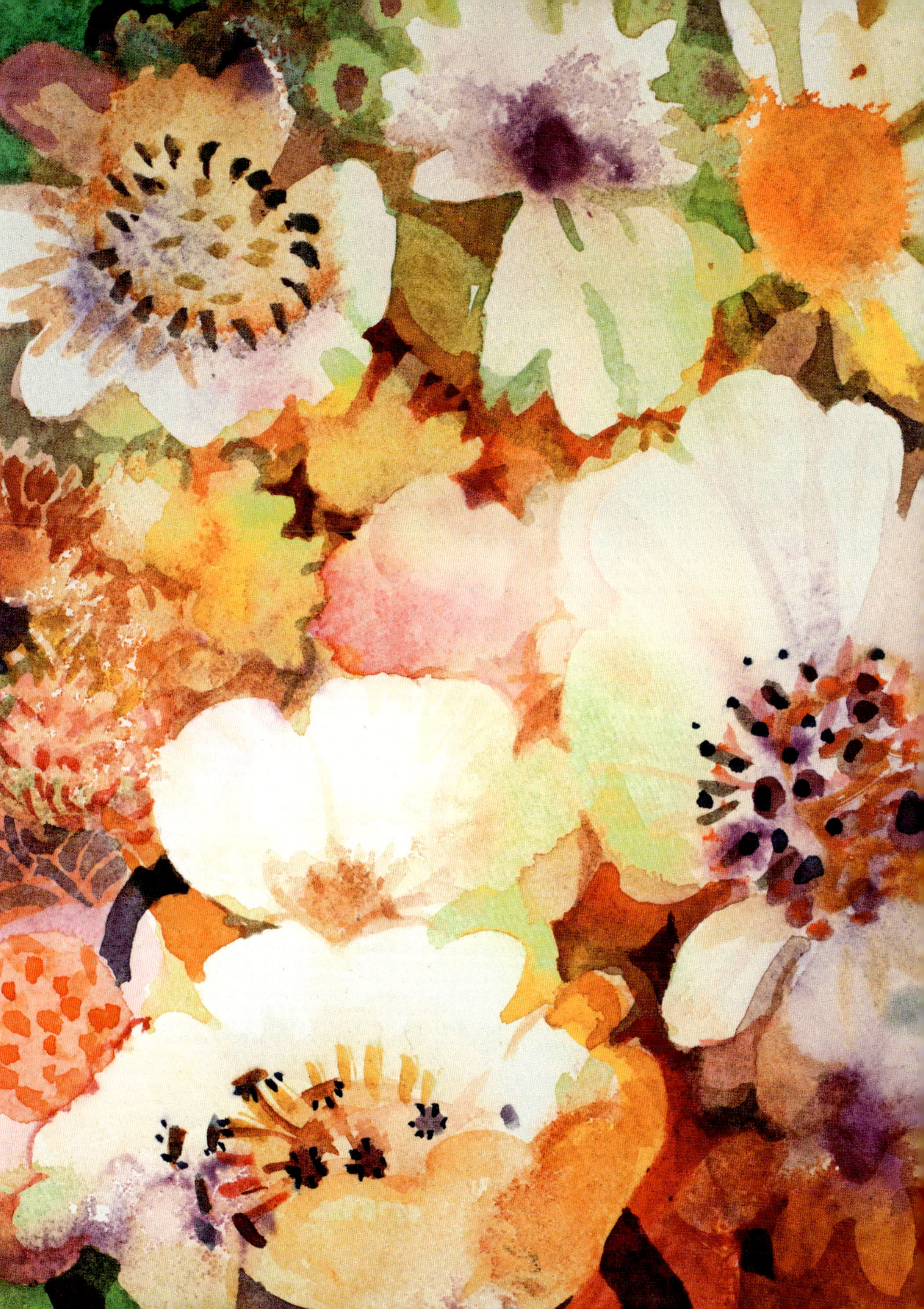

Demonstration: Painting Flowers in Watercolor

The Approach

My garden calls to me and I choose it as my subject location throughout the spring, summer, and fall. It's the color and shape of my flowers that I like the best. I like to watch the garden change throughout the day as the light shifts, affecting the flowers and foliage. I pick the time of day when the color shows best.

PHOTOGRAPHY

Step 1. The moments when I usually feel that rush of excitement and go searching for my camera are when the morning sun is coming at an angle across the foliage and blossoms. Sunny mid-mornings are a fabulous time to be in the garden. The blossoms are opening wider. There may still be dew in the crook of a leaf. Often the shadows act as dark cool backgrounds and make the blossoms appear to jump out.

I like it when there is enough sun to highlight the colors without bleaching them or tinting them yellow. For New Hampshire, it's mid morning. I try to record the light changes with my camera.

My first challenge in approaching a flower is to determine exactly what I like about it and its foliage. This seems obvious, but I don't know how many times I've gotten three-quarters of the way through a painting and then realized I was really only interested in one small part. With the nasturtiums I am interested in the big circular leaves, the thin turning stems, and the intensity of the color of the blooms.

STARTING TO PENCIL SKETCH

Step 2. I bring my trusty outdoor sketchbook with the big spiral binding into the garden and pull up close to the nasturtiums spilling from a planter. I have my graphite pencil and eraser ready. This is a non-pressure, intimate, getting-to-know the plants time. I admire their leaves and stems. I marvel at their color and the tiny veins on their petals. I notice the interplay of leaf shadows, one on top of another.

I draw blind contour sketches. I put my pencil point on the paper and as my eyes follow the length of the stem, my pencil point traces it automatically on the paper. I'm falling in love with their delicate strength and vitality.

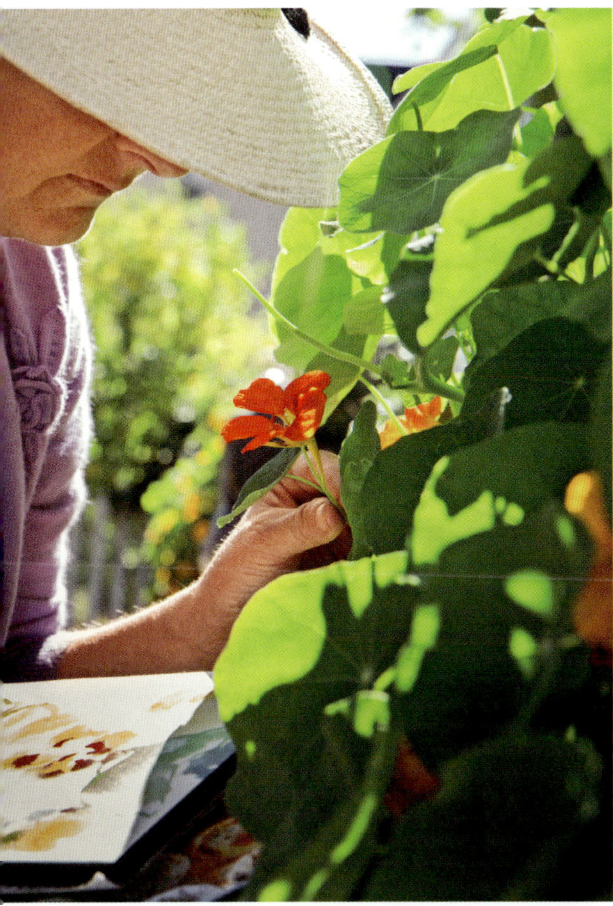

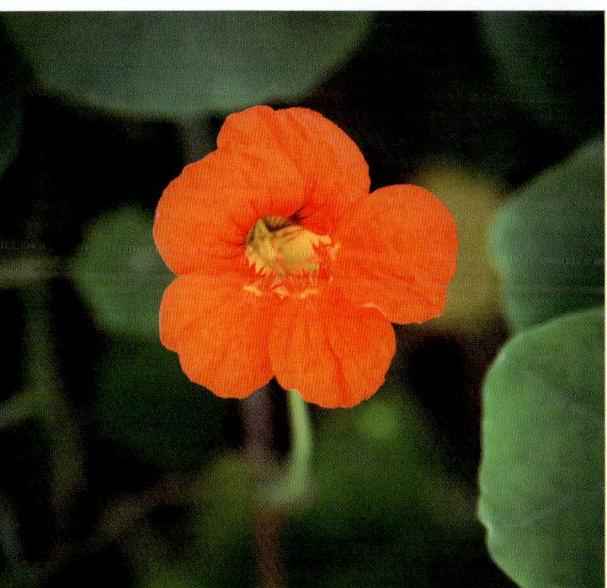

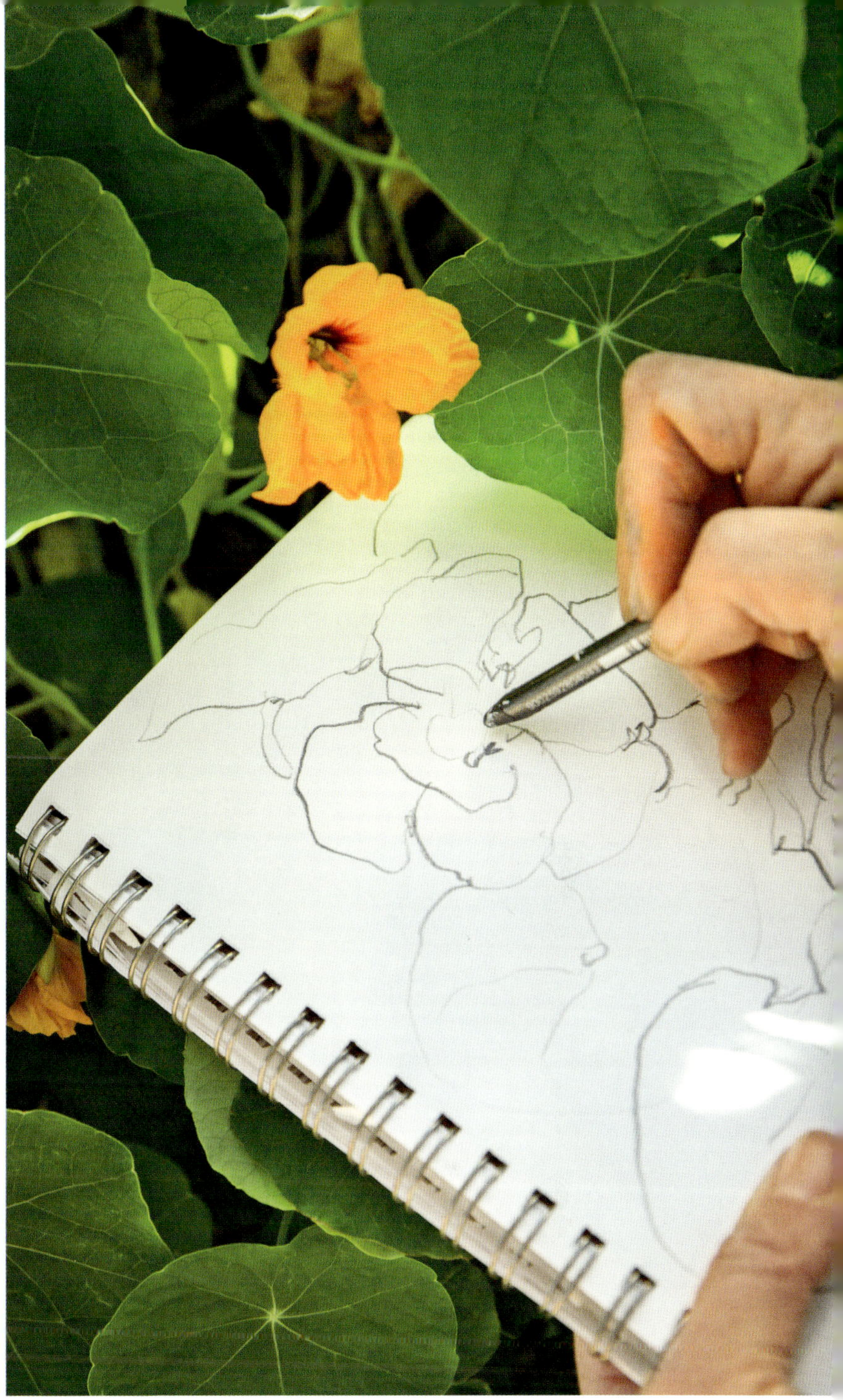

ABOVE LEFT: I'm definitely an amateur gardener. My garden is a tangle, often more foliage than flowers, but I kind of like that. For me, finding the bright spots of color tucked into the abundant green just calls attention to how important each part of the garden is.

BELOW LEFT: I like flowers, such as these nasturtiums, with intense color and interesting silhouettes.

ABOVE: Sketching allows me to really enjoy looking at the beauty of a flower.

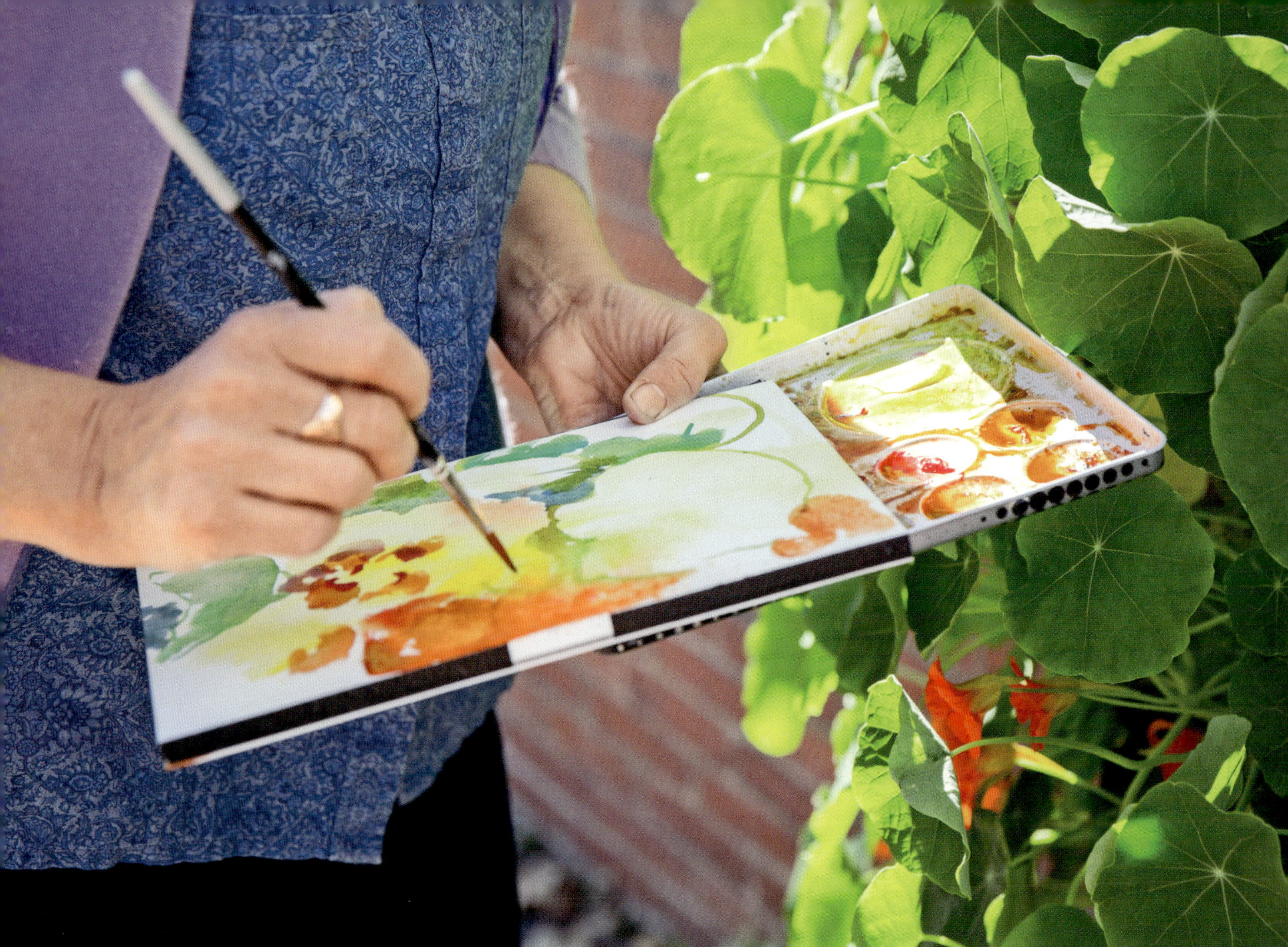

ABOVE: My abbreviated watercolor kit allows me to hold everything and paint at the same time.

OPPOSITE: *Impression of Nasturtiums.* Watercolor. 9" x 12" (23 x 30.5 cm).

ON-SITE WATERCOLOR

Step 3. When my pencil sketching has helped me clarify what I want to capture in the painting, it's time for me to transition to color. Much as I did with my on-site color sketch of the woods, I put together an abbreviated palette of colors, water, brushes, and an 8" x 10" (20 x 25.5 cm) Arches hot press watercolor block to work with on site. I often use two or three of these watercolor blocks when I sketch outdoors. That way I can work on several color sketches at a time, while I wait for the first ones to dry.

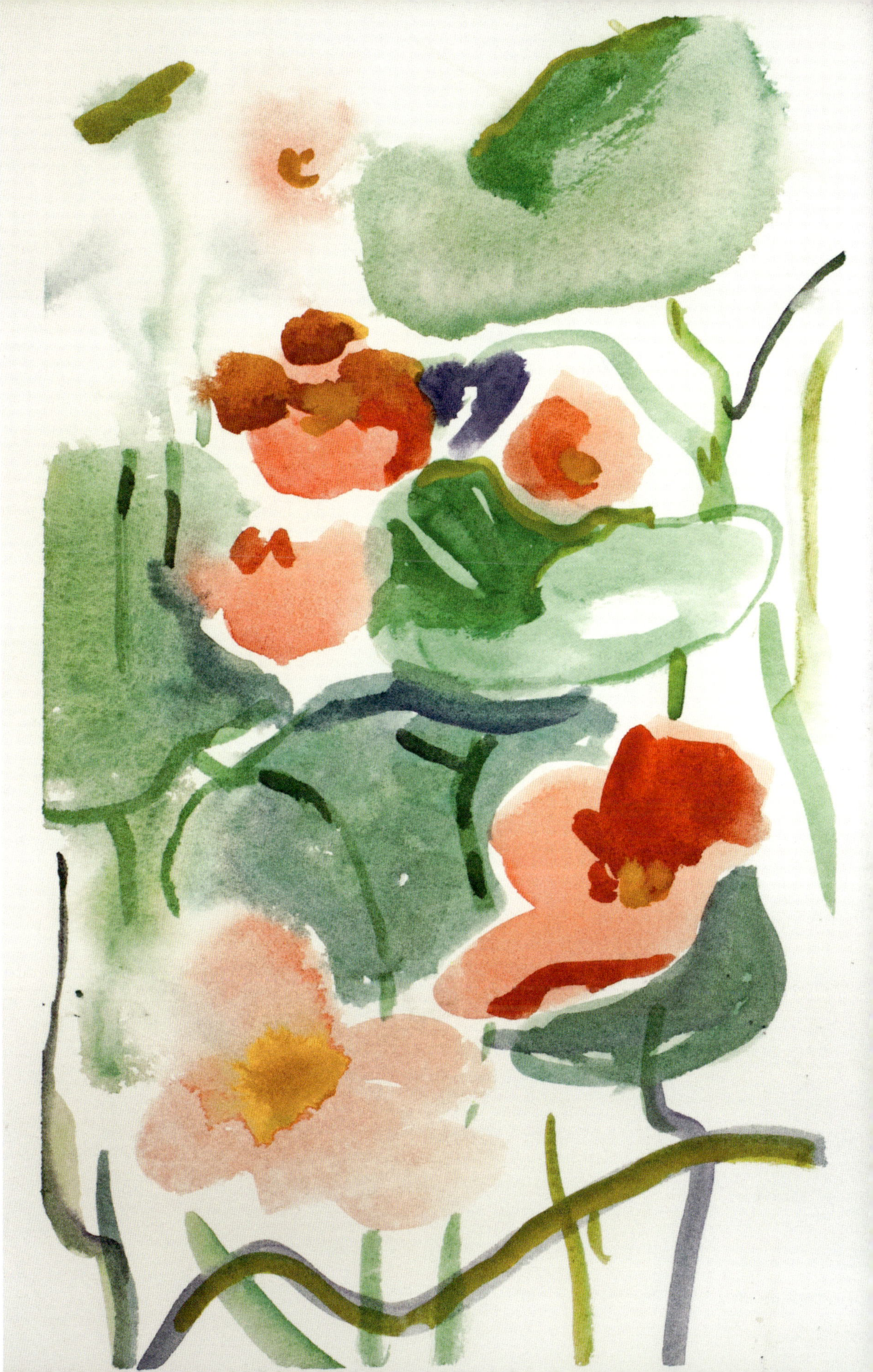

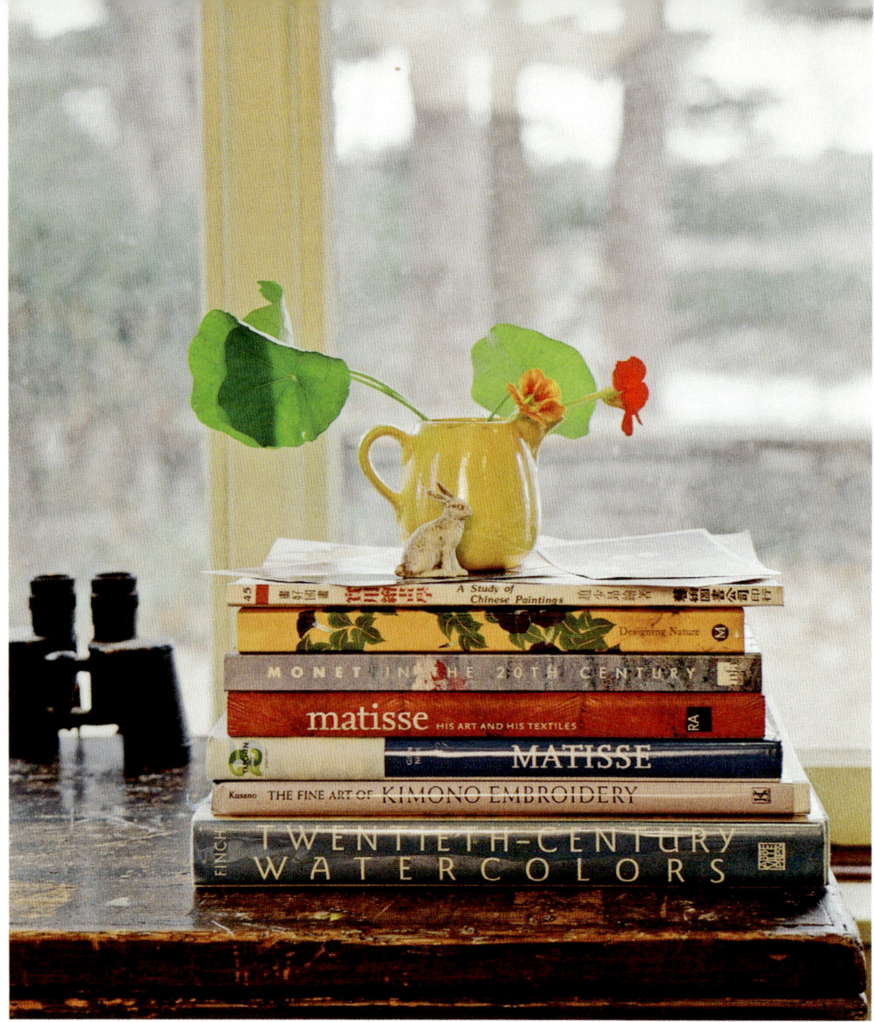

A quiet moment

In the Studio

I take everything back to the studio and spread out my sketches and photographs on the floor. My dog, Lilly, is glad to get in from the sun and watches me from her nest under a table. I feel rich with so many choices.

Moving inside quiets my mind. I have more control over the environment. It's just me and my impressions. The choices I make are my own. There isn't much in life that's like that. It's an open candy shop of possibilities.

Often each sketch and photo has a different look and feel depending on how densely the flowers are arranged, how many stems and leaves appear, or whether the background color is light or dark. Sometimes, when I notice that I have a slew of photos and sketches of a single image, it dawns on me: I already know how I want this painting to go.

For this painting, I create two story boards, one with a large sheet of paper taped into rectangles, and the other with the paper taped into squares. I find this particularly helpful with flower paintings because I like to play with the composition of foliage and blossoms. Starting out with two story boards, I can go back and forth between them, trying out both formats simultaneously. I also like to have a lot of story board frames for flower paintings because the first color I put down for each flower is the most intense, delicate, and transparent that I will achieve. The pigment is pristine on the clean white paper. Every time I go back into the blossom, even if I use the same color, the surface will become a tiny bit cloudier and, sometimes, drastically more opaque and gray. The first color I put down for my blossoms has to be what I want: practice helps me decide.

Step 1. Design. I like the feeling of being surrounded by foliage and flowers, as if my nose is right there next to them, causing the shapes to blur a bit. To create that feeling, I pick up my pencil and make an all-over design without any reference to the sky or horizon. Everything is close to the foreground.

Within the close-up space I've drawn, I've made a complex design of overlapping shapes. I keep in mind considerations like variations in size and make a point of varying the sizes of the flower shapes. I create a big round flower in the center left as a focus. The overall design is a soft curve from the bottom left up along the right side and back across the top. I put smaller blossoms at the top and crop the bigger blossom on the lower edge as if I've come in very close to it and can't see the whole blossom at once.

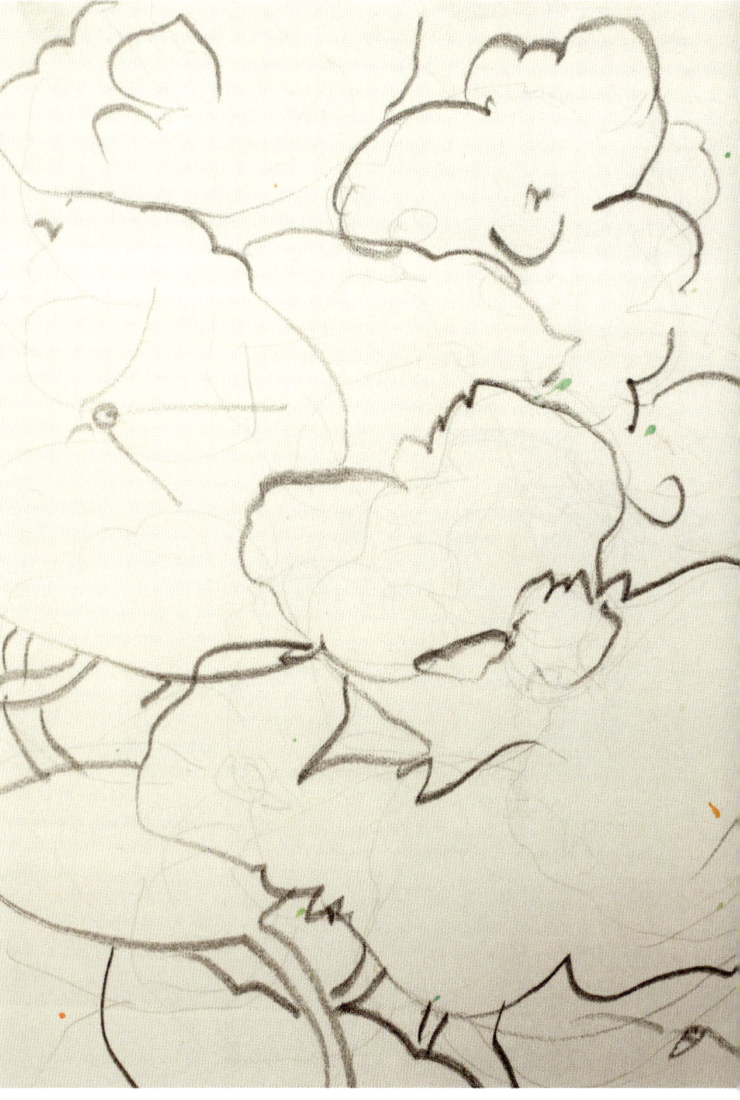

First studio sketch

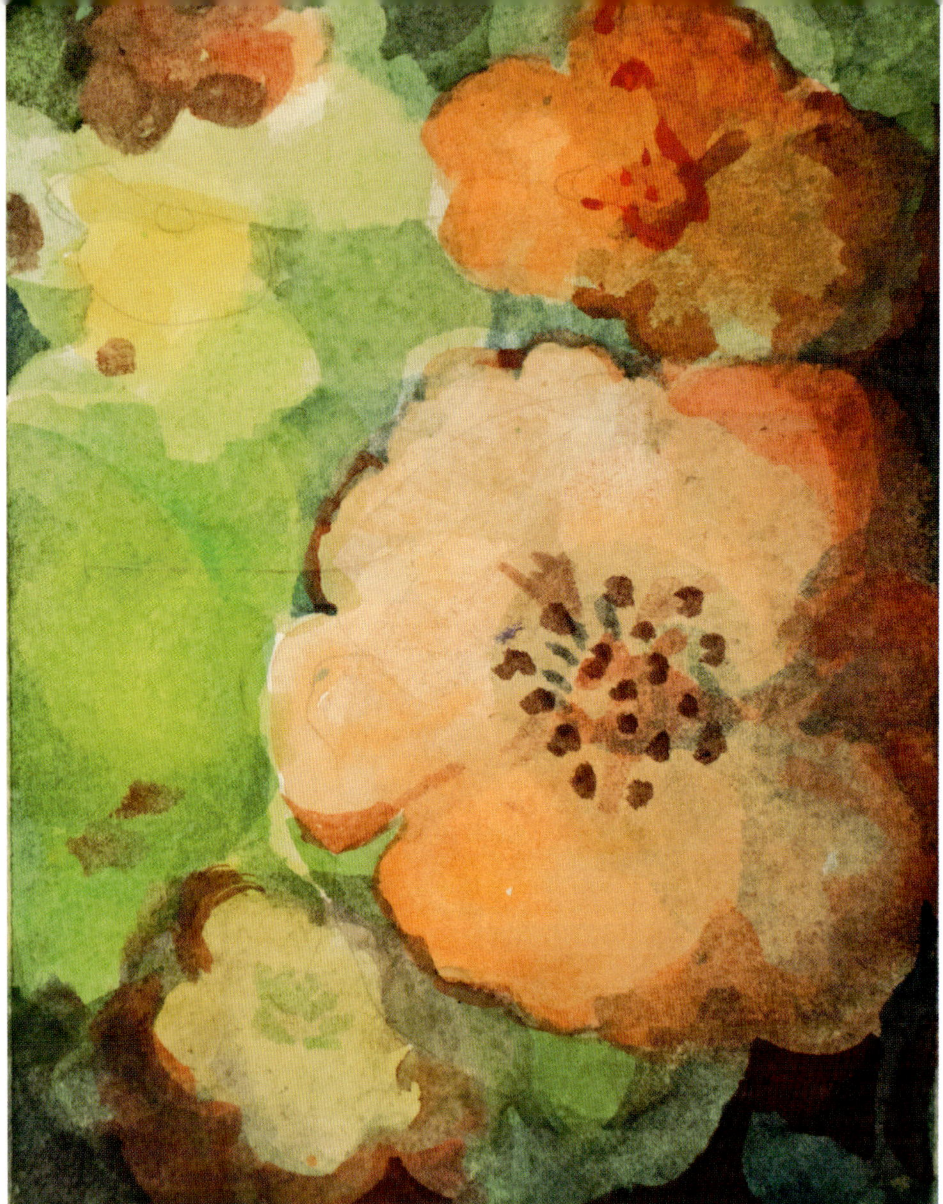

Step 2. Value. I'm ready to work on the value sketch just as I did with the woodland painting, but I'm using the values differently this time. I'm not going to show the direction of the sunlight in this painting. This time it's about color not atmosphere.

I'm already thinking about colors, but first I need to decide where I will keep the painting lighter and where it will be darker. The light areas will be pure, bright color, and the darker areas, more opaque mixes. I plan where the paint will go on in a single layer and where it will be mixed or overlaid.

There's a saying that values are the cake and color is the frosting of a good painting. The values are the structure that holds the painting together. The most important thing for me in this design is to keep the composition light in the center. I want the center to lift up toward me, fresh and fragrant, as if it will brush my nose. So I will darken the design around the edges and keep the center light.

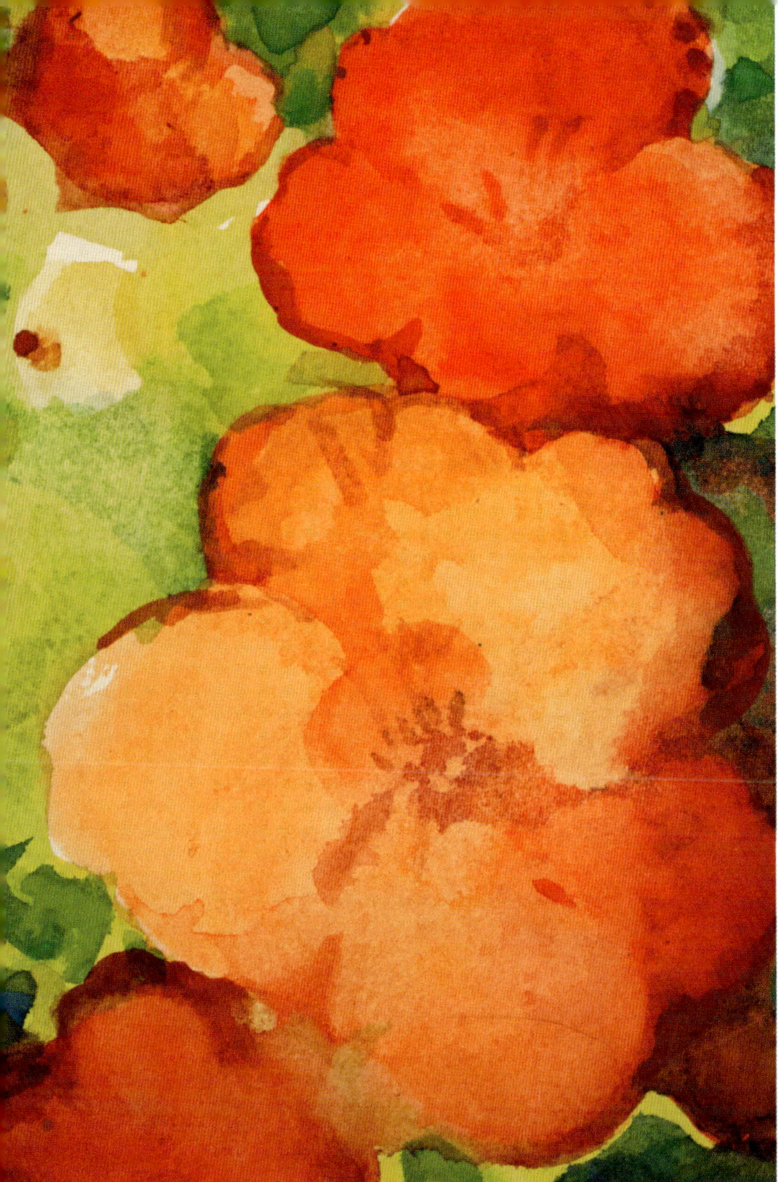

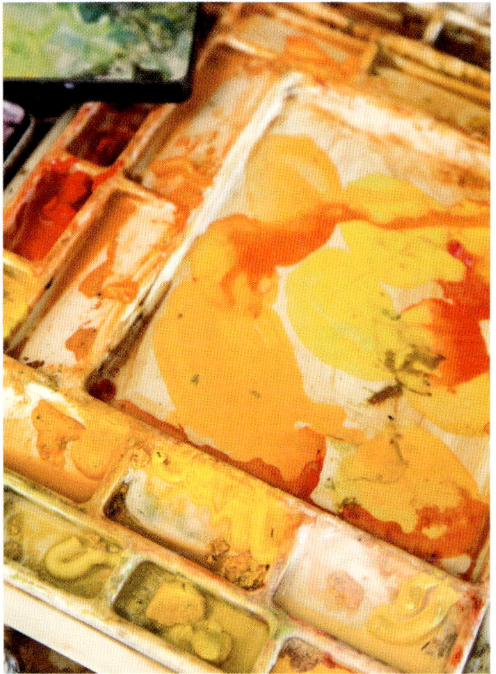

OPPOSITE: I decide to darken the edges and keep the center light in my value sketch.

LEFT: When I work out my colors I go for bright warmth: cadmium yellow light, Winsor red, cadmium red, and cadmium orange for the blossoms. Cobalt turquoise and cobalt blue will mix to give me a good range of greens.

ABOVE: Several yellows mix together on my palette.

Step 3. Color. I use a lot of yellow in all my watercolor paintings. It has a very light value, so it doesn't change the value range of the white paper too much. As an under-painting, it unifies the finished work with a common ancestor. If glimpses show through, they are all part of the same color family.

I have a large palette with only yellows on it. I put five of one yellow in a row. As I work on the painting, and return to the five, they pick up other colors from the paint and become different yellows.

For this painting I'm using the cadmium yellow light as the first color. I mix a puddle with clear water until the color is light. I also make a puddle of cadmium orange. I can control the intensity of the colors by adding either more pigment or more water. I have one water container to rinse off a dirty brush and another of clean water to dilute clean colors. I am using one brush for the yellow and one for orange to start. I will put the pure yellows and oranges in first.

ABOVE: My first light wash of pure color is a lemony yellow, reaching toward green. I also use orange, which I've mixed on my palette using the yellows and some cadmium red.

OPPOSITE: I add a range of happy greens.

Step 4. First wash. I begin by lightly washing in the background colors, reminding myself that I want to arrange the darks around the edges and to keep the center lighter. I use a lot of water and a soft, round brush. The size of the brush depends on the size of paper. I'm working on a small piece of paper so I select a #8 brush.

I brush the clear water on first in a simple round shape, a little smaller than I think the flower will be. Then I drop the color into the center and watch as the color spreads out into the wet shape. This is a wet-on-wet watercolor technique.

In other areas of the painting I will load up a brush with the water and color I've mixed on my palette and paint directly onto the dry paper. This is wet-onto-dry painting. When you're painting, use whichever technique you prefer, wherever you want, both in the same painting if you like, and make up variations of your own to get the look you want.

Step 5. Second wash. I let the first wash dry before proceeding. In this round, I begin establishing the foliage shapes in the center by letting some yellows and wet turquoise blues blend together on the paper. I stay away from the flowers and work only with my greens and blues.

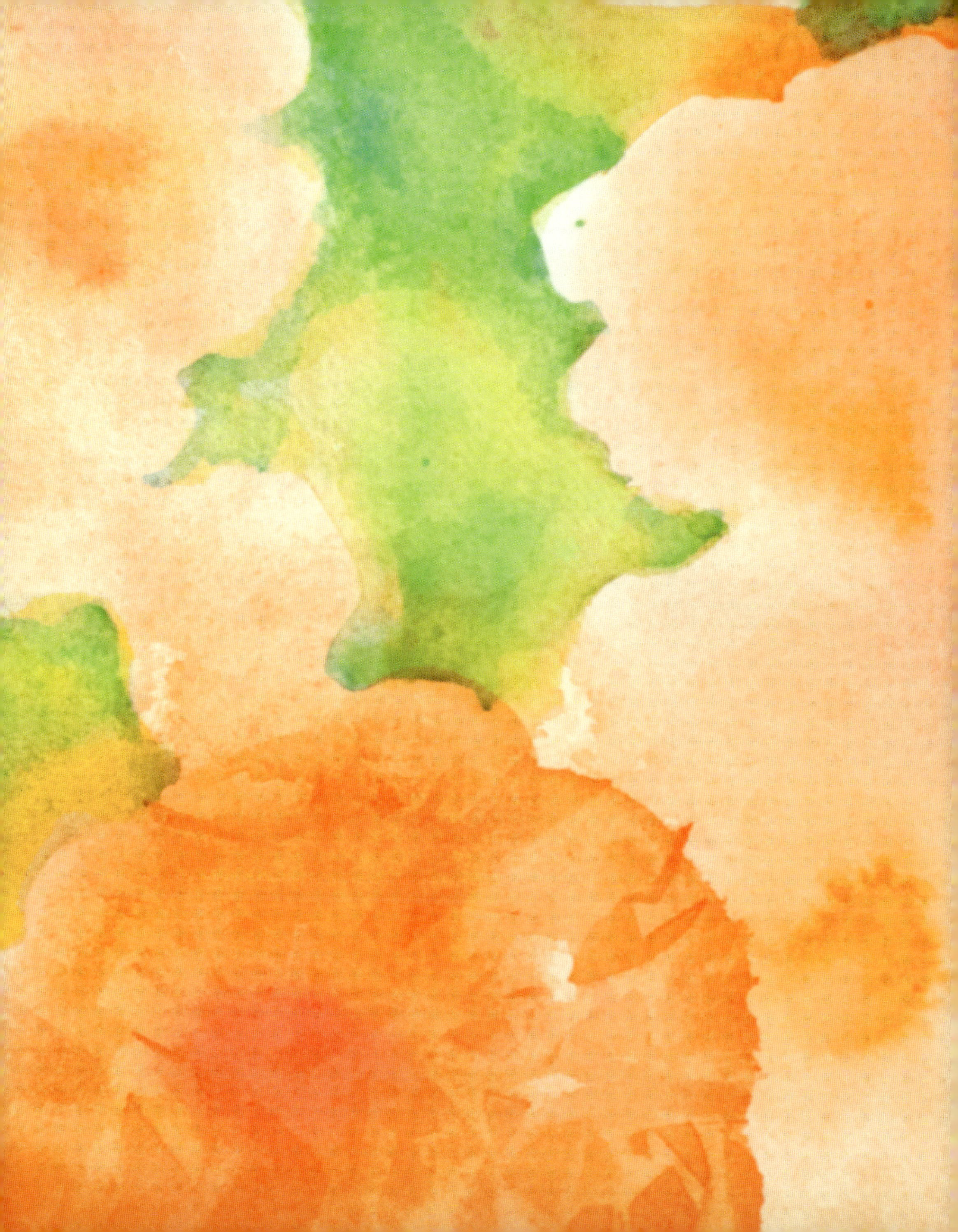

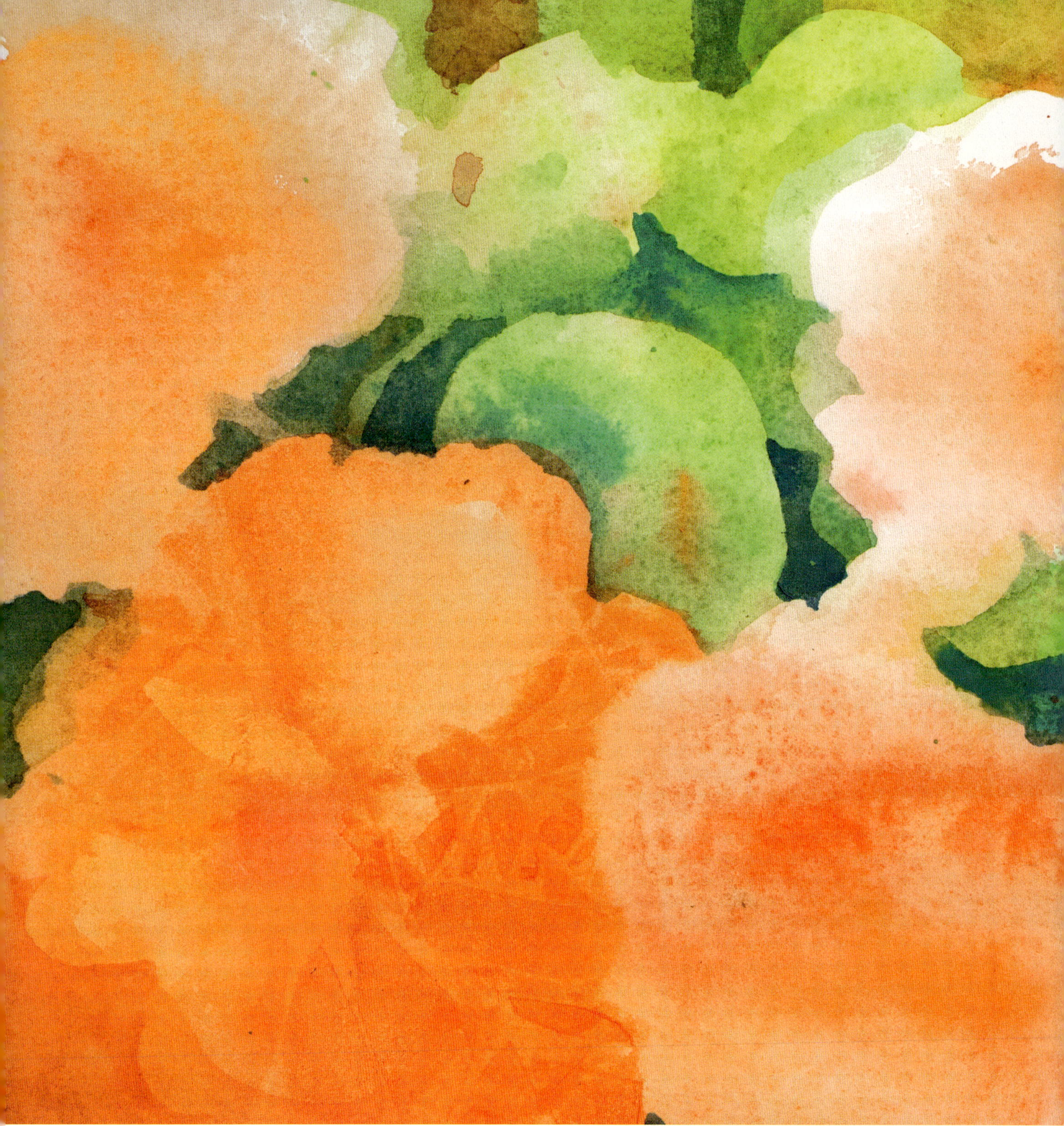

I give more form to the green foliage by shaping leaves and stems.

Step 6. Adding foliage. I continue developing the foliage while avoiding the drying blossoms. I mix several different greens on my palette. The contrast between the greens and the oranges should be striking. If I used only one orange and only one green, the contrasts would look flat. The time spent mixing the variations of blues and yellows and greens is time very well spent. Watercolor pigments do not all mix the same. Each pigment, and even each brand, has a slightly different chemical formula causing it to dilute, granulate, and dissipate its own way.

I use a yellow green in the center of the painting to connect the blossoms visually. I use fresh water and brushes to make sure the oranges and reds do not mix with my greens. If the orange mixes with the green, I will get a brown green, which can be beautiful, but it's not what I want here. I mix a bluer green for foliage around the edges of the painting, always supporting my original idea of light and warmth in the center of the design.

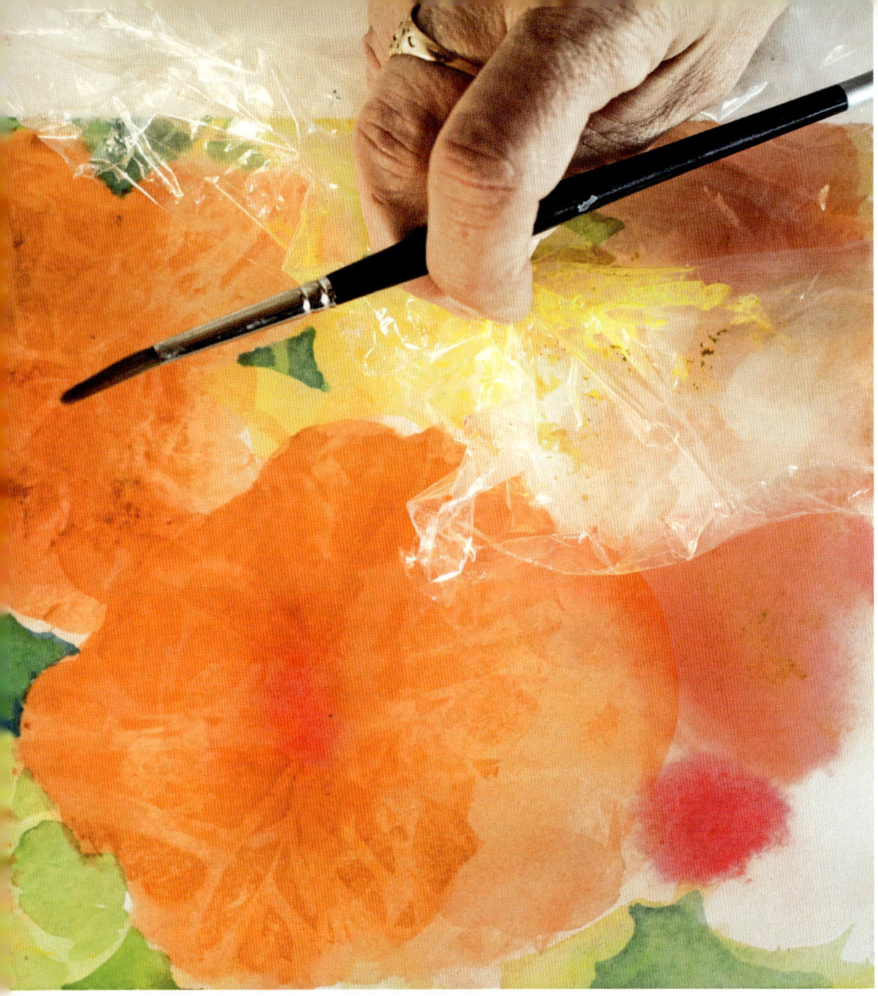

LEFT: I use plastic wrap to add delicate details to the petals.

OPPOSITE: I can go back into the patterns made with the plastic wrap to soften some and darken others.

Step 7. Adding texture to the flowers.

Once the feeling of depth is suggested by the variations of greens in the foliage, I go back to add richer oranges to my flowers.

I get clean water, rinse my brushes, and rewet the yellows and oranges on my palette. I want to begin adding delicate texture to the petals, but I don't want to get too fussy. I decide to use plastic wrap to create the feeling of the folds and veins in the petals. (See pages 74 to 77 for details on the plastic wrap technique.)

Step 8. Adding details to the foliage.

While I wait for the paint to dry under the plastic wrap, I make some decisions about the foliage. I've already decided I want it bright and cheerful, but the amount of detail I put into the foliage will determine the degree of attention it will attract.

Often it's the background that determines the volume and tempo of a painting. If I describe every leaf and indicate every stem, the painting will be visually demanding. If I blur the leaves and indicate only the bits of stems, the painting will relax and it will feel as though the air is moving through it. I decide to blur the leaves and suddenly the painting relaxes.

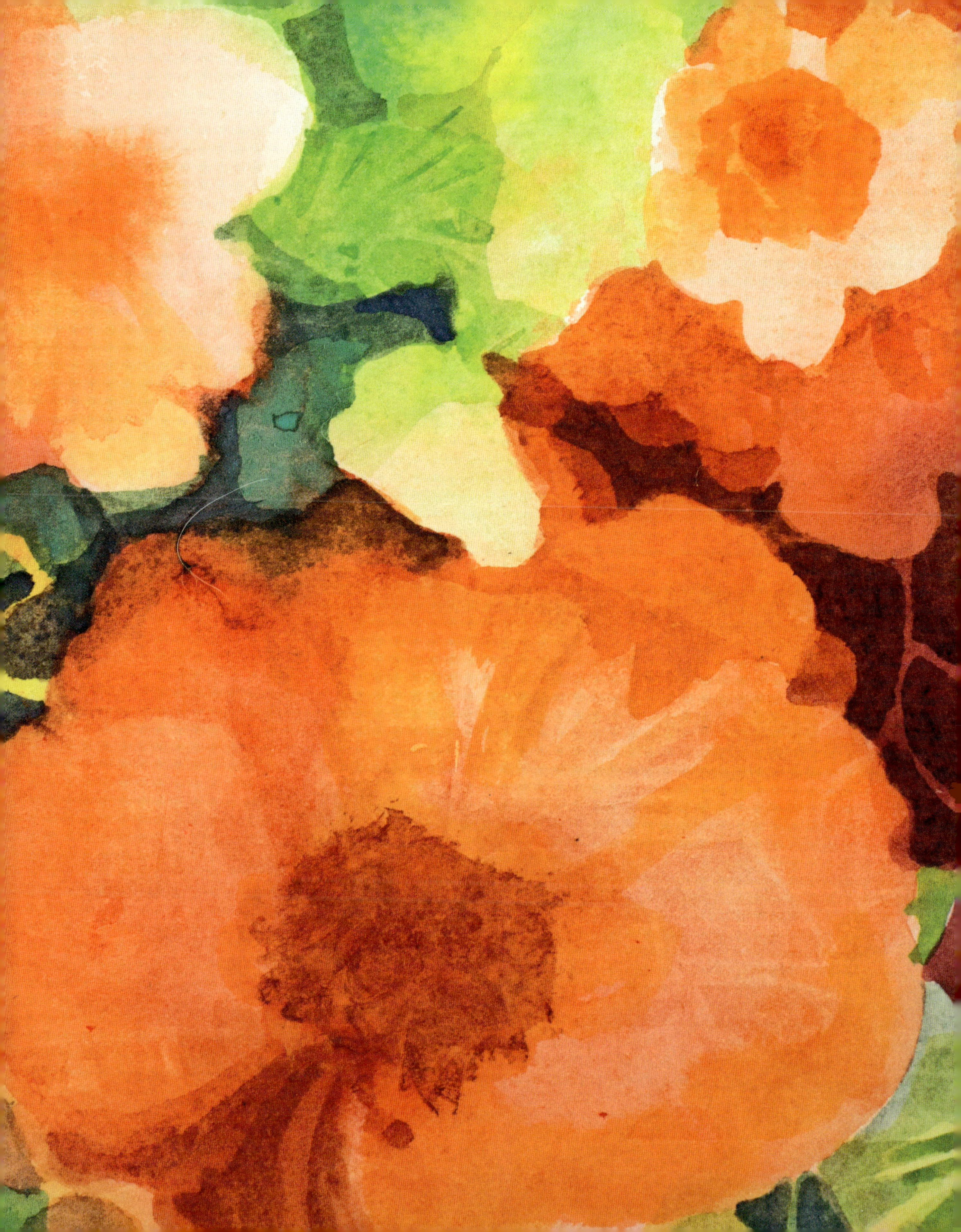

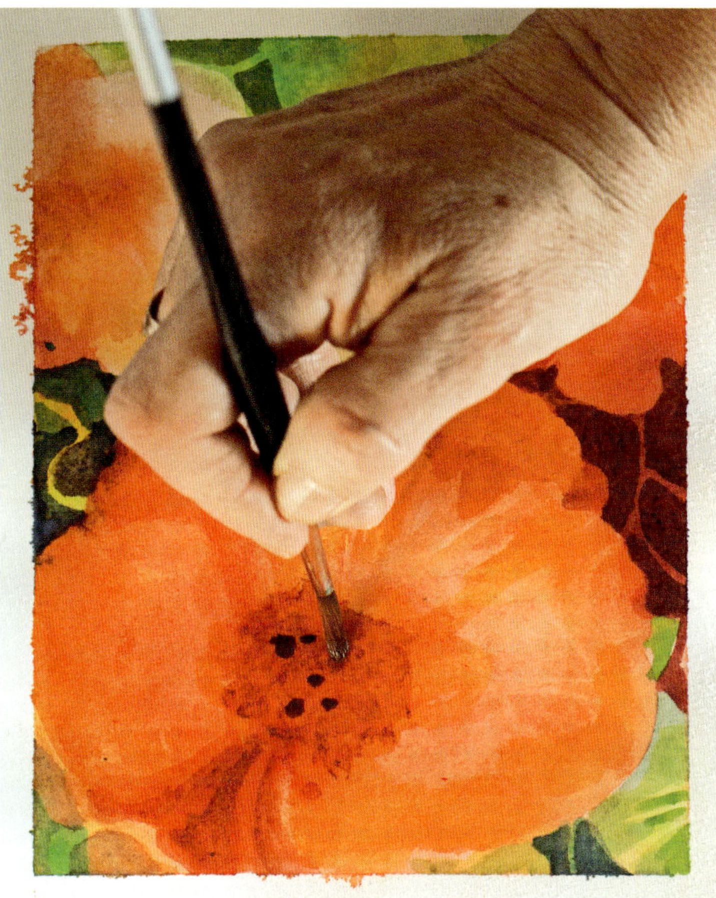

LEFT: Adding the final details to the centers of the flowers.

OPPOSITE: The finished watercolor

Step 9. The reveal. I get fresh water and go back to consider the flowers. I'm eager to see the effect of the wrap. I gently lift off the plastic. Each blossom is different. I admire the way the darker reds and oranges make a fluted pattern across the delicate first washes. I touch the textured paint to make sure it's completely dry before moving on.

As I adjust the details of the blossoms, I am careful not to cover the first wash or lose the crispness of the plastic-wrap imprint. This is not the time for big gestural brushwork. Using a small brush, such as #1 round, I add a darker area, never more than a third of the blossom. I can't stress enough the importance of using clean water when working with flower colors. Even the slightest amount of green or blue in the water will mute the orange, and I want the color to stay bright.

To finish up I add dots of varying sizes and colors to create the center of the flowers. I place them so that the flowers appear to turn in to face each other.

Step 10. Standing out. I squint at the painting, which allows me to see the overall composition and value relationships. I let my mind slip back to the feelings I had leaning into the bright glory of the blossoms, hearing the buzz of the busy honeybee, feeling the sun's heat on my back. The square watercolor I've been working on (opposite) really captures the impression I am hoping for.

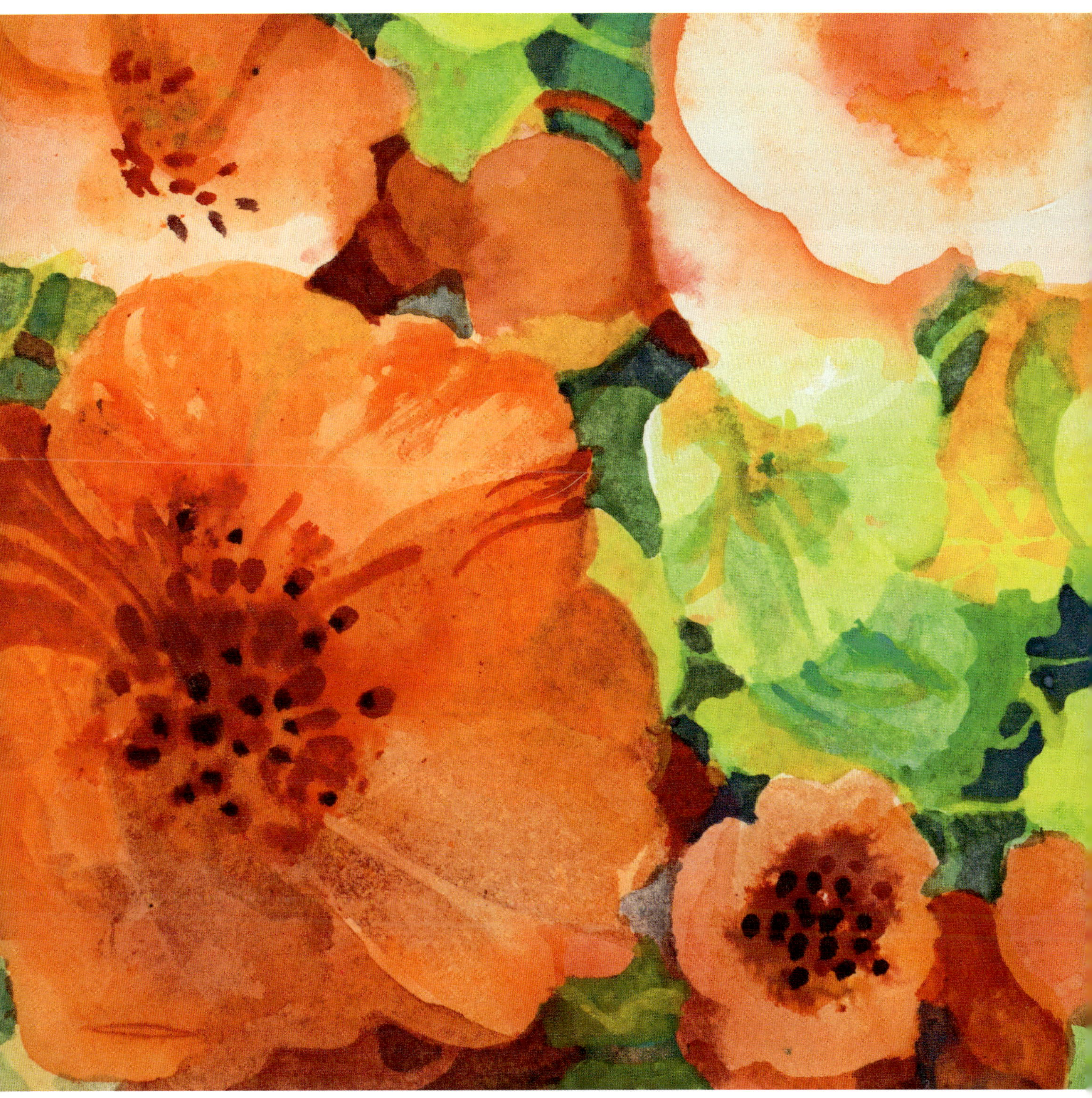

Special Watercolor Technique: Plastic Wrap

Creating Texture

Plastic kitchen wrap is a staple for every watercolorist. I avoided using it for many years because I thought it was too gimmicky. But I discovered in time that if you use it properly, it can add a level of delicate detail to even the most expert watercolors.

You'll need clingy kitchen wrap, clean water (a spritzer helps), a round brush, and several colors of paint. I've decided to try it on some more nasturtiums and have chosen cadmium yellow light, pyrrole orange, cadmium orange, and cadmium red.

In this process, you'll use plastic wrap to create a crinkled pattern in the paint. Once it dries, you can then use the thirsty brush technique (pages 38 to 41) to add washes and lift out color in the textured pattern.

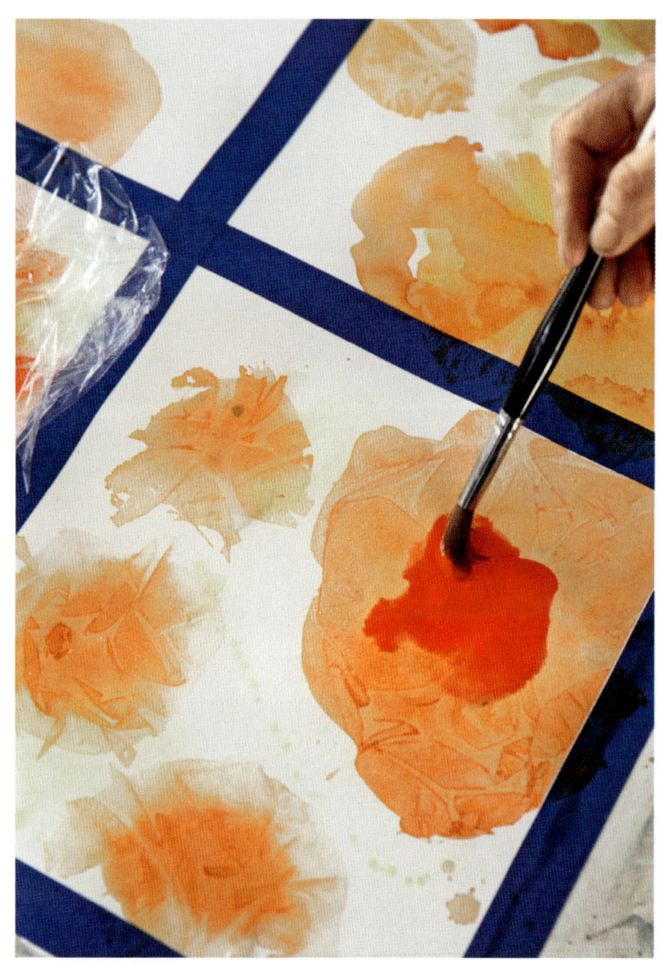

Step 1. Spritz or brush a thin puddle of water on the paper where you want to create the flowers. Drop some bright yellow into the water and watch the color spread. When the yellow dries, make another puddle of clear water over the first and drop in some orange or red where the center of the blossom will be.

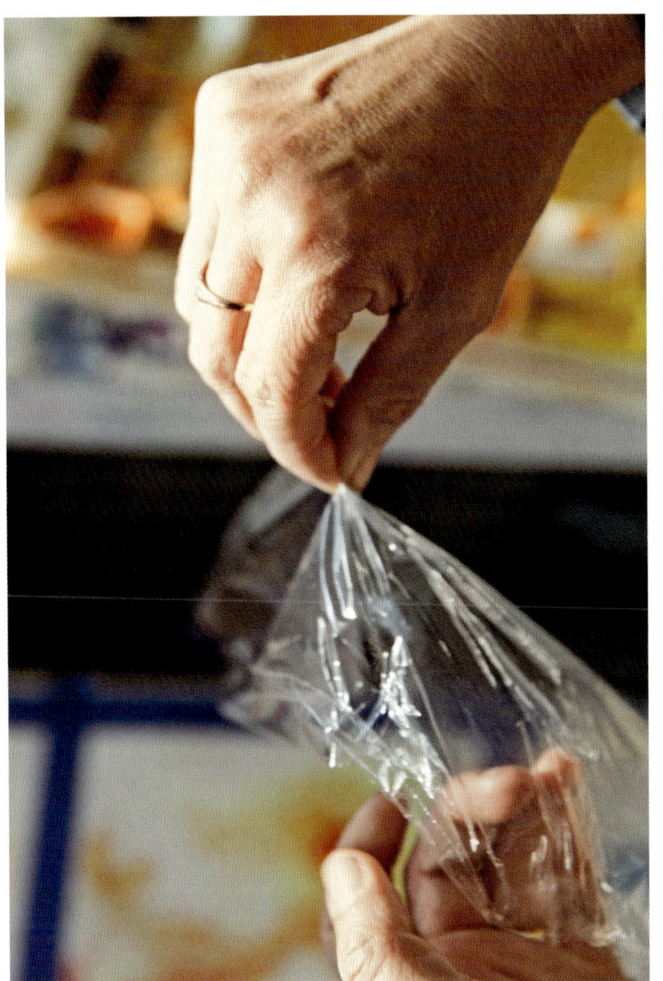

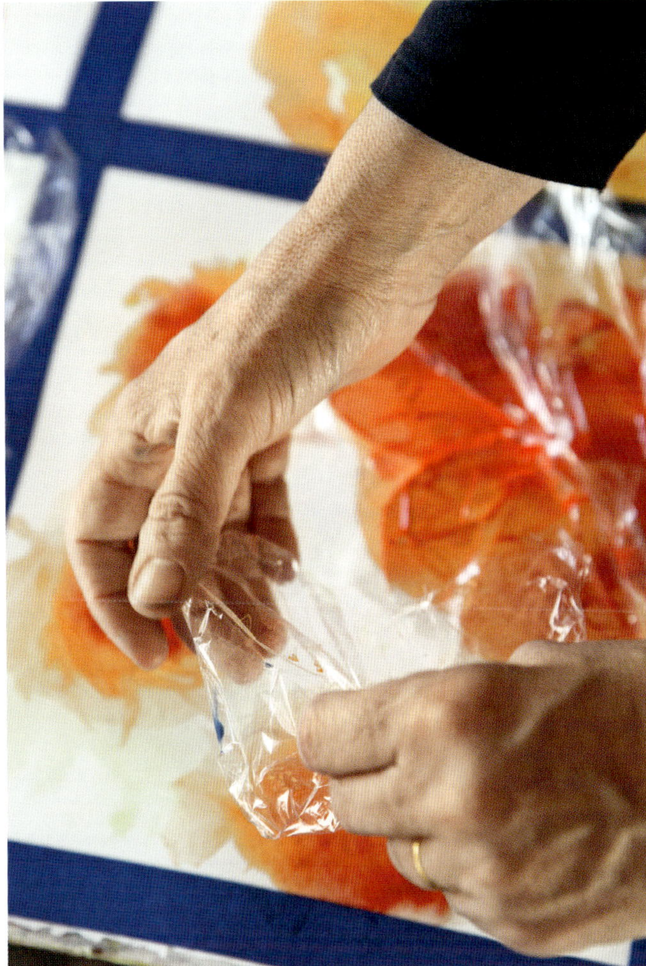

Step 2. While the orange paint is still quite wet, tear a square of plastic wrap double the size of the blossom. Pinch the center of the plastic square and pull out the edges so that it is pleated from the center outward.

Step 3. Once the pleats and creases are arranged, place the square of plastic over the wet orange paint. Press lightly; you will see the orange paint squish into the creases of the plastic wrap.

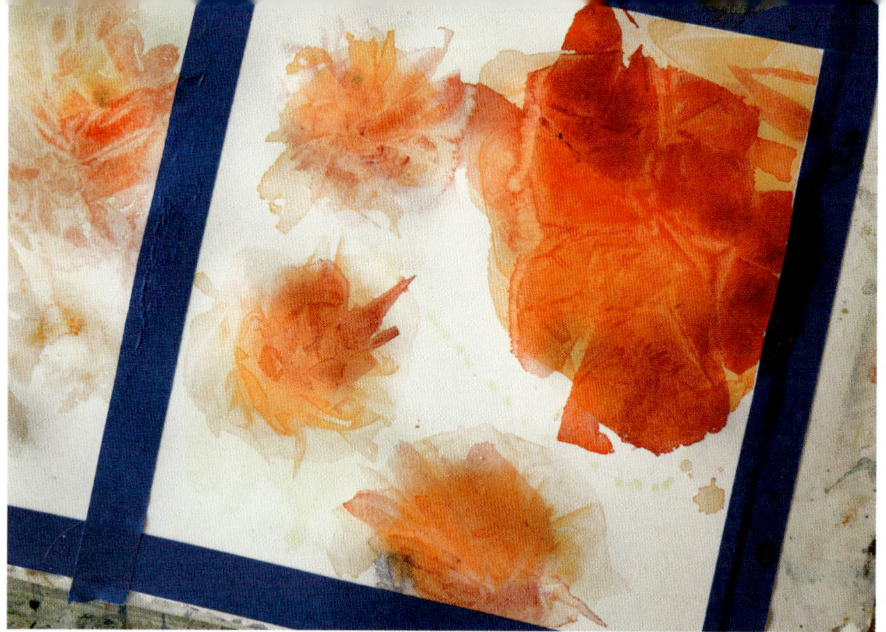

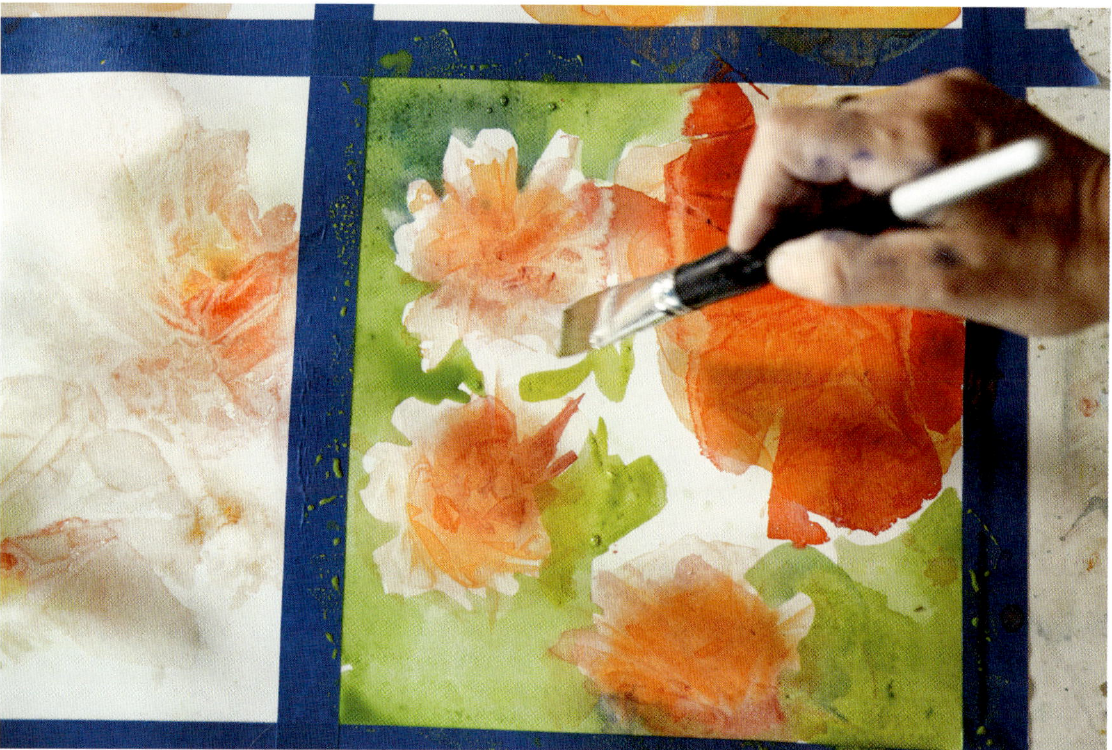

Step 4. Allow the paint to dry completely before shifting or removing the plastic wrap. The best way to tell whether the paint is dry without removing the plastic is to blow on it. If the plastic slides off the paper, the paint is dry.

Step 5. Now you can go back into your painting and add foliage as well as details.

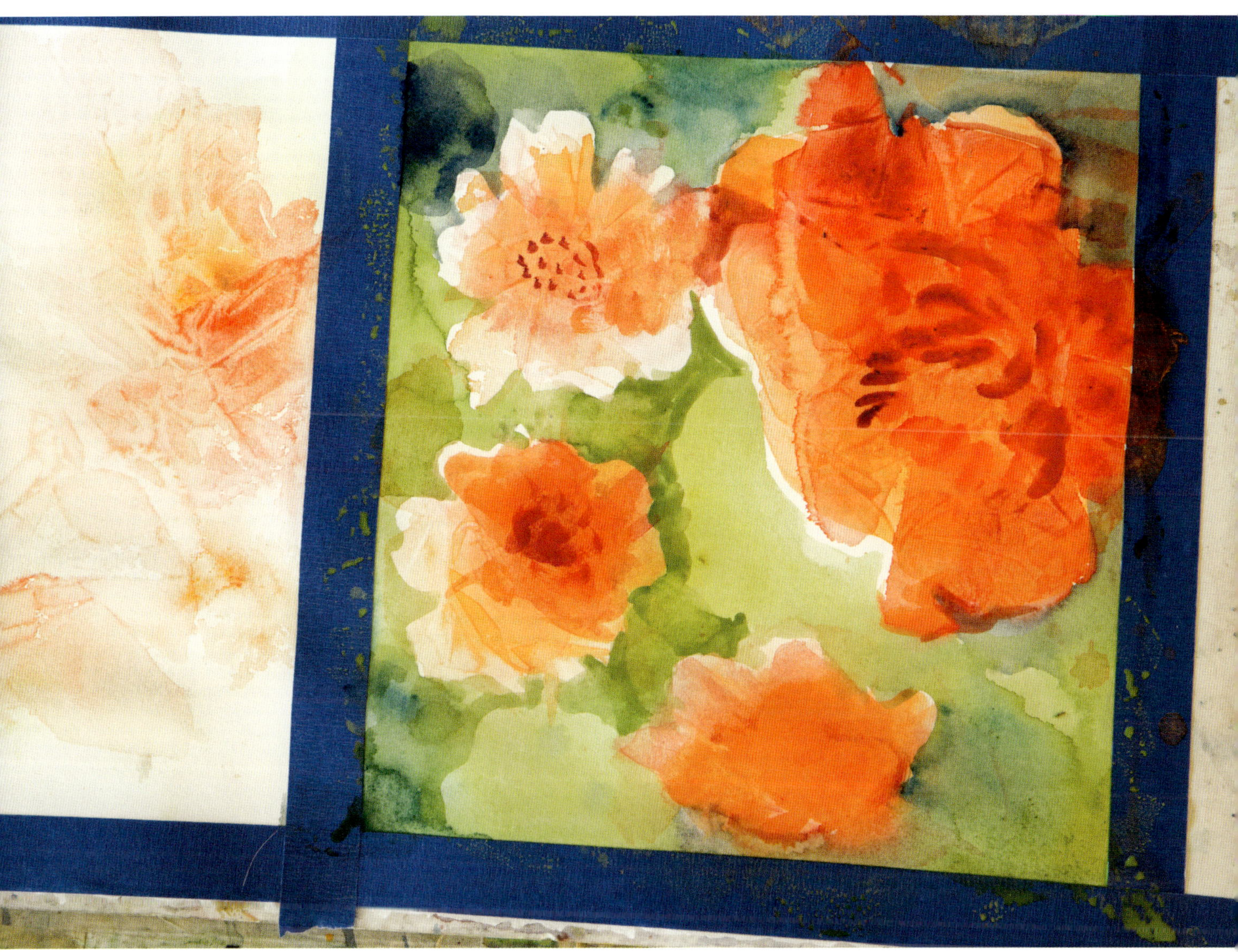

Step 6. The drier the paper and pigment, the crisper the pattern will be. Once your pattern is dry, you can paint over it with darker washes or lift out areas to create contour in the petals.

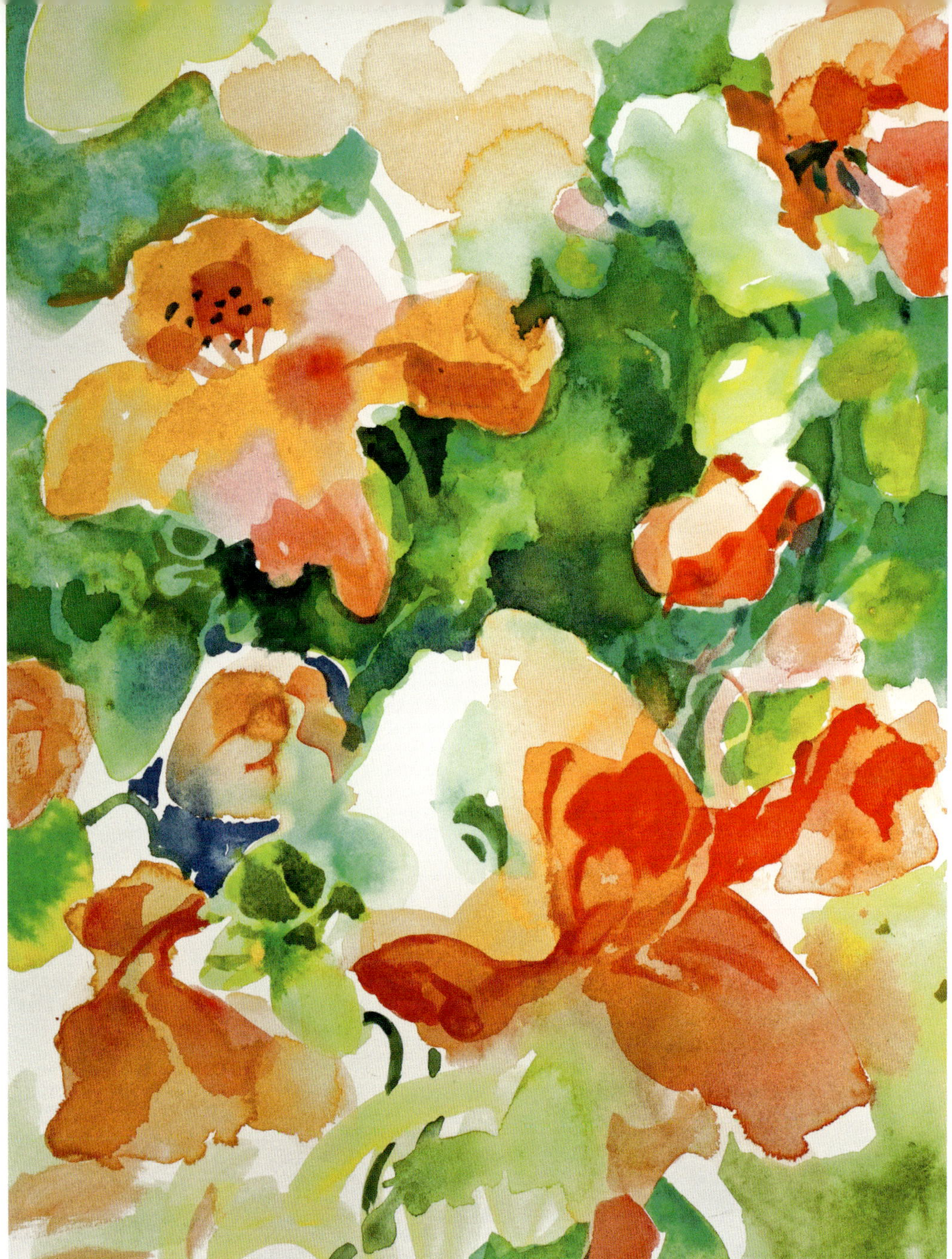

ABOVE: *Impressions of Nasturtiums.* Watercolor. 22" x 12" (56 x 30.5 cm).

OPPOSITE: *Moonlight on Peonies.* Watercolor. 22" x 11" (56 x 28 cm).

Gallery

Flowers are gloriously varied in shape, color, and details. These finished paintings celebrate the beauty of the flower.

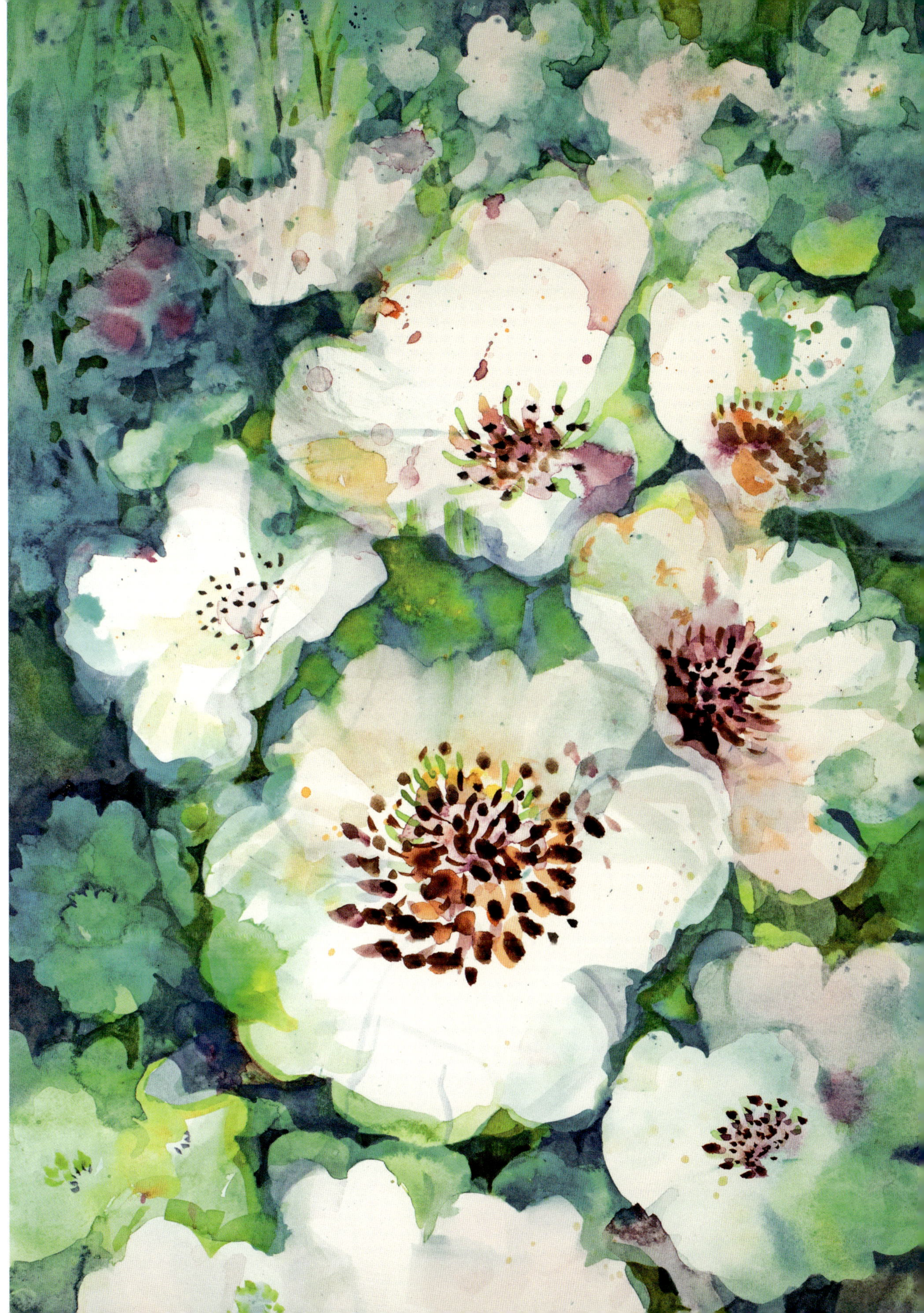

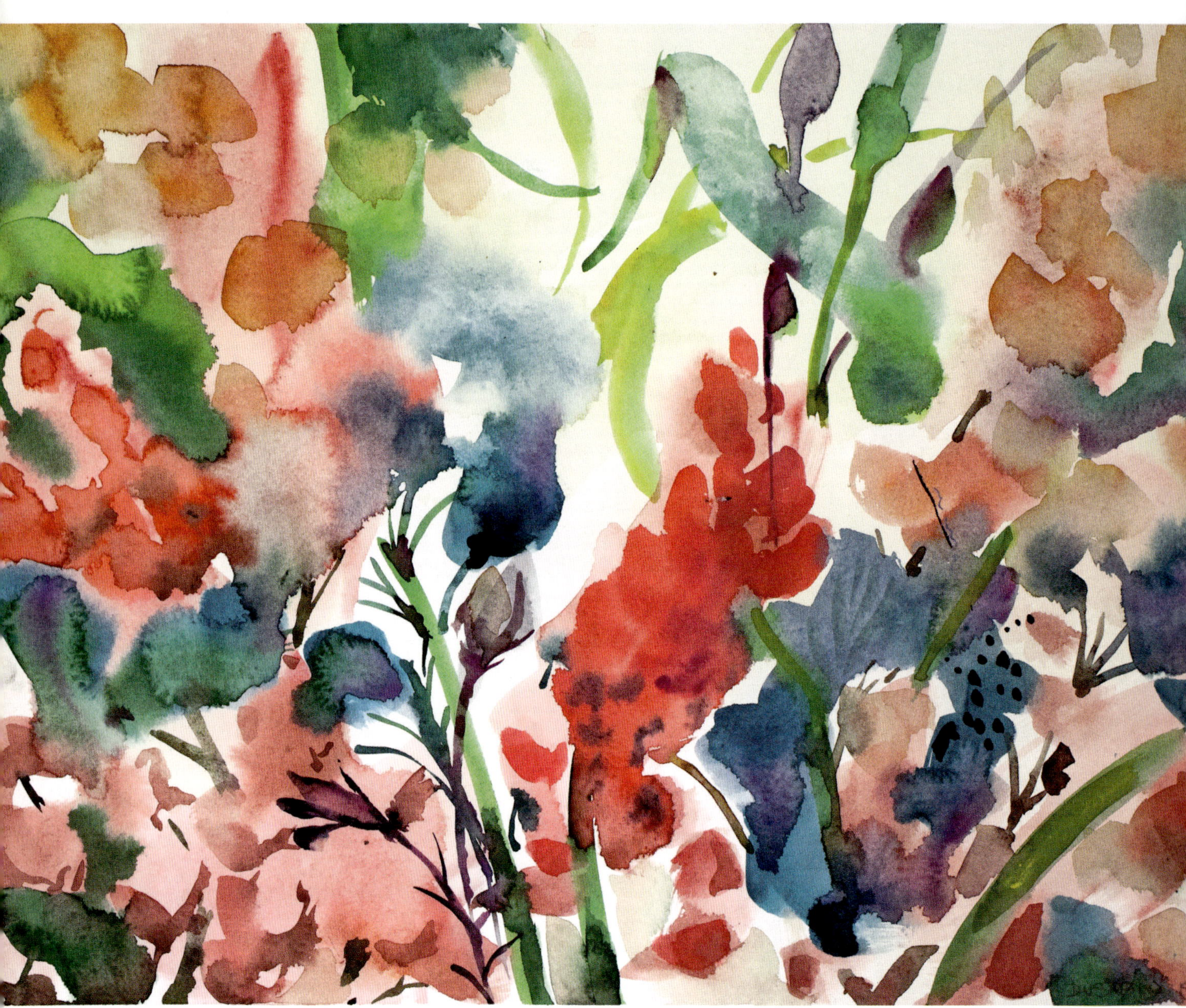

ABOVE: *Morning Garden in June*. Watercolor.
11" x 22" (28 x 56 cm).

OPPOSITE: *Golden Melody*. Watercolor.
22" x 12" (56 x 30.5 cm).

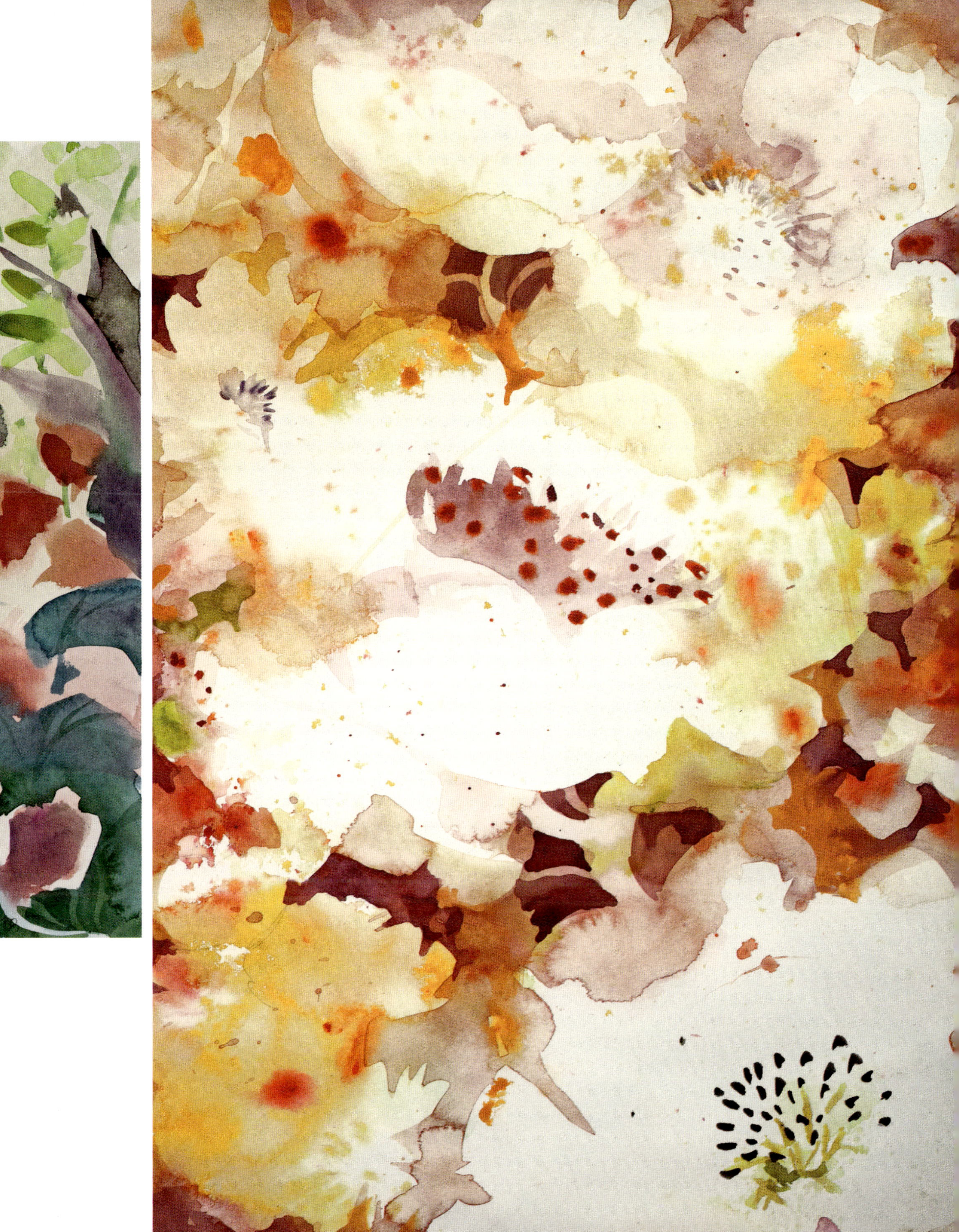

Demonstration: Painting Flowers in Acrylic

When I think of flower paintings on canvas, Monet's water lilies and fields of poppies come to mind. Let's add Van Gogh's sunflowers and irises and Renoir's enormous vases of rust and gold chrysanthemums. These artists knew what it was like to have their noses right up close to the blossom. That's my favorite view, too. I am still intrigued with the idea that I started in watercolor.

Working with acrylic on canvas, however, offers me greater flexibility in the painting process and a physical presence beyond the watercolors. The color dries where I put it, and by dragging and scumbling the paint, I can build up tactile layers, allowing dozens of colors to sit in close proximity. When close up, you can see all the tiny bits of the individual colors. Step away and the colors blend into three-dimensional forms. Monet's water lilies are a perfect example.

As I approach the idea of beginning a painting in acrylic, I'm thinking it would be great to build up a complex physical surface in one area of the painting and a smooth, thin surface of a single color in another. I'll need to pay attention to the thin layers of paint that provide the transparency of the petals without making them so thin that I lose the big happy orange color. As in the watercolor painting, I intend to use the plastic-wrap technique to suggest a pattern of thin veins on the petals.

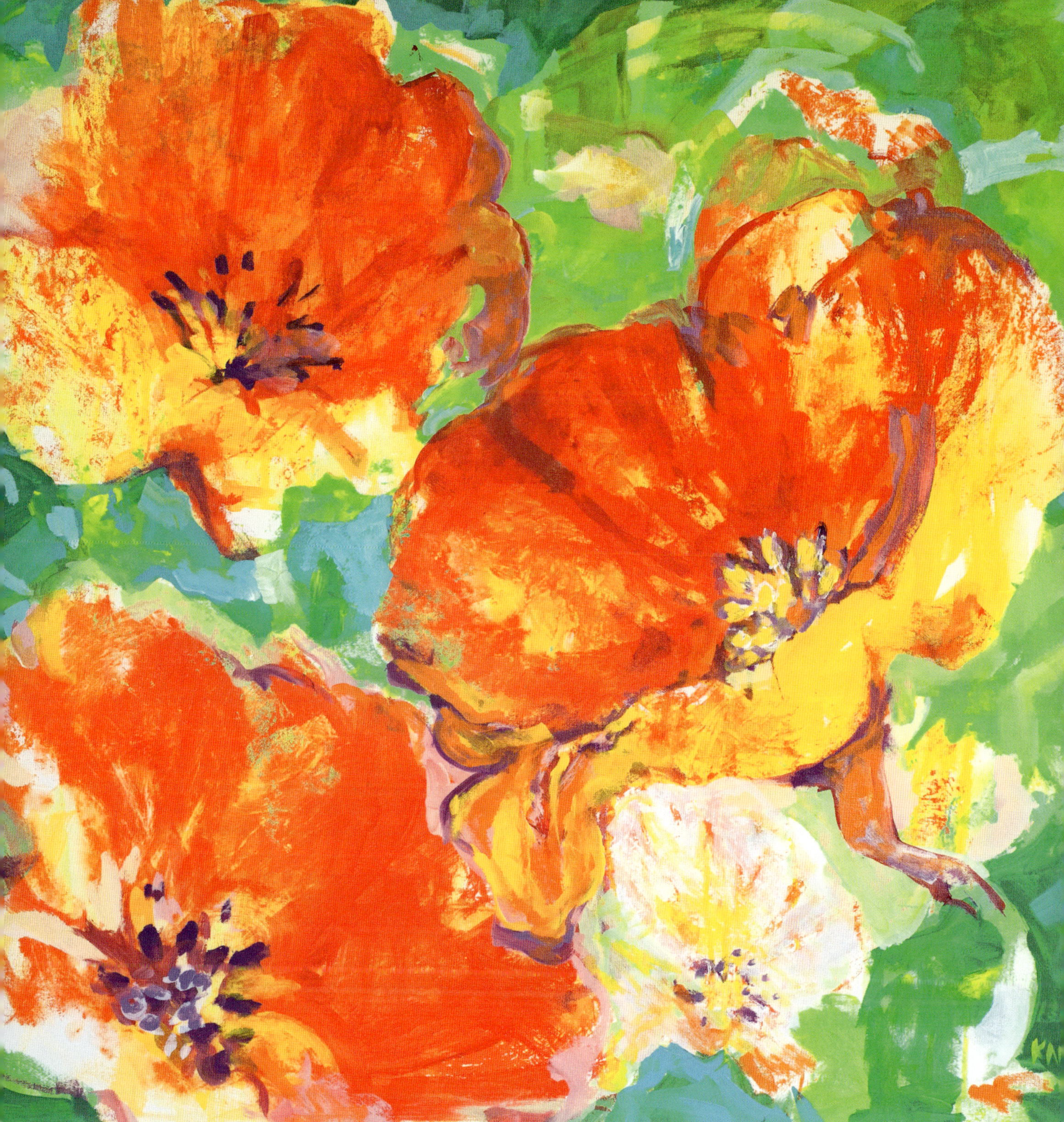

Big, Bold and Beautiful. Acrylic on canvas. 36" x 36" (91.5 x 91.5 cm).

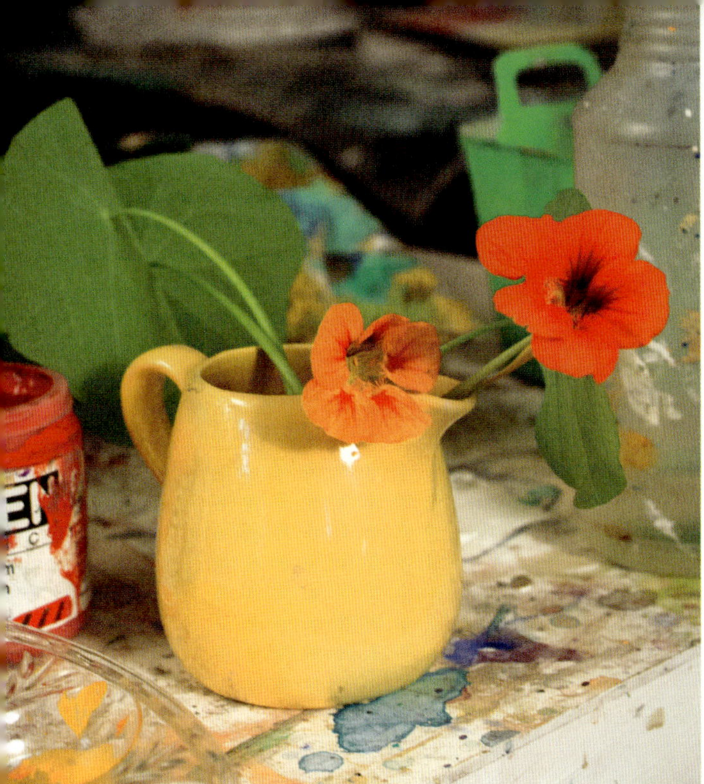

Color inspiration in the studio

Getting Ready

I put away my watercolor gear and bring out my acrylic water buckets, synthetic brushes, and jars and tubes of acrylic paint. I also gather old plastic lids and plastic plates to use as palettes, a roll of plastic wrap, and paper towels.

I want to keep the bright, warm reds and oranges that I used in the watercolor, so for my floral colors, I choose cadmium red light and cadmium red medium. Cadmium yellow and lemony aureolin yellow will add warmth. I'll also use titanium white, burnt umber, and a darker red (perhaps a pyrrole red or alizarin crimson) for the deeper tones. I want this painting to make me cheerful, so I will contrast the bright orange flowers with green. Choosing turquoise for my greens will make the reds and oranges pop, but I also want cobalt blue for a cooler green mixture.

In the Studio

Step 1. Setting up an acrylic palette is different than setting up a watercolor palette. Professional watercolor paints are pigment-intense. They are thinner and quickly settle into a flat puddle when you squeeze them out. Acrylics have more filler and binder, giving them a full-body, toothpaste texture.

I squeeze out a generous blob of cadmium yellow and a blob of titanium white. I won't put out all the colors I intend to use because they dry so quickly. I begin with the yellow and white, leaving lots of room on the palette to mix and move the paints. Acrylic does not flow like watercolor. I have to drag the paints together. As with watercolor, I use separate brushes, one for oranges and yellows, and the other for greens. I also use separate water containers for each.

I put the pre-stretched and gessoed canvas on my easel and choose a hefty #12 synthetic round brush. This is a durable, flexible brush that holds a lot of paint and allows for a wet application of paint.

I rarely start acrylic paintings with pencil sketches, but instead start directly with paint. With acrylic, I can always go back over an area to change it. In this case, with my sketches as models, I have my design clear in my mind.

I brush large circles of bright (but not thick) yellow paint onto the canvas and let it dry. While it sets, I squirt out cadmium orange and an additional blob of white on my palette. On another palette, I set out my greens—using yellows, turquoise, cobalt blue, and white. I add pale orange loosely in areas over the yellow and sketch in with green where I want important pieces of foliage to be.

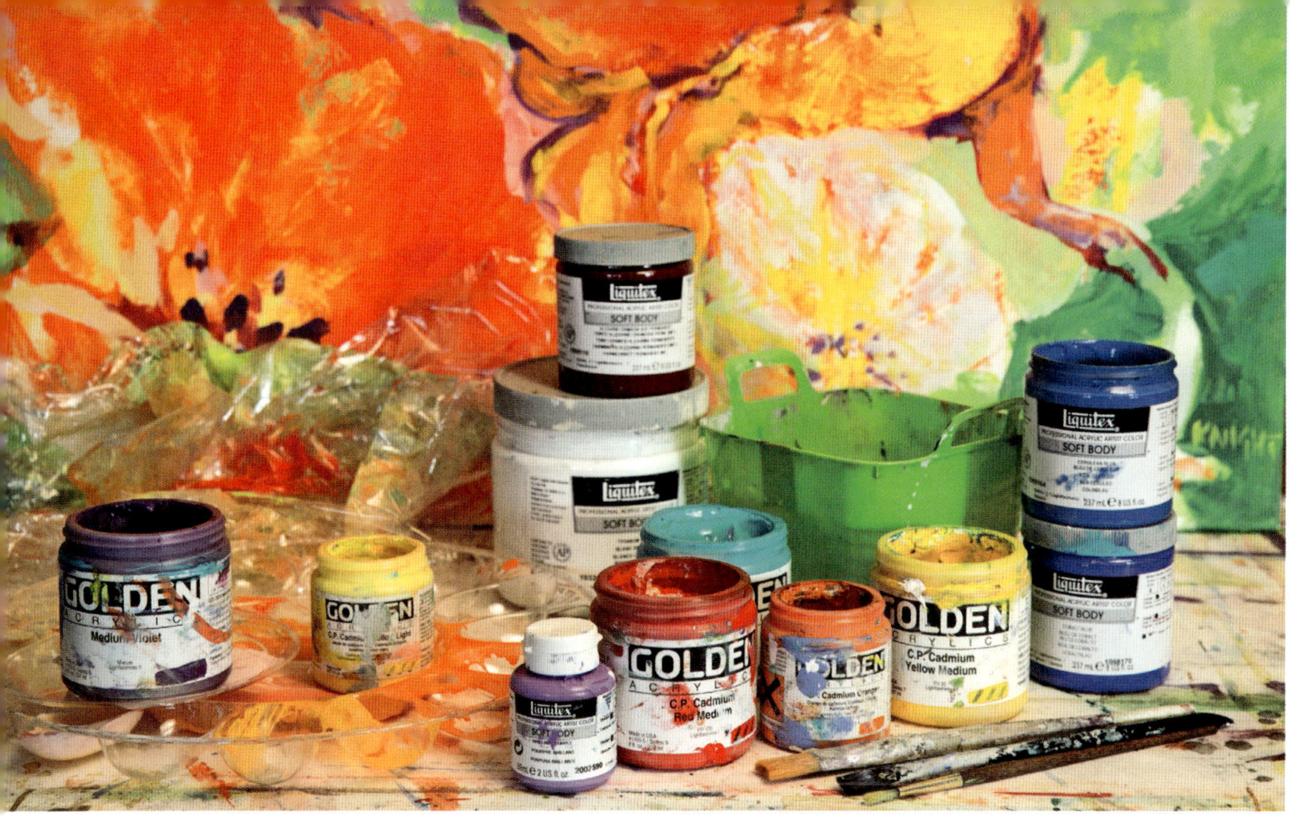

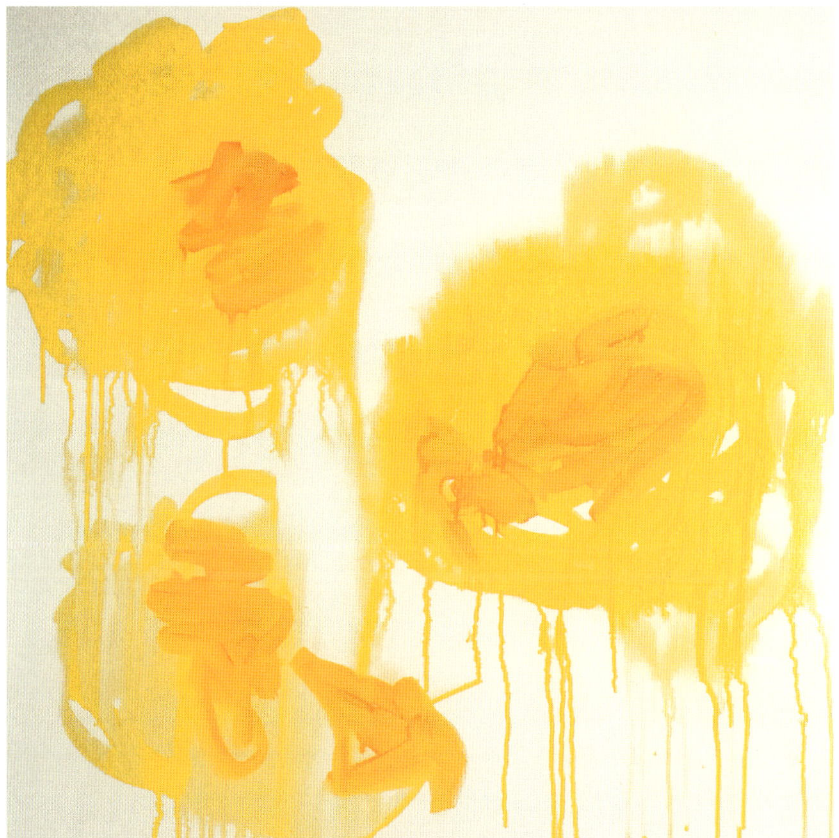

ABOVE: Materials include Golden and Liquitex acrylic paints, a plastic water bucket, and acrylic paint brushes.

LEFT: First loose, bold washes

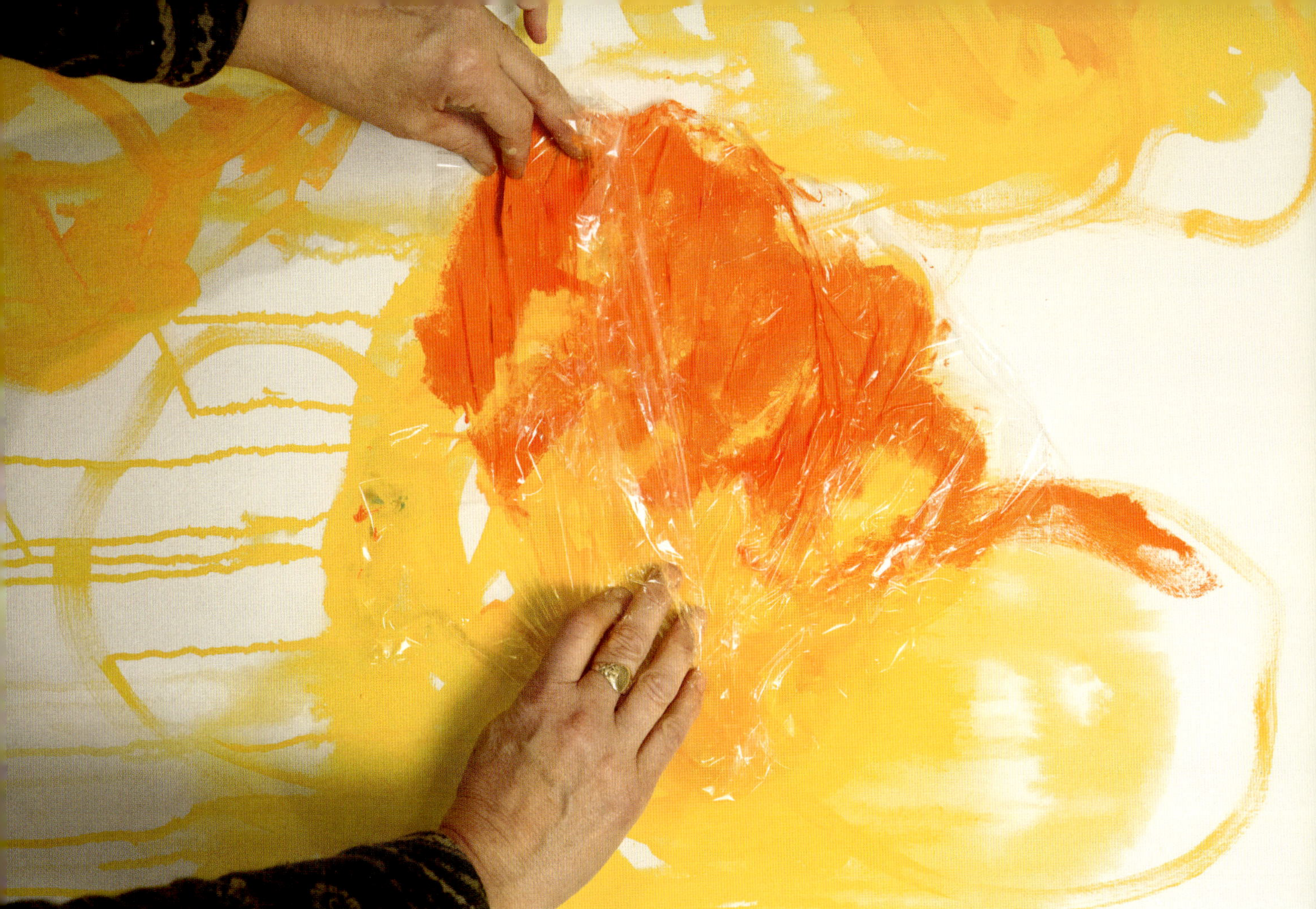

Place the plastic wrap onto the wet acrylic paint and arrange the crinkles and pleats to suggest petal details.

Step 2. When the paint is dry, I'm ready to use the plastic wrap, in the same way as I do with watercolors (see pages 74 to 77). This will be easiest if I lay the canvas flat on the floor or on a large work surface. I mix a red-orange on a palette and brush it over the yellow flowers, trying to stay within the flower shape, and piling the paint thickly at the center. I cut a piece of plastic wrap larger than the area I want to cover and pinch the center of the wrap to create a pattern of wrinkles and folds. I place it over the wet paint and gently press down, encouraging the thick red-orange paint to move into the folds of the wrap, and then I leave it to dry.

NOTE: To get the clearest, most delicate striations of texture from plastic wrap, it's best to use the technique only once for each flower. Later, as the painting progresses, you can return and repeat the process in smaller areas. You can do this at any time. Overdoing it with the plastic-wrap technique can cause the texture to become confusing, losing the feeling of the delicate flower. A single application is best.

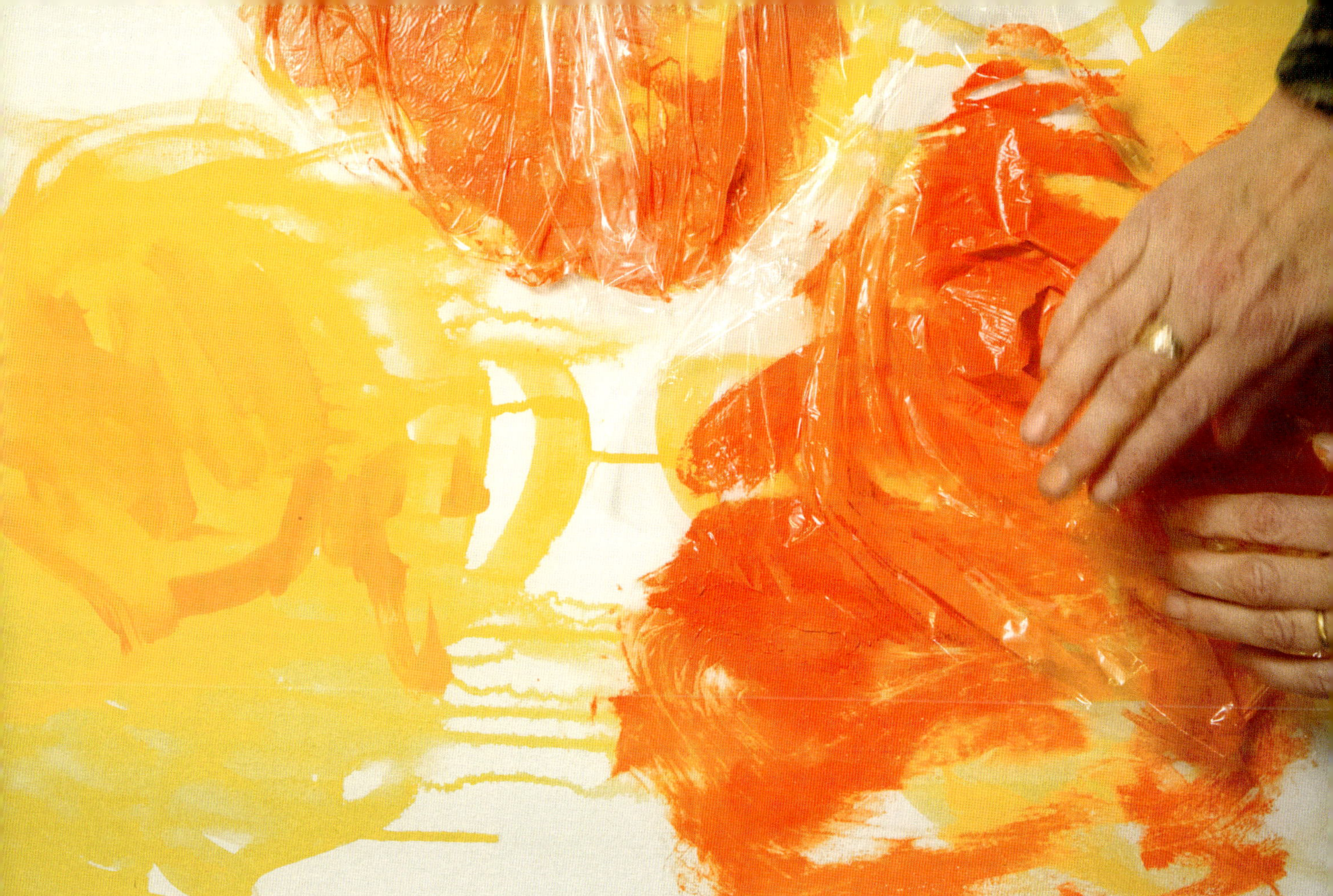

Smooth some of the creases to blend the colors.

Step 3. While the paint is drying under the plastic wrap, I work on the foliage. In the earlier watercolor painting, I painted "negatively," filling in the shapes around the lighter leaves. With acrylic, that's not necessary; I can paint the leaves in front and the foliage in back at the same time.

What I need to keep in mind is that the leaves in front will be lighter and yellow-green. The leaves behind them will be darker and bluer. I can mix my greens in an orderly way by thinking in terms of light, medium, and dark, and moving from warm yellows to cooler blues.

I squeeze cadmium yellow light and turquoise onto my palette, along with white. For a cooler blue green, I add a squeeze of cobalt. (My palette is covered with many coin size piles of various greens.) Then I mix, trying different variations, sometimes mixing all the different greens together. I want to capture the rich variety of greens I see in the garden.

Always mix colors until you like them. Everyone has a slightly different color taste. It's what makes your art yours.

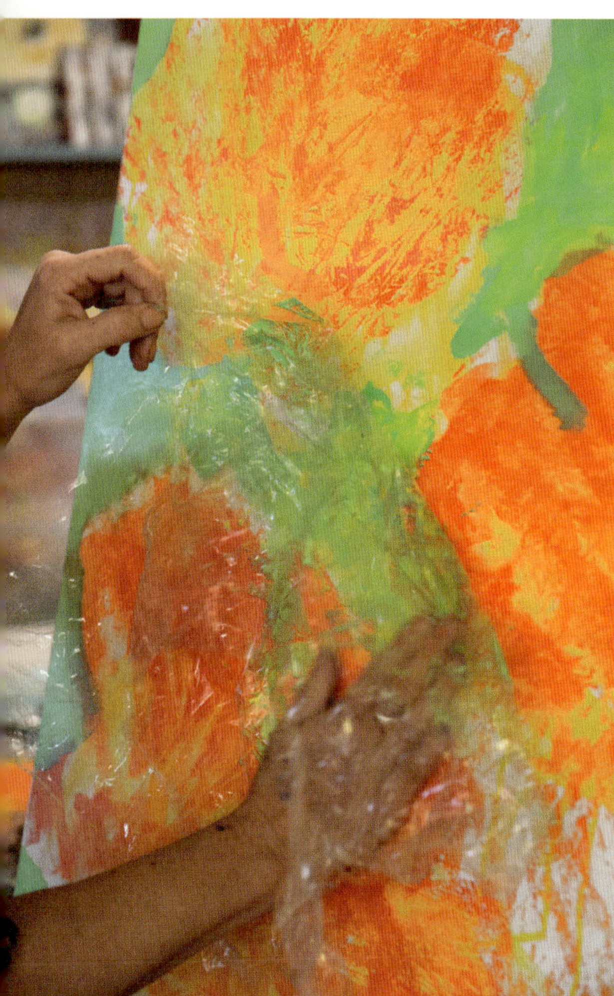

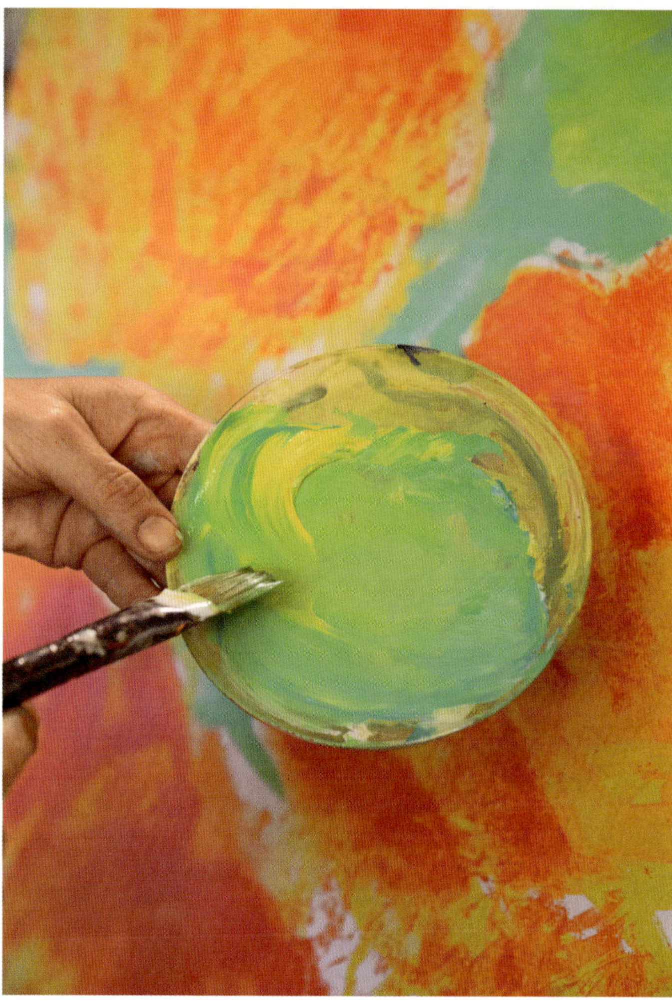

ABOVE LEFT: Repeat the plastic-wrap technique on the leaves.

ABOVE RIGHT: Mix some greens, keeping variations on the palette.

Step 4. I repeat the plastic-wrap process on the foliage. Building up rich variations in the color and textures of the foliage is critical for this painting. I can remove the plastic wrap within minutes of putting it on if the paint is thick, or I can leave it on all afternoon. I vary my timing to see what I like. The flexibility of the acrylic allows me to make big and small adjustments throughout the painting process.

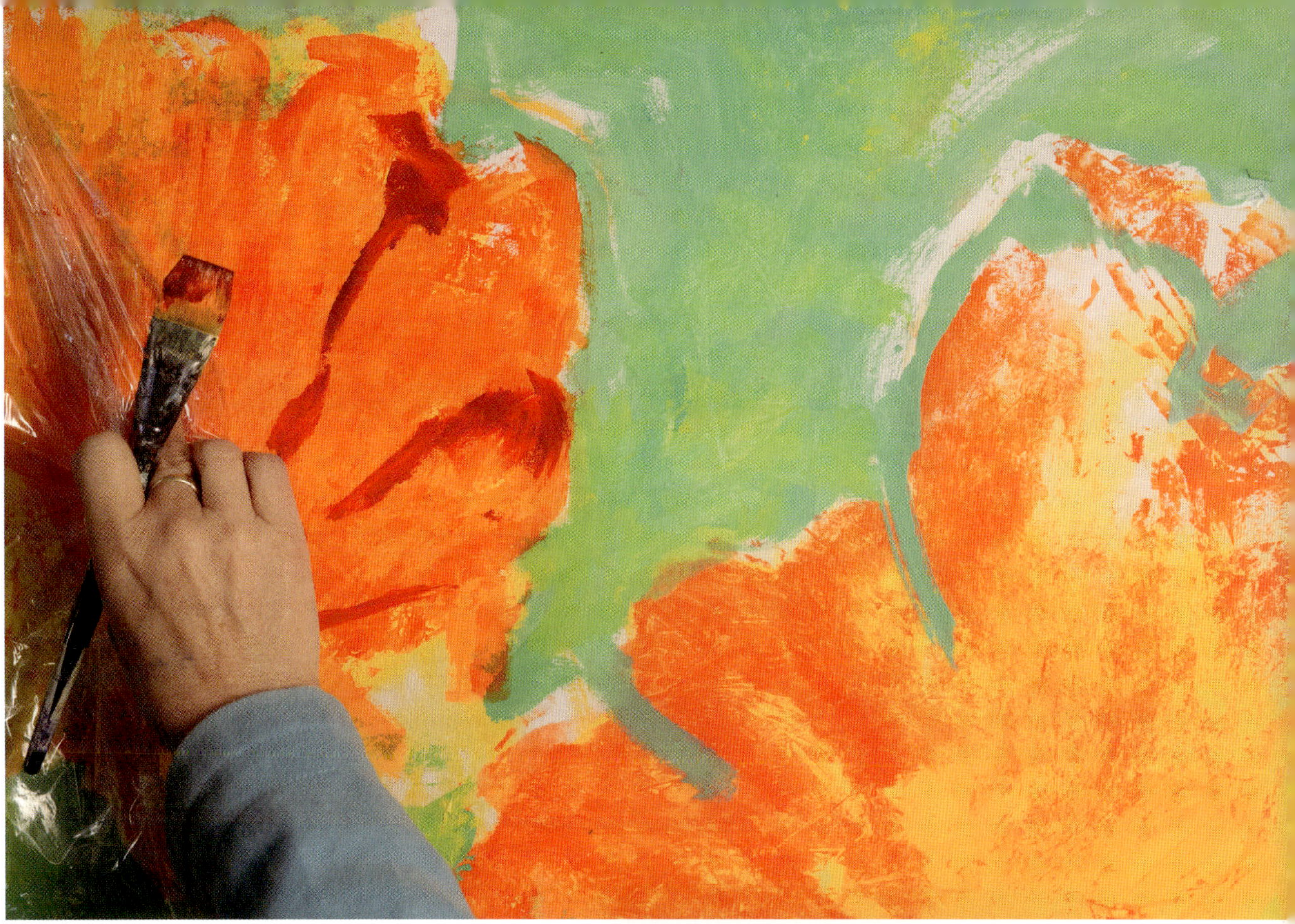

ABOVE: I build up layers of orange, yellow, and deep red.

RIGHT: I lightly tap some orange across the yellow to suggest the thin, delicate impression of the petals.

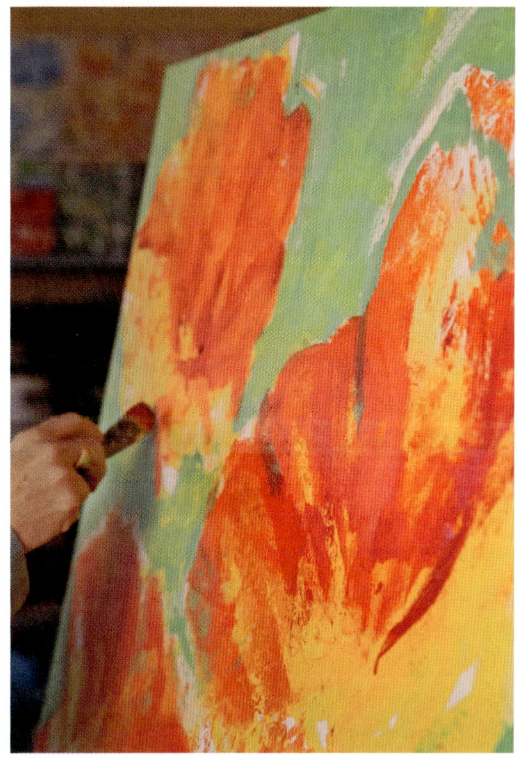

Step 5. As I shape and blend my foliage colors, I simultaneously refine the flower shapes by bringing the green up to the orange. I think about bringing the leaves under the flowers. I remember the layers and layers of leaves and stems under the flowers in my nasturtium garden. I think about the delicate edges of the flower against the rich, thicker foliage.

I like the tangle of leaves and tendrils. They've created the impression I wanted, but I do need a focus in the painting to draw the eye. I squeeze alizarin crimson onto the palette and use a smaller brush to dab a darker center on each flower so the flowers seem to talk to each other—as I did for my in-studio watercolor painting.

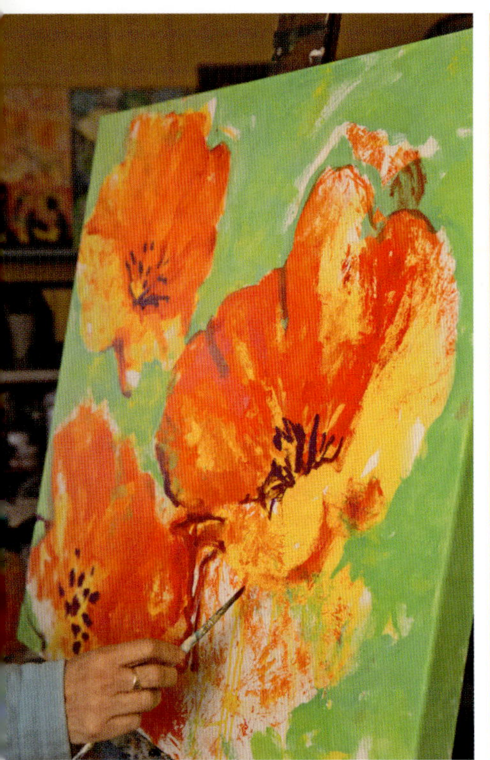

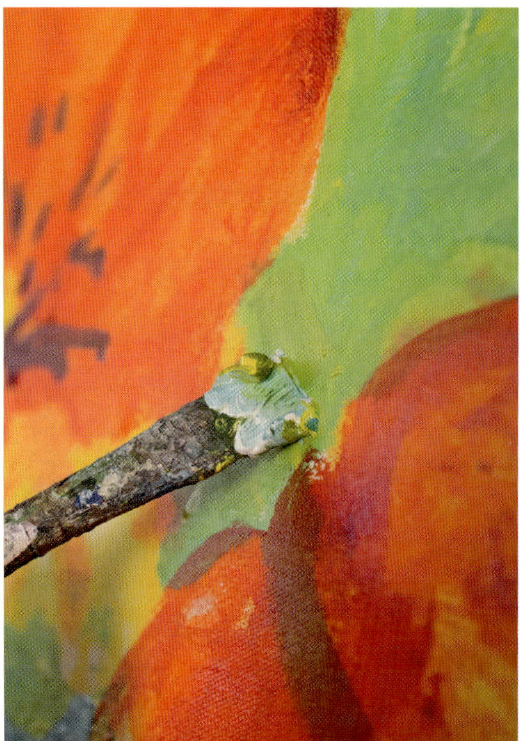

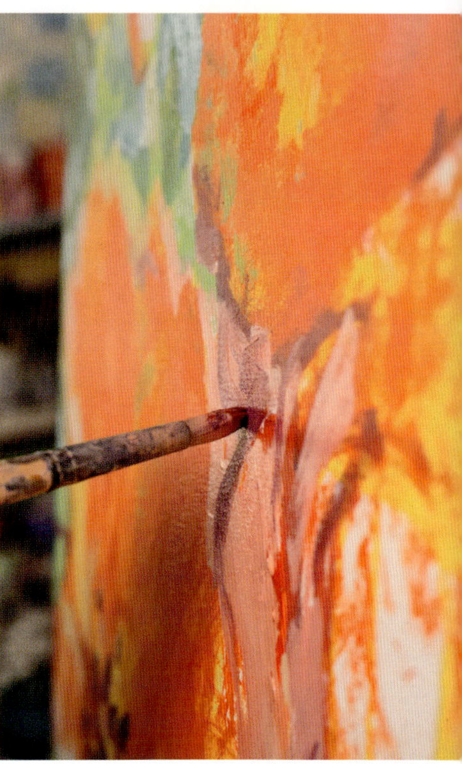

ABOVE LEFT: Detailing reds

CENTER: Working in the greens

ABOVE RIGHT: Painting details with a small, round brush

Step 6. Art is a wonderful process of starting with a loose idea, making decisions about it, and then refining it until you know it's done. I have made most of the big decisions about this painting. The process isn't over yet, but now I can relax and have fun refining the blossoms further.

I use smaller brushes—small, synthetic flats. I make a point of using new brushes now, so I can achieve a tidy edge. My brushstrokes become smaller. I continue to clean up the blossom edges by outlining them with various light, dark, and yellow greens. Yellow greens are for the foliage tucked around the petals. The darker blue green is for the small spaces between the lighter leaves and around the edges of the design.

Step 7. I take a break to sit in my big studio chair and "listen" to the painting. What is it saying? Does it need something here? Is it too busy there? Can I feel the delicate vitality of the petals?

Step 8. Finishing up this acrylic is a wonderful slow dance of adding glimpses of detail among the leaves. I add a graceful bending stem of the curve of a shadowed petal. I also add more dark details to the centers. I look for the most "talkative" blossom, the one that the others seem to be listening to.

I adjust the flowers' strengths by varying detail and contrast. The most important flowers have the darkest, most dramatic centers, and the less important may have just a few spots of body color. The centers of the flowers become less dramatic as the eye moves away from the center of the painting. I've tried to capture the feeling that I am leaning into these flowers and leaves.

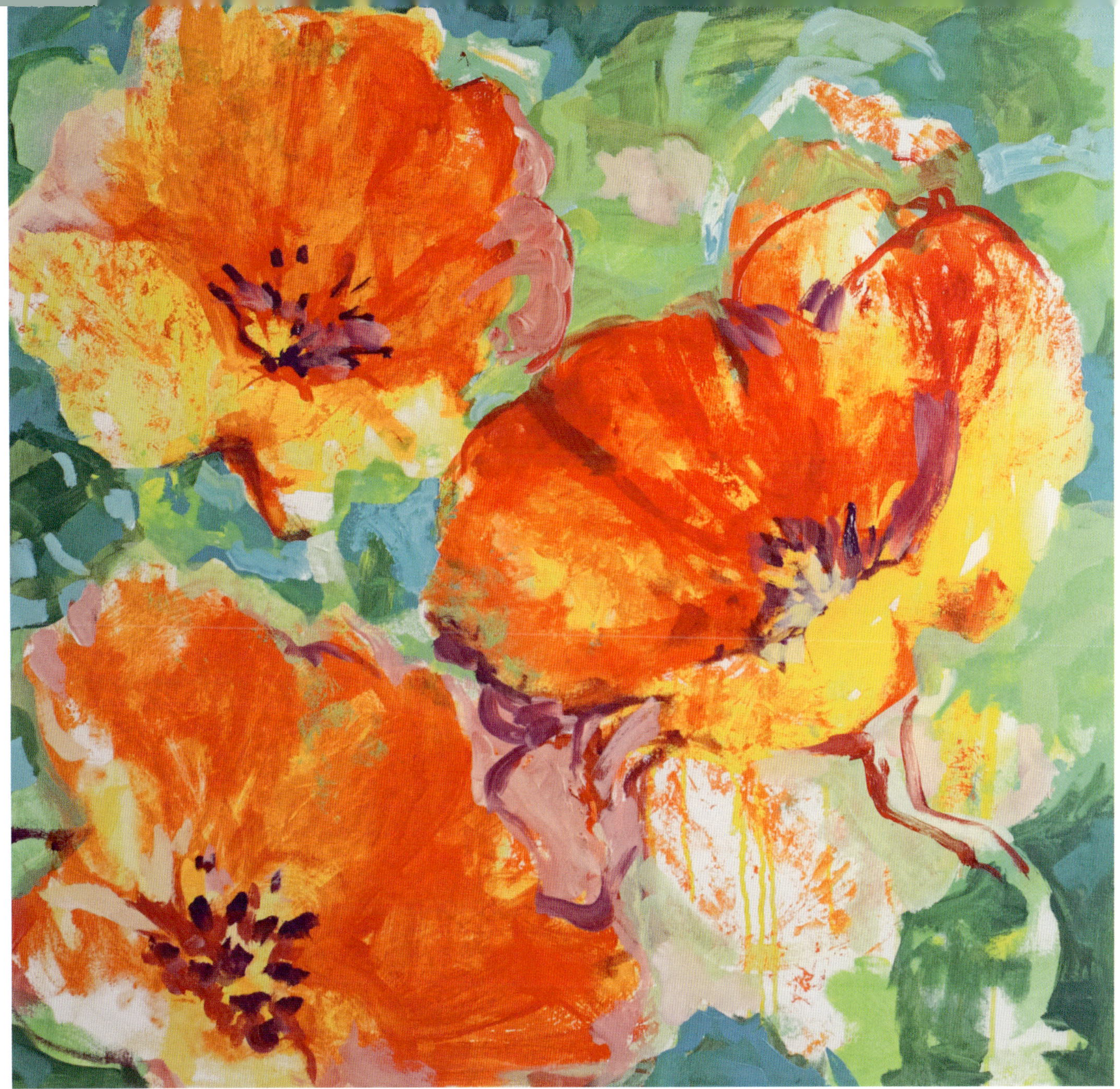

As I finish up, I use crisp drawn lines of bright red to refine the shapes.

Step 9. I'm happy with the outcome of this painting. It has the bright colors and interesting design of my earlier watercolor plus the physical texture and presence of acrylic. It seems to call out "come look at me" when you walk into its space. That's what attracted me to the nasturtiums, when I photographed them in the garden.

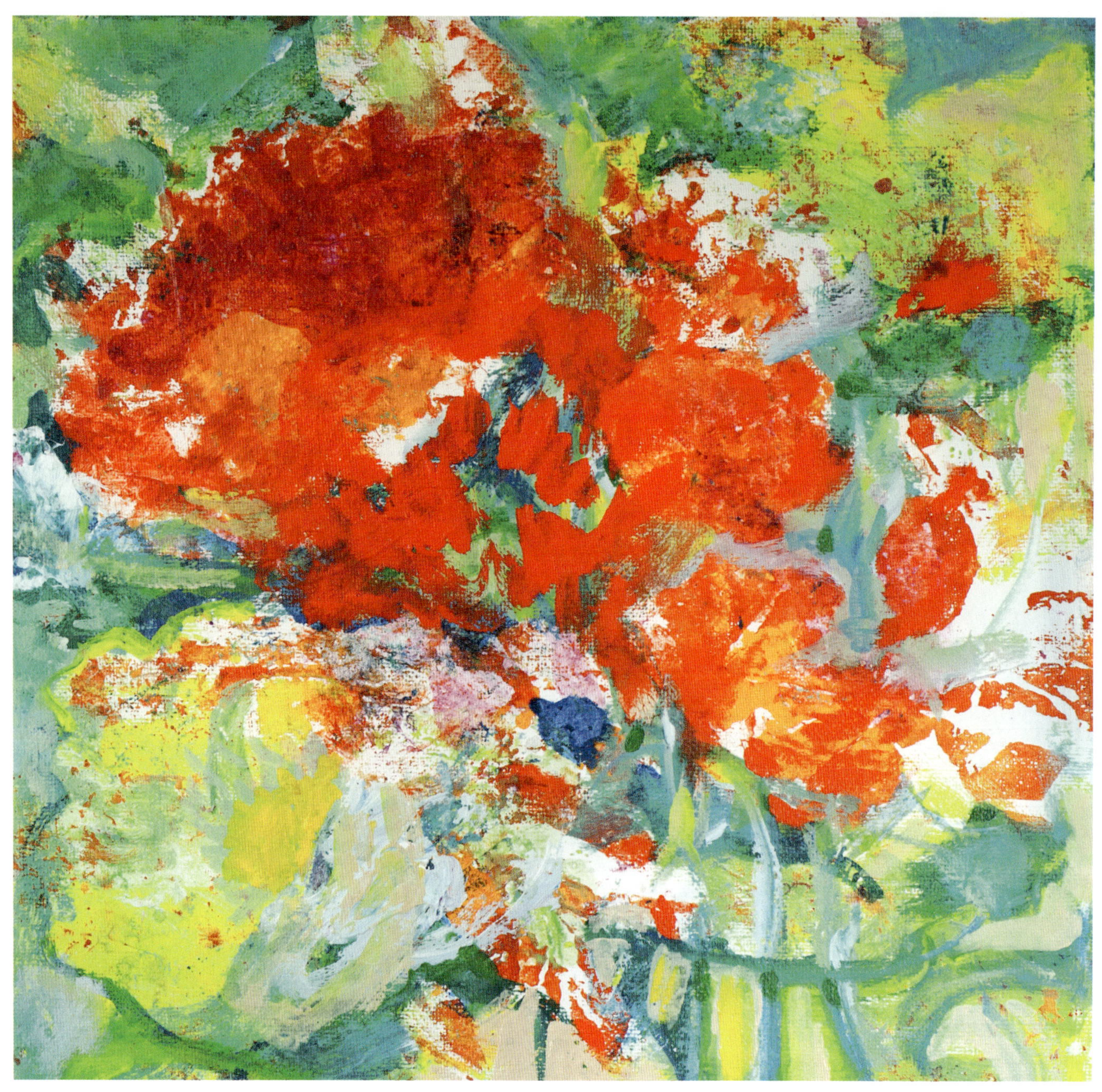

Geraniums. Acrylic on canvas. 20" x 20" (51 x 51 cm).

Gallery

Here are some other acrylic paintings of flowers from my garden.

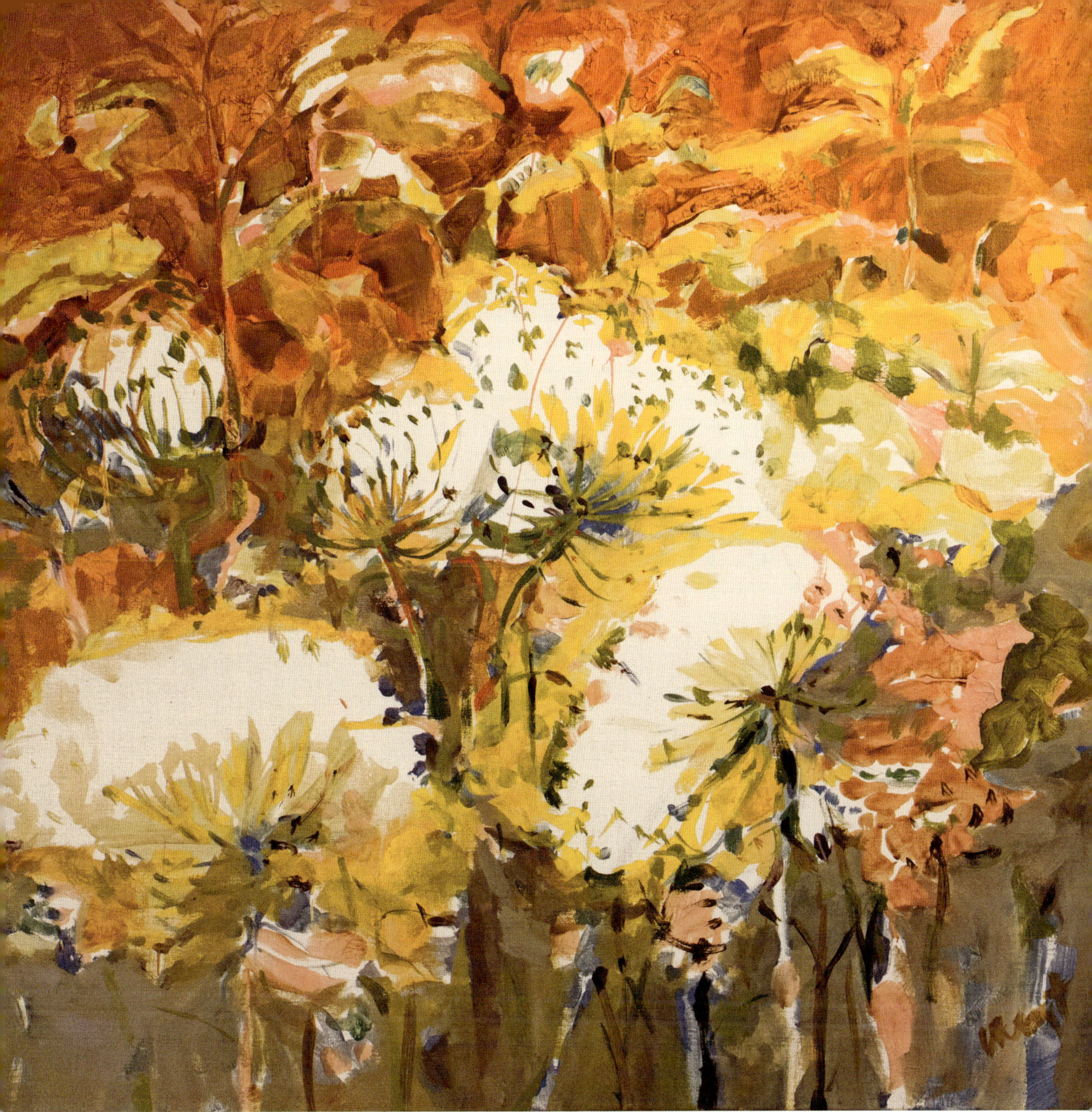

Queen Anne's Lace Evening. Acrylic on canvas. 30" x 30" (76 x 76 cm).

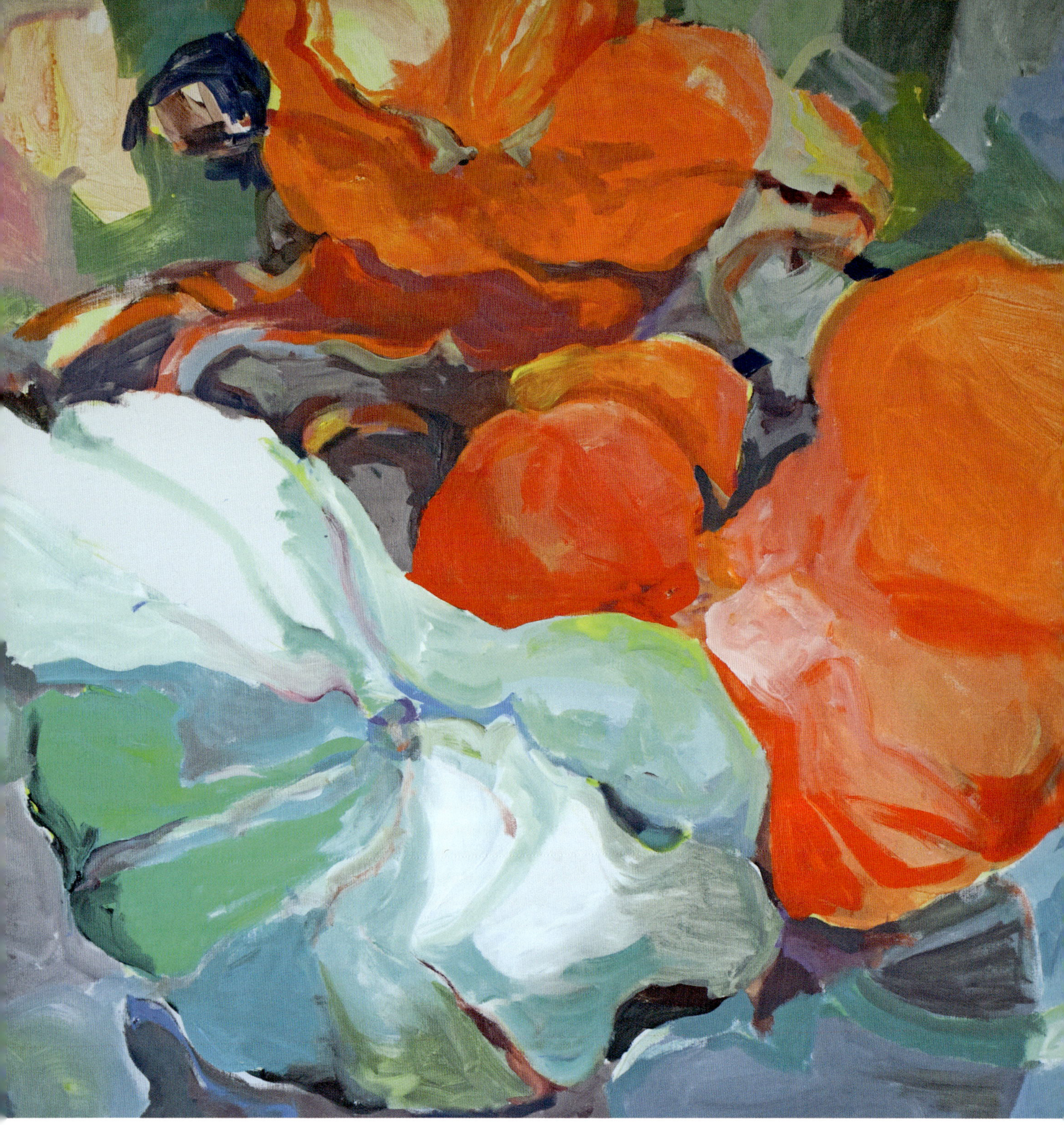

Nasturtiums #5. Acrylic on canvas. 30" x 30" (76 x 76 cm).

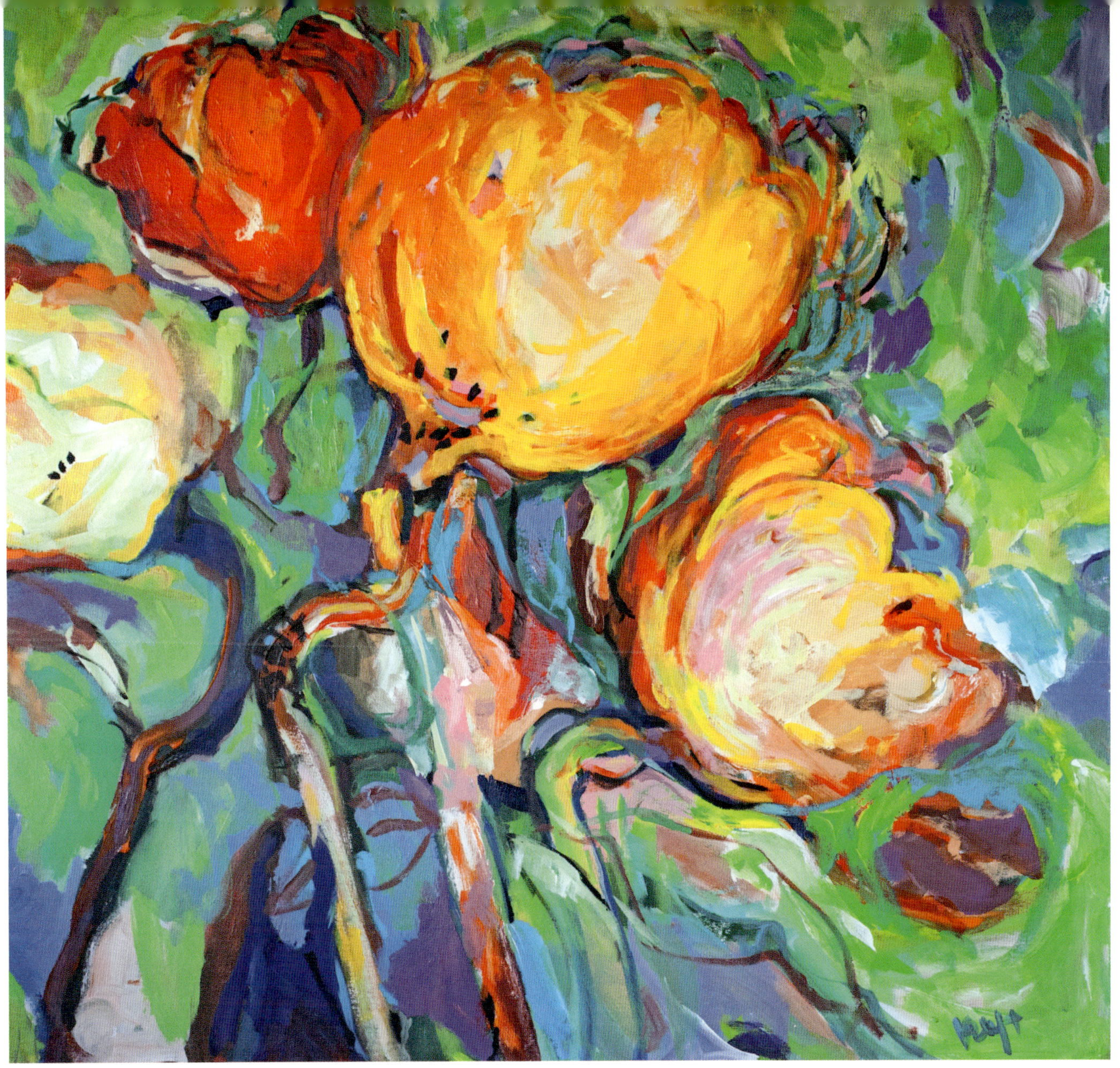

Tulip Tango #2. Acrylic on canvas. 30" x 30" (76 x 76 cm).

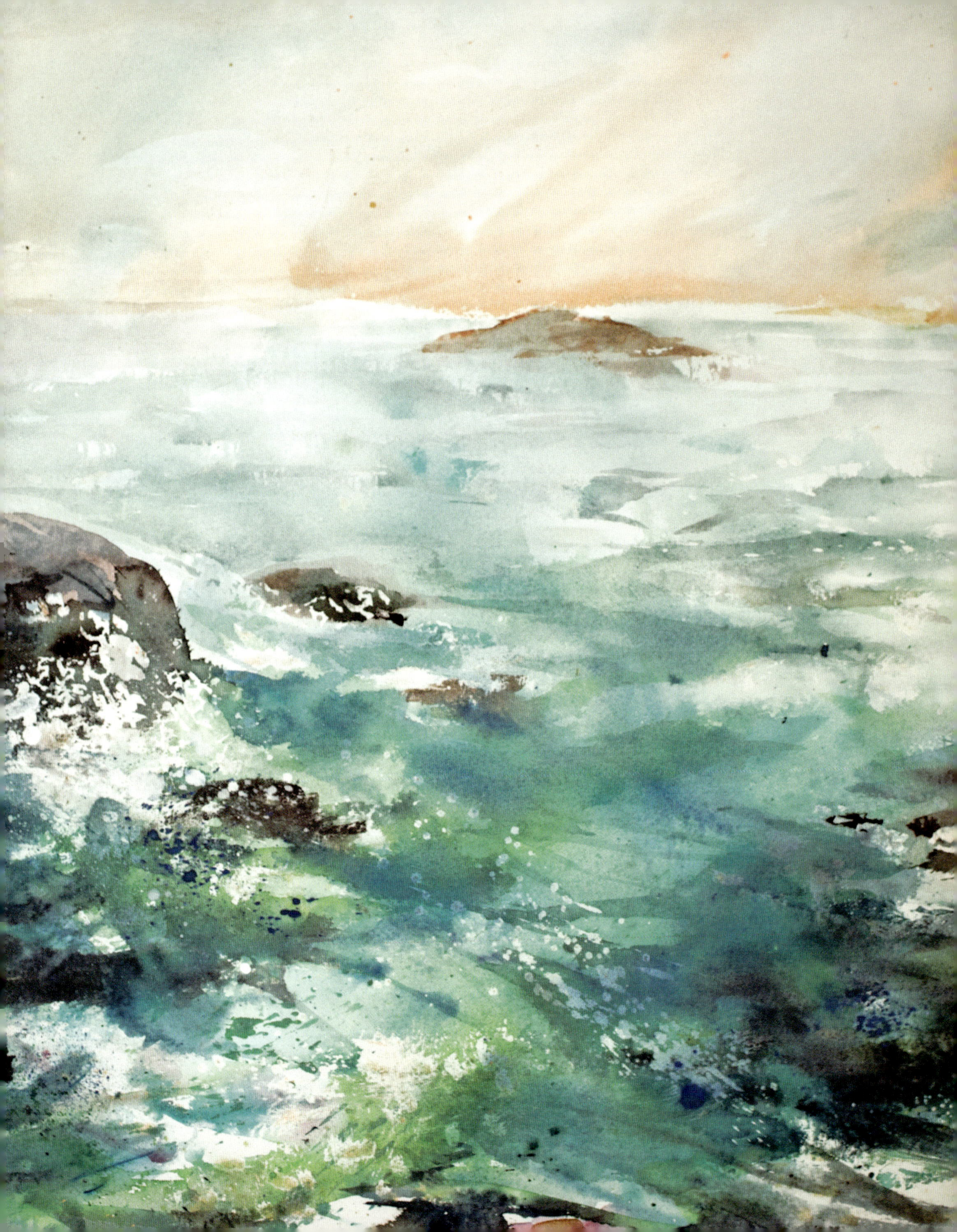

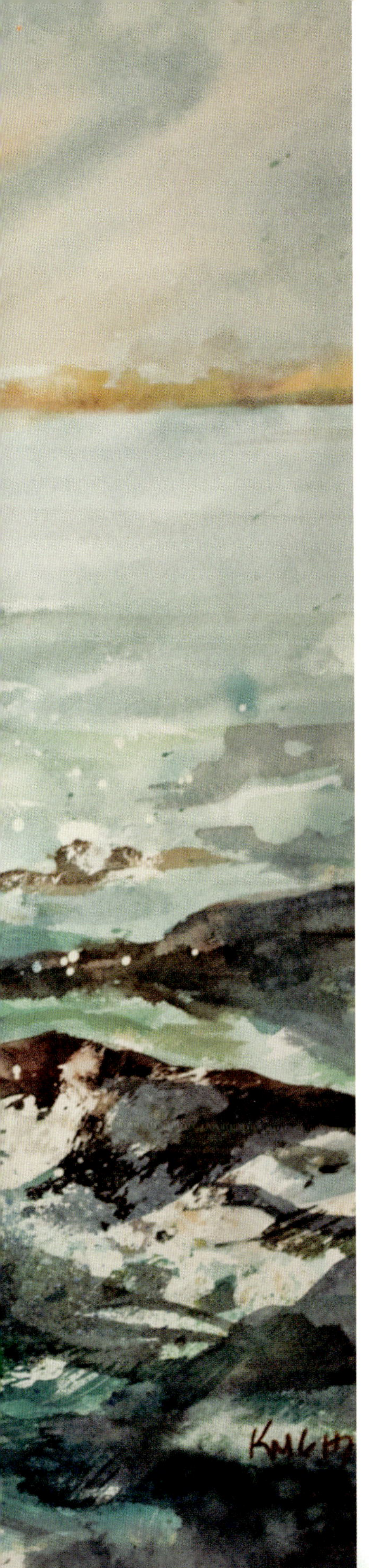

PAINTING THE ROCKS AND SEA

I AM ATTRACTED TO THE VARIATIONS OF WATER MOVEMENT. Sometimes, in a garden pool, for instance, the movement is nearly invisible. In contrast, the movement of a pounding ocean wave is almost overwhelming, happening everywhere at once with different colors and textures and patterns. It's easy to compare the variability of water's movement to so many different kinds of music, from lullaby to parade band to full symphony orchestra.

Painting pictures of water is always a good idea. There are so many aspects to appreciate. I love looking at the light and shadows in the moving water, the flow of the current splitting around a rock, the shifting reflections of the clouds and distant shoreline rippling across the surface, and the fish and pebbles beneath it. Along the shore, our green-ochre seaweed called "rockweed" wraps and swirls above and below the surface with each breaking wave. For me, it's mesmerizing.

One of my favorite subjects to paint is New Castle's ocean shoreline. I have done it many times. I've attempted to capture my impression of the different aspects of the ocean—sometimes more successfully than other times. My experience growing up here, searching the rocks and tidal pools for starfish and sea urchins, made me imagine crevices of hidden treasures. The possibility of a slip on the rocks and an unceremonious dunking into the very cold, rock-weed camouflaged pools, however shallow, made the experience fraught with hazard. The Atlantic Ocean off of New England is always cold, even in the summer.

Early Island Morning. Watercolor. 20" x 30" (51 x 76 cm).

One of the most challenging aspects of painting water is, unsurprisingly, its movement. There are many ways to paint ocean waves. Some artists seem to "freeze" the wave in mid-tumble. The French Impressionists were captivated by patterns of the waves heaving and cresting from a distance. They portrayed them moving with blurred edges and myriad colors reflecting the sunlight and sky.

Similarly, Winslow Homer, perhaps the best American painter of water and waves, captured moving power and splattering foam in his Prouts Neck ocean paintings. He chose to forgo the anatomical rendering of a wave and instead portrayed the impression of pouring, spilling water and rugged rocks.

When I start thinking about painting the ocean I remind myself to simplify my impressions. The compositional elements, light and dark relationships, and color choices become important to expressing the feelings I hope to convey.

Composition is particularly important in creating the mood. Will the picture seem to tilt and loom or balance evenly and peacefully? The more dramatic the angles, the more exciting the painting. But perhaps I want an entirely different feeling, one of relaxation and escape. If I stretch a straight unbroken horizon line midway through my paper, the feeling is stable and relaxing.

My palette is equally important. Will the colors vary dramatically between light and dark? Will I choose colors that are saturated and intense, or muted, softly blended grays?

The way I convey energy in my brushwork will have a big effect. If the strokes are blended and nearly invisible, the feeling will be calm. If the brushwork is plainly visible, abrupt, and going in all directions, the image will be energized and more dramatic.

If I want to share the exciting impression of being practically in the water, I will leave out the horizon line and fill the images with active diagonals of white foam and intense color.

Water can express so many emotions, it is no wonder it is such a popular painting subject. Deciding how dramatic or calm I want a water scape to feel is the first step in creating a strong painting.

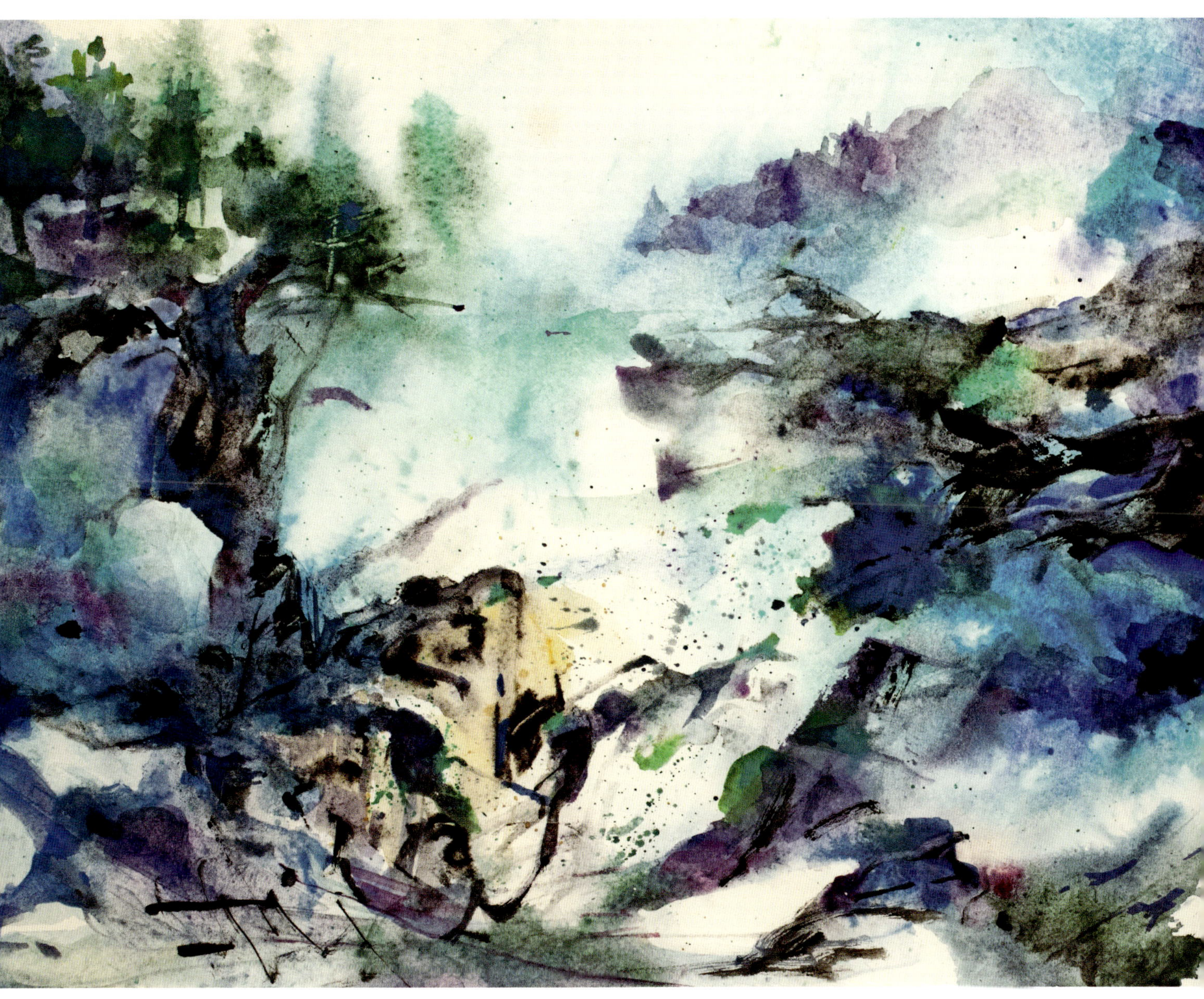

Morning Chop. Watercolor. 22" x 30" (56 x 76 cm).

Demonstration: Painting the Rocks and Sea in Watercolor

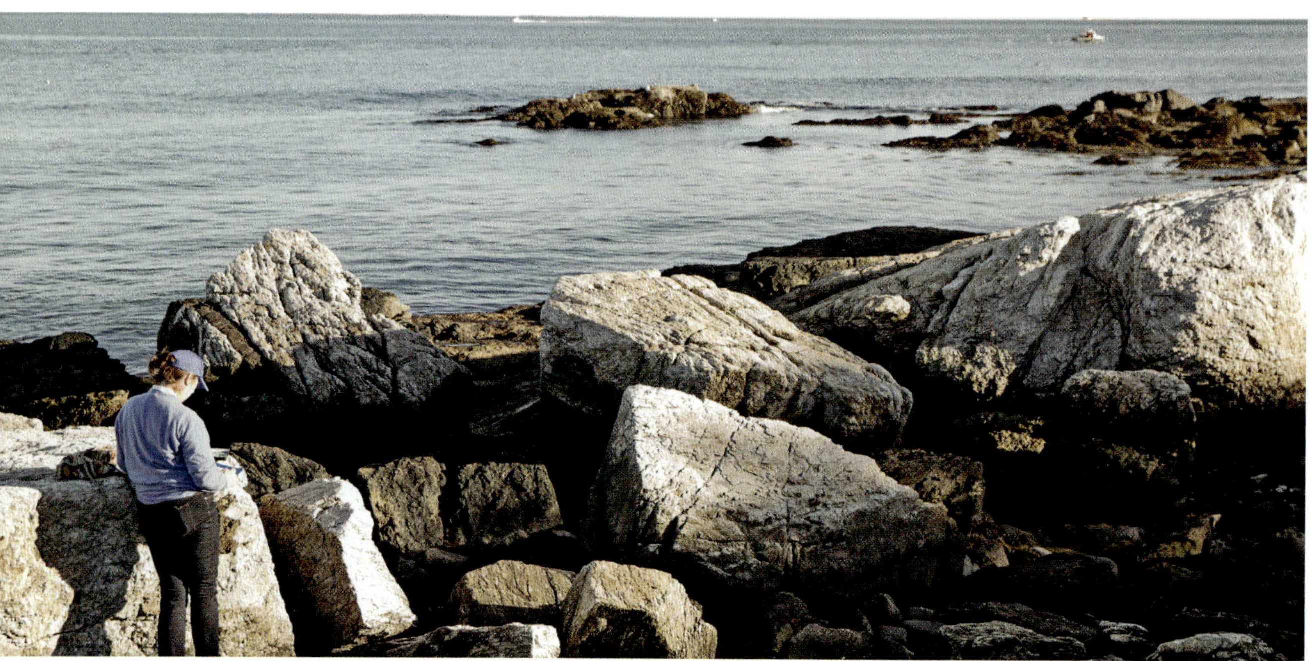

On the ocean side of the island

Most of our shoreline in coastal New Hampshire is rocky. When I think of choosing a specific site for a watercolor demonstration, there is one special place on the island that comes to mind.

A historic fort still stands guard on the southeast side of the island. The rocks along its shore are huge and rough. They are a chaotic mix of black, rounded shapes with white, bleached tops, dark red blocks that shatter into rectangles, and soft gray lumps that seem to melt a bit under each wave. It's a glorious place. There are seldom any people there because of the rough walking. I can sit undisturbed until the tide comes in.

I spend extra time just being there, breathing the salt air. I close my eyes and try to differentiate between the smell of the ocean and the rafts of drying sea weed on the higher rocks. I sit listening until I can

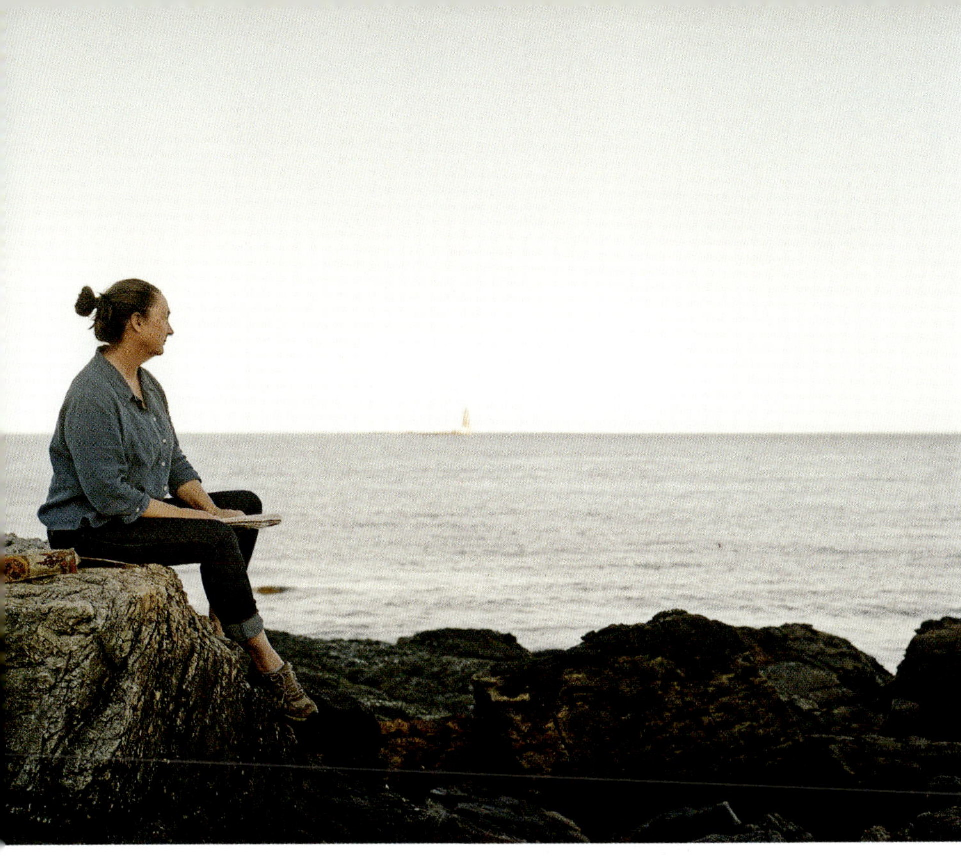

Sometimes I forget to sketch and just sit, lost in "seeing."

hear the waves hitting in a sequence around me: the boom that echoes from a low overhang, the crack of the breaker just off shore, and the hiss as the wave pulls back across the smaller rocks. Sometimes I have to make an effort to open my eyes again. Being able to take the time to not only be there, but to *experience* being there, is one of the greatest perks of being an artist.

Eventually sitting on the rough surface of the rocks becomes uncomfortable enough to pull me from my reveries and push me toward my work.

The Approach

PHOTOGRAPHY

Step 1. I pull out my camera and start snapping photos, looking at different angles. I crouch to view the white rocks above me, climb high to look down into a wide crevice, or sit still to snap a panorama of the rocks, breaking waves, and distant horizon—with or without the obliging lobster boat and lighthouse.

I take photos in series, trying to catch the foam on the rocks at the best moment. It's harder than I thought, and I begin to think that painting it might be easier than trying to capture it with a camera.

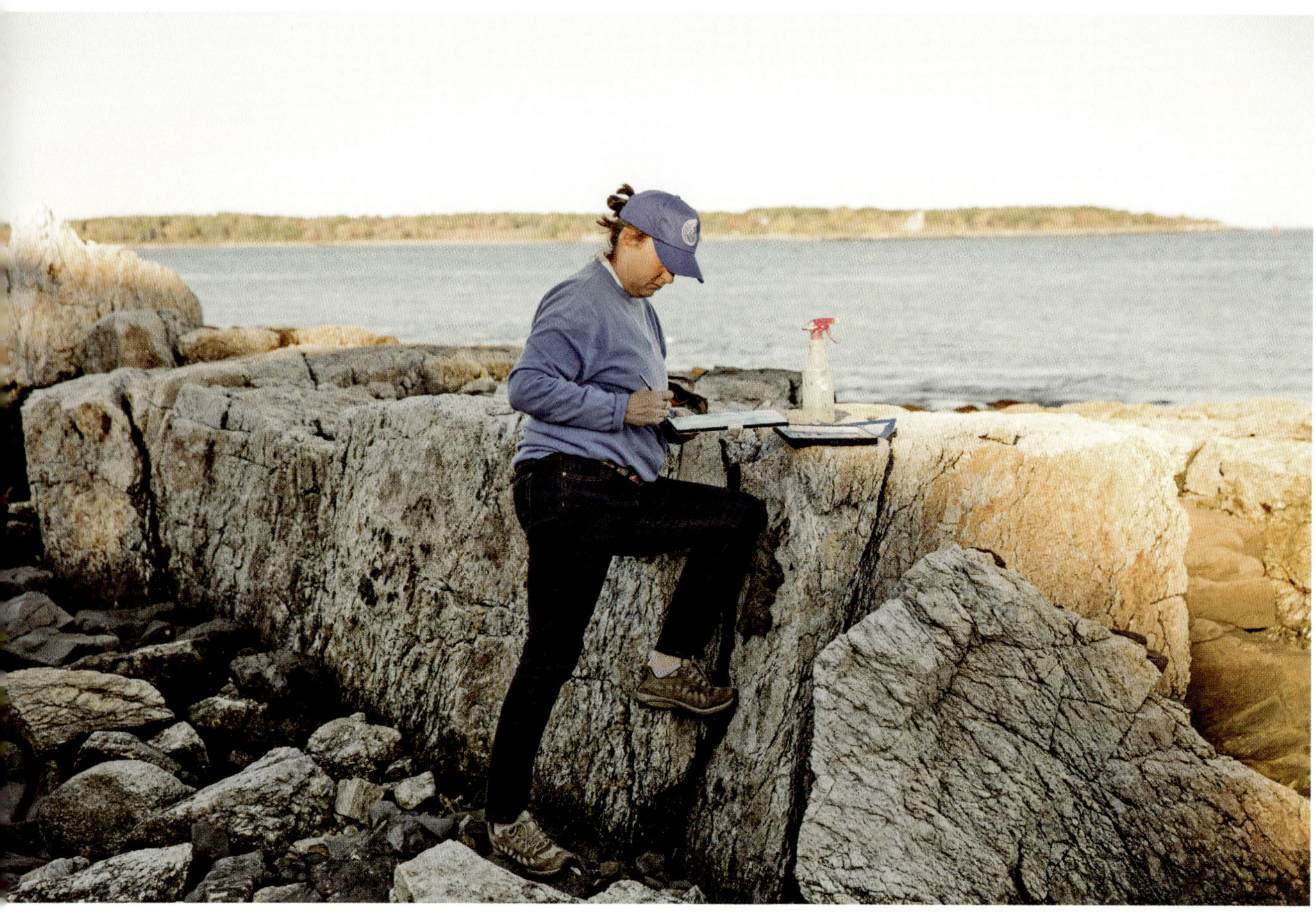

Capturing quick impressions of the rocks and sea

PENCIL SKETCHING

Step 2. I'm glad I brought both my camera and my drawing tools today. I have my spiral-bound sketchbook, graphite pencil, and eraser. I move about quickly, sketching in the larger shapes and shading the sides with smudges or crosshatching. Immediately it becomes clear to me that one of the more intriguing aspects of the scene is the heavy mass of the rocks and the fluid transparency of the water. That is what I want to try to capture.

I know from experience that my outlines of the rock shapes need to be clearly defined so that when I get back to the studio they still retain the quality of being specific rocks.

Rocks are interesting. They have layers of color and fascinating striation patterns because of their constant abuse from the waves. I have to remind myself to resist the temptation to detail the surfaces until I've sketched their shapes. It's like a fellow wearing a bright pink paisley shirt: I have to sketch the fellow before I get to the paisley.

I try to capture the rock's weight in my drawing. I chant "rock, rock, rock" to myself as I sketch and try to feel its solidity and size as if I were the rock itself. It helps. By reminding myself that the rocks are darker on the bottom and lighter on the top with a boxy mass, my sketches capture the impression I'm looking for.

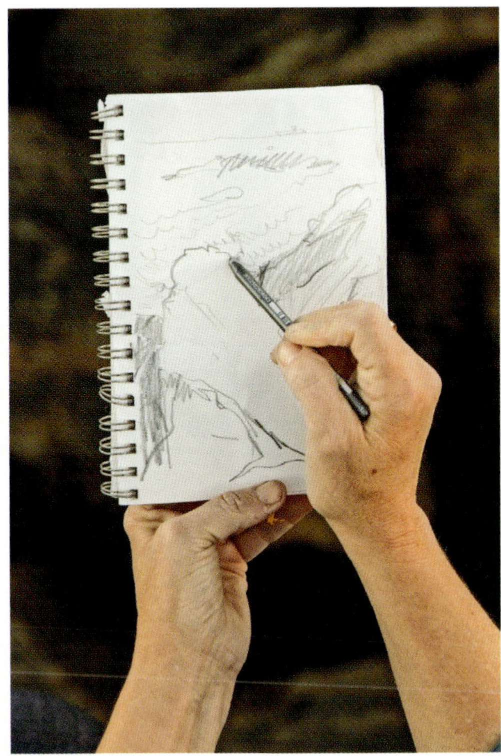

Step 3. I have to clear my mind and change gears as I start to sketch the waves. Their nature is the opposite of the rocks. As I sketch quick lines that represent the current flowing in, I imagine the force of the water sweeping around the far rock and spilling over the smaller ledges before swirling back on itself.

It's critical that I understand the nature of that flow; the way it pushes back against itself. It bursts into a high spray when it hits the farthest rock first and then dies down as it's dragged from beneath by the shoreline. I catch myself making sounds like the waves as I sketch them; it's just as well there are no other people around.

ABOVE: Keep the pencil sketch loose and let the moment inspire you.

BELOW: My outdoor watercolor kit wedged between ocean shore rocks

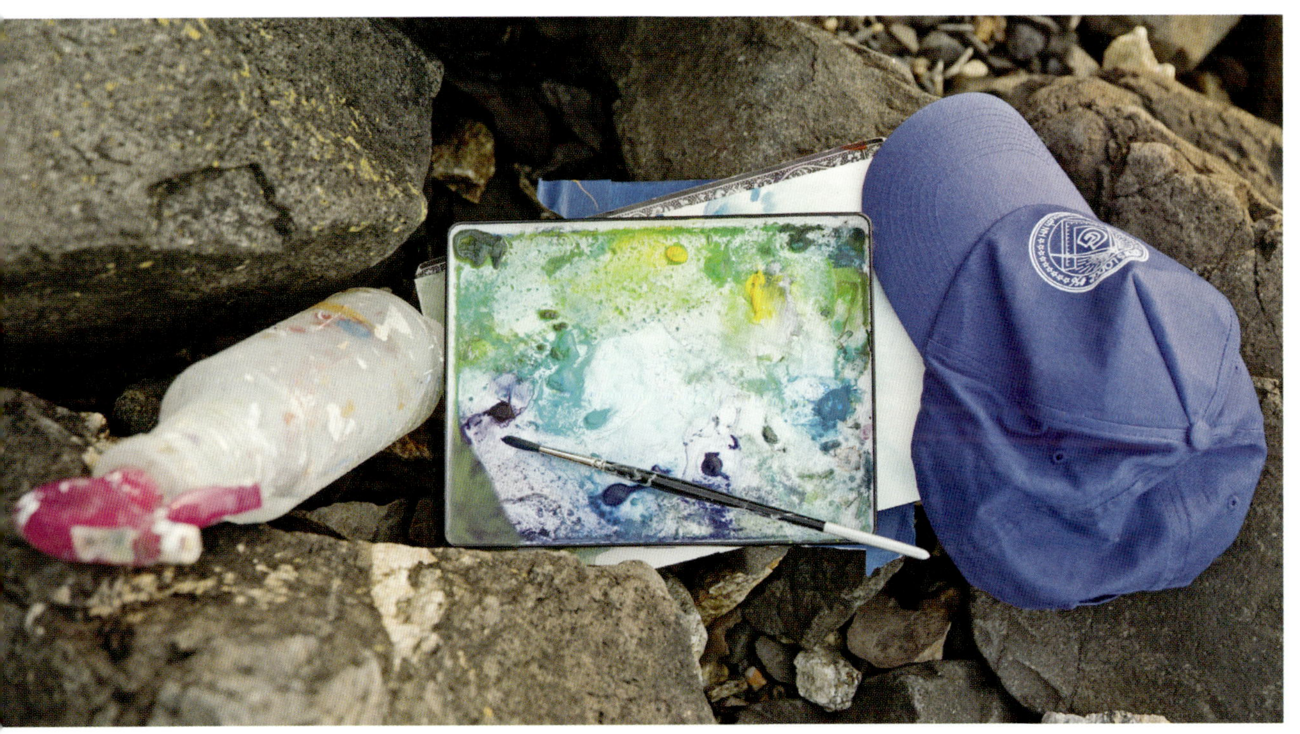

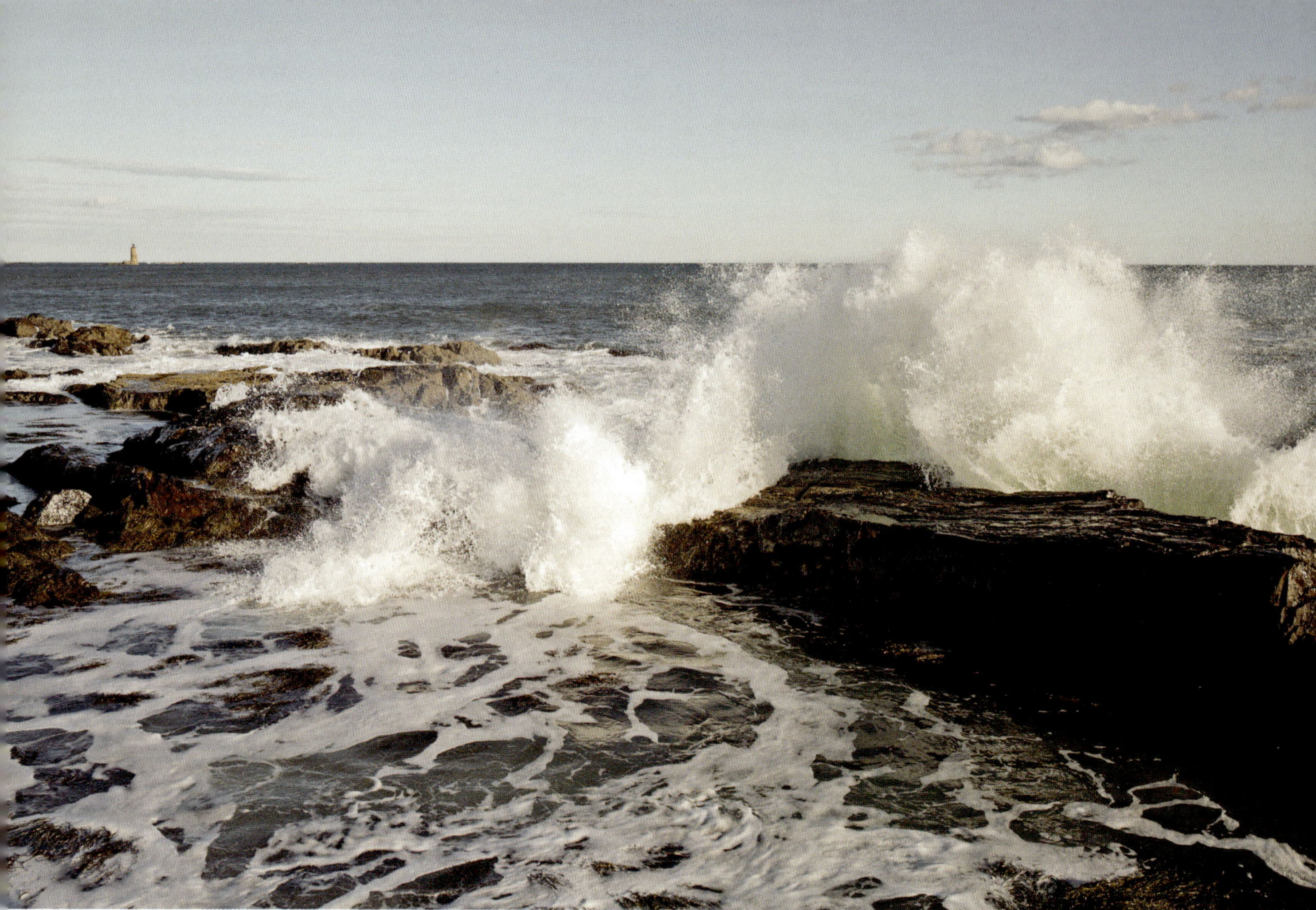

Breaking waves

WATERCOLOR SKETCHING

Step 4. Luckily, the next morning the weather has not changed too much. I try to get back to the site when the tide is about the same as the day before. I have my traveling watercolor kit with me: yellow, red, and blue paint dried on a little plastic palette, my spray bottle and a small round brush. I've brought along two 8" x 10" (20 x 25 cm) blocks of Arches hot press 140 lb (300 g/m^2) paper. It can be extremely windy on the shore, so I've brought minimal supplies and only things that can't blow away. I've carried everything in a cross-body painting satchel; I need my hands free when I move around.

I begin realistically, choosing colors that come close to what is there. The rocks are so beautiful I have to consciously tight the temptation to focus on their striations. Maybe someday I will come back and paint just the rocks, but today I want the broader seascape feeling.

The color of the rockweed as it undulates in the current is a mix of yellow, red, and blue. It glows against the grayed darkness of the rocks. I try to get a feel for the color of the water as it breaks over the rocks and swirls in the shallows. I try to capture the color of the falling edge of foam as the waves break against the rocks. I head back to the studio inspired.

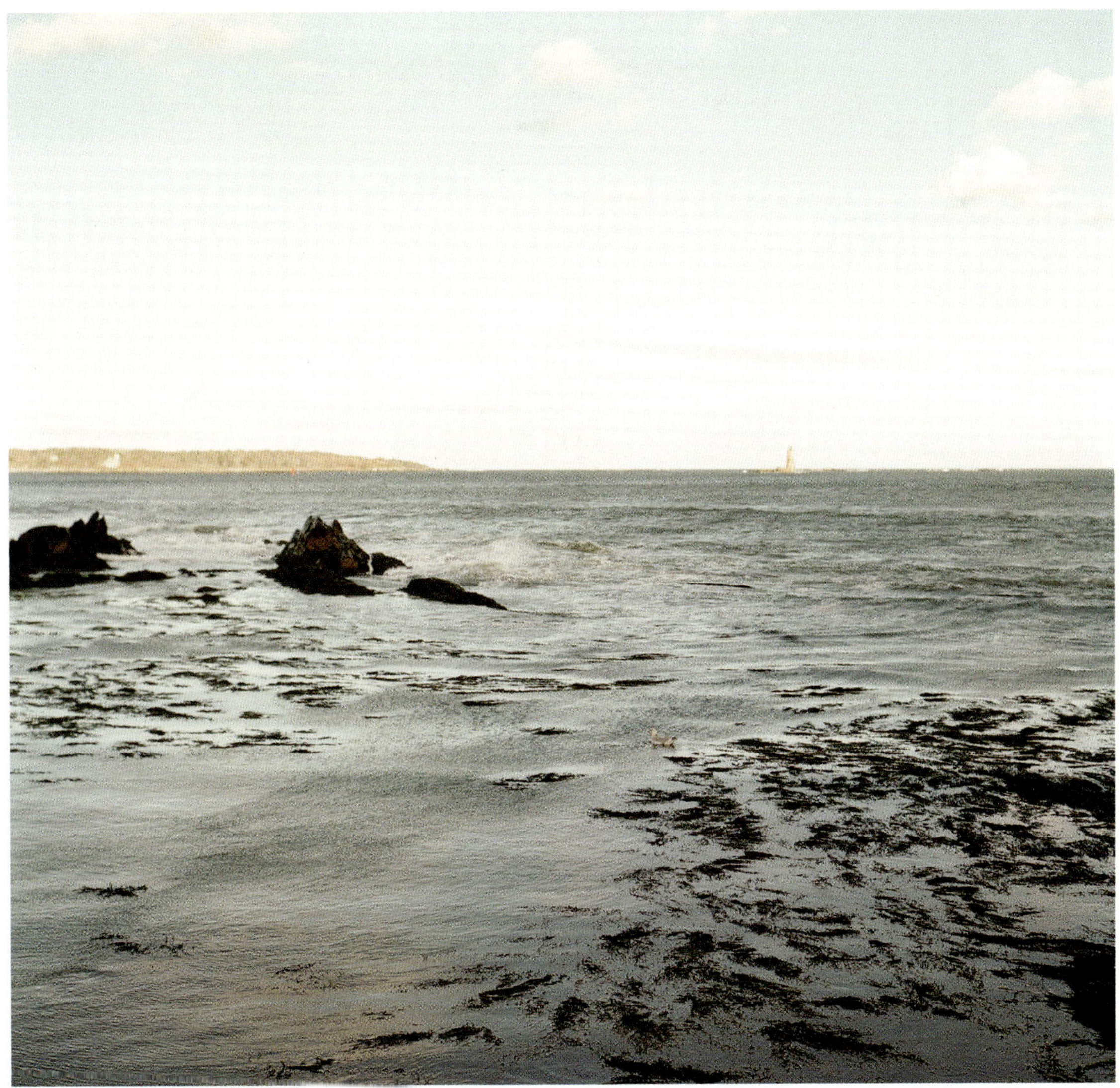

Patterns of rockweed, roiling in from the waves

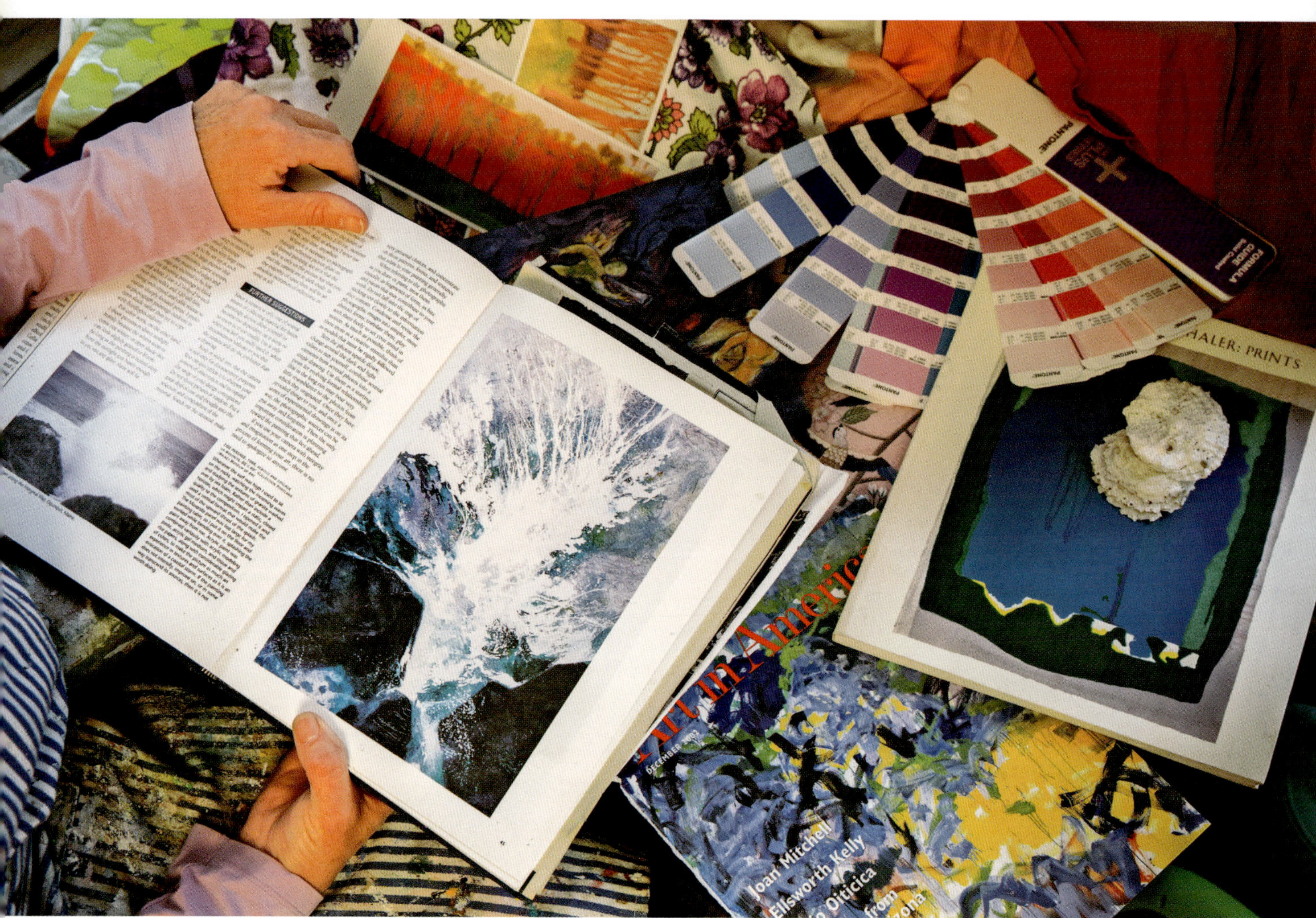

Inspiration from painters Ed Betts, Joan Mitchell, Helen Frankenthaler, and Wolf Kahn

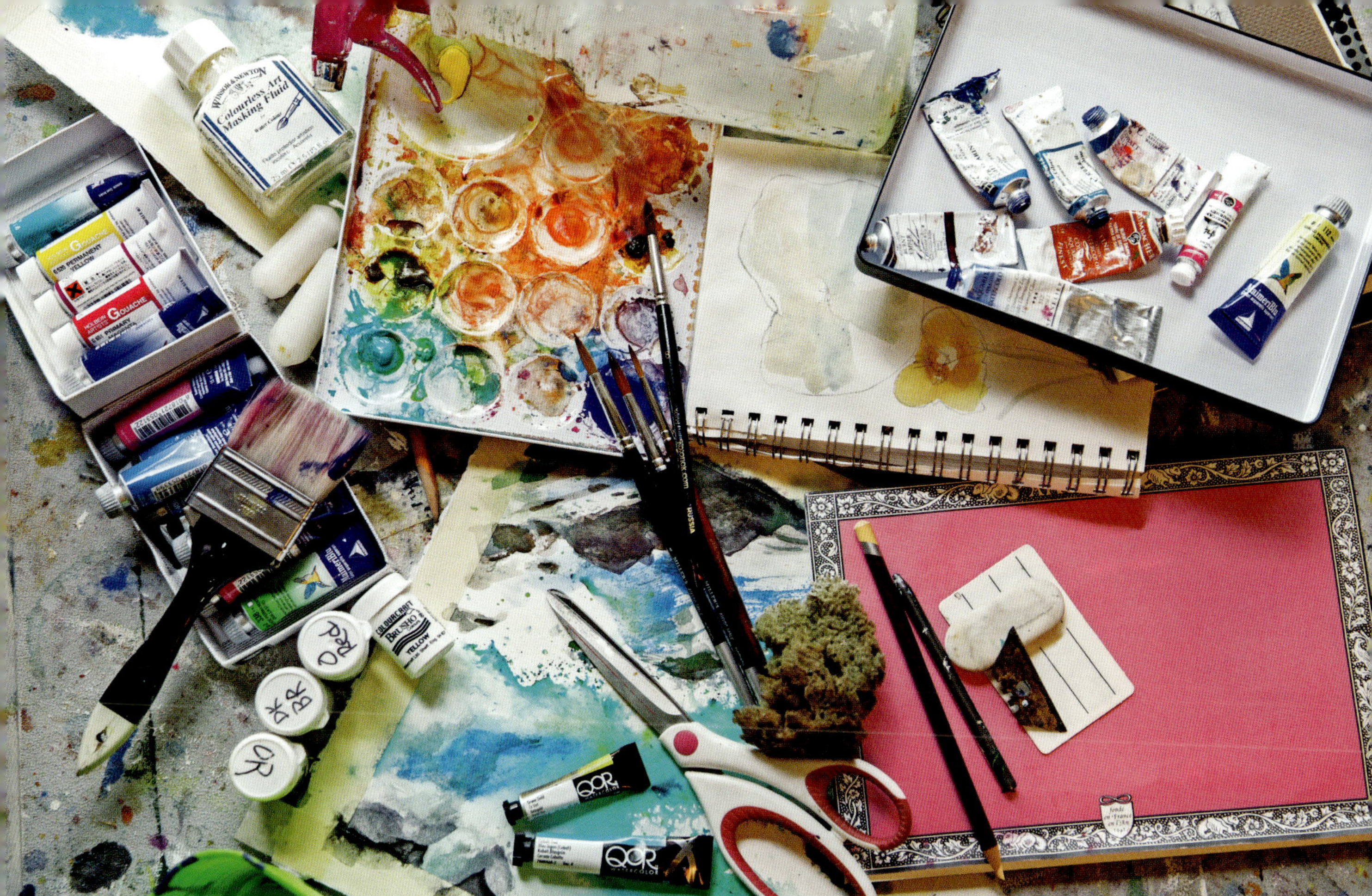

Collecting materials for the in-studio watercolor painting

In the Studio

It takes longer than usual to adjust to being inside, probably because of the rush of sea air I've been breathing. I take my time, in part because I'm a little overwhelmed by the idea of trying to paint the swirling, crashing energy of the waves. How did I do it before? How have other artists done it?

I dig into my stacks of books and art magazines and I look through mountains of my older watercolors, trying to connect with previous ideas. I'm unconsciously sorting through my impressions of the experience and am confident that what comes out in the end will be stronger because of this process.

I realize that it's the simplicity of my desired composition—one that is solely waves and rocks with no sky or beach—that makes proceeding difficult.

I want the feeling of energy in the waves. I want to feel the sting of the sea spray on my cheek when I look at my final painting. Can I achieve that?

I tape a grid onto a large sheet of watercolor paper with that goal in mind. I also assemble plastic wrap, a single-edge razor blade, a white candle stub for wax resist, an old toothbrush, a small watercolor sponge, a spray bottle of clean water, and paper towels.

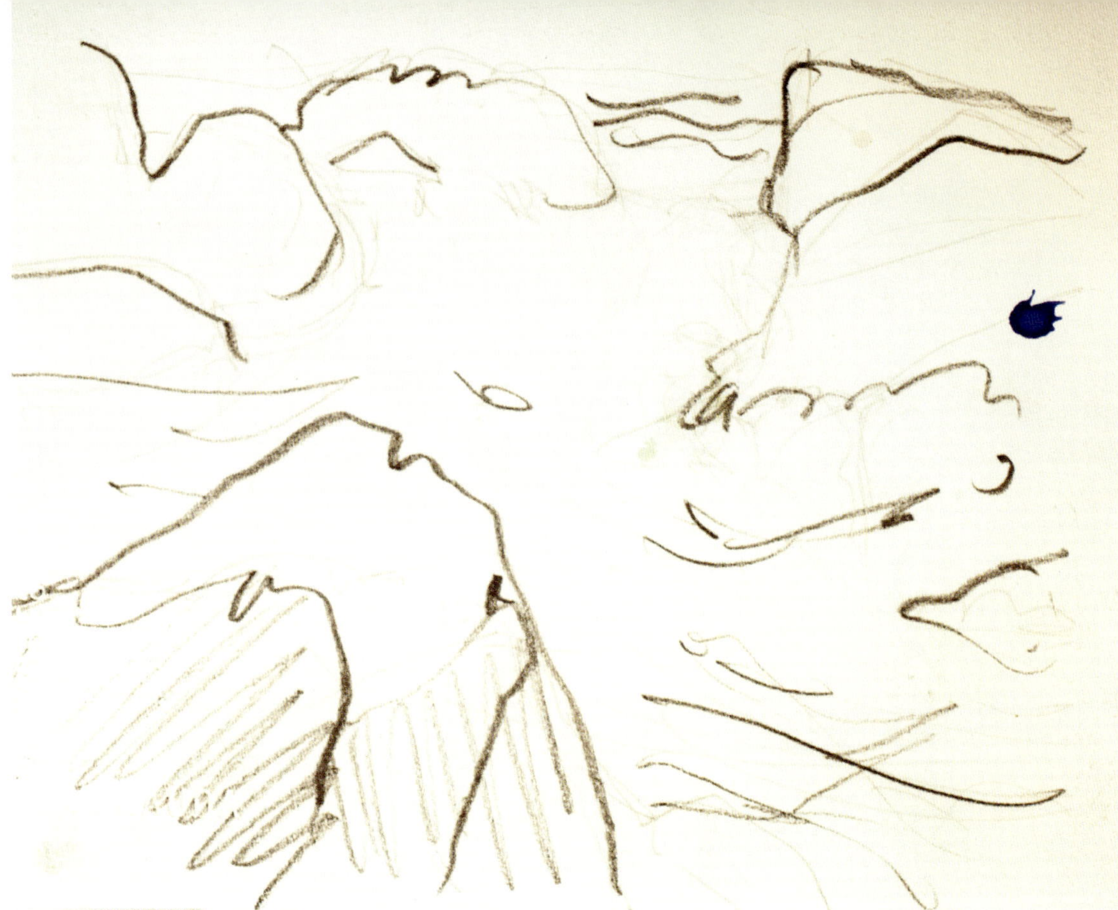

ABOVE: I do a quick studio sketch to simplify my impressions into a solid composition. This is my design sketch.

OPPOSITE: The light of the foaming water should be in high contrast against the dark rocks. This is my value sketch.

Step 1. Design. I start with a light pencil sketch, trying to capture the movement and rhythm of the waves. The placement of the rocks is critical to the design. If they huddle along the lower half of the composition, they feel tame. If they rise to the height of the format, they become looming forces.

I decide to start with a big, a medium, and a small shape. I position my rocks so that they recede in space. The large rock in the foreground gives the viewer a place to stand. I'll open one side of the composition for the water to flow through. The back-and-forth jostling of the water will contrast with the solidness of the rocks.

Two rocks anchor the corners and squeeze the rushing water toward the bottom right. The rocks hold the design like thumbtacks holding rippling silk. The water will command attention as it pours through the center of the design, bumping into the rocks and erupting into spray. To add to the energy of the painting, I zoom in close, eliminating the sky completely.

This is just one possible composition. It expresses one level of drama. When you set out to do a seascape— or any painting for that matter—try all sorts of compositions and be aware of what intensifies or relaxes the drama of the image. I'll be working on several different versions at once, as I did earlier in the book.

Step 2. Value. One of the interesting things that happens when I look at my design for this painting is the way my eye goes back and forth from rocks to water. At first, the rocks are the positive objects and the water runs around them. At second glance, it's the water that is the positive force and the rocks are shadowy elements.

When you come across this kind of back and forth in a design, consider both aspects to decide which one you want to emphasize. In the value sketch, I look at the light and the dark. The light of the foaming water is in high contrast to the dark rocks.

You can subtly make the rocks more important and have the water be the background around them, or decide the water will be the most interesting part, with lovely colors and splatters of foam. I scribble a note in the margin to remind myself that it's the water that will be my focus.

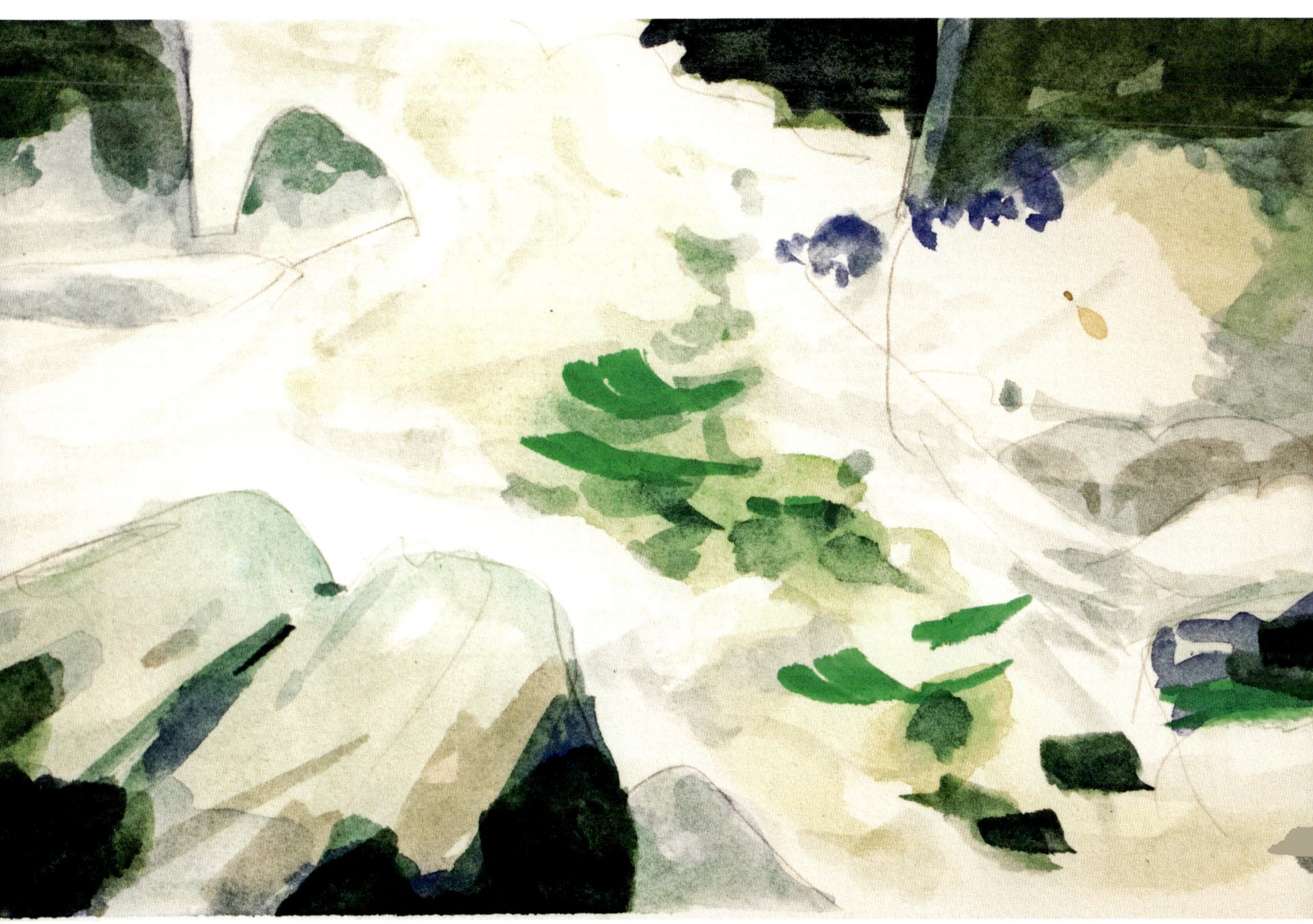

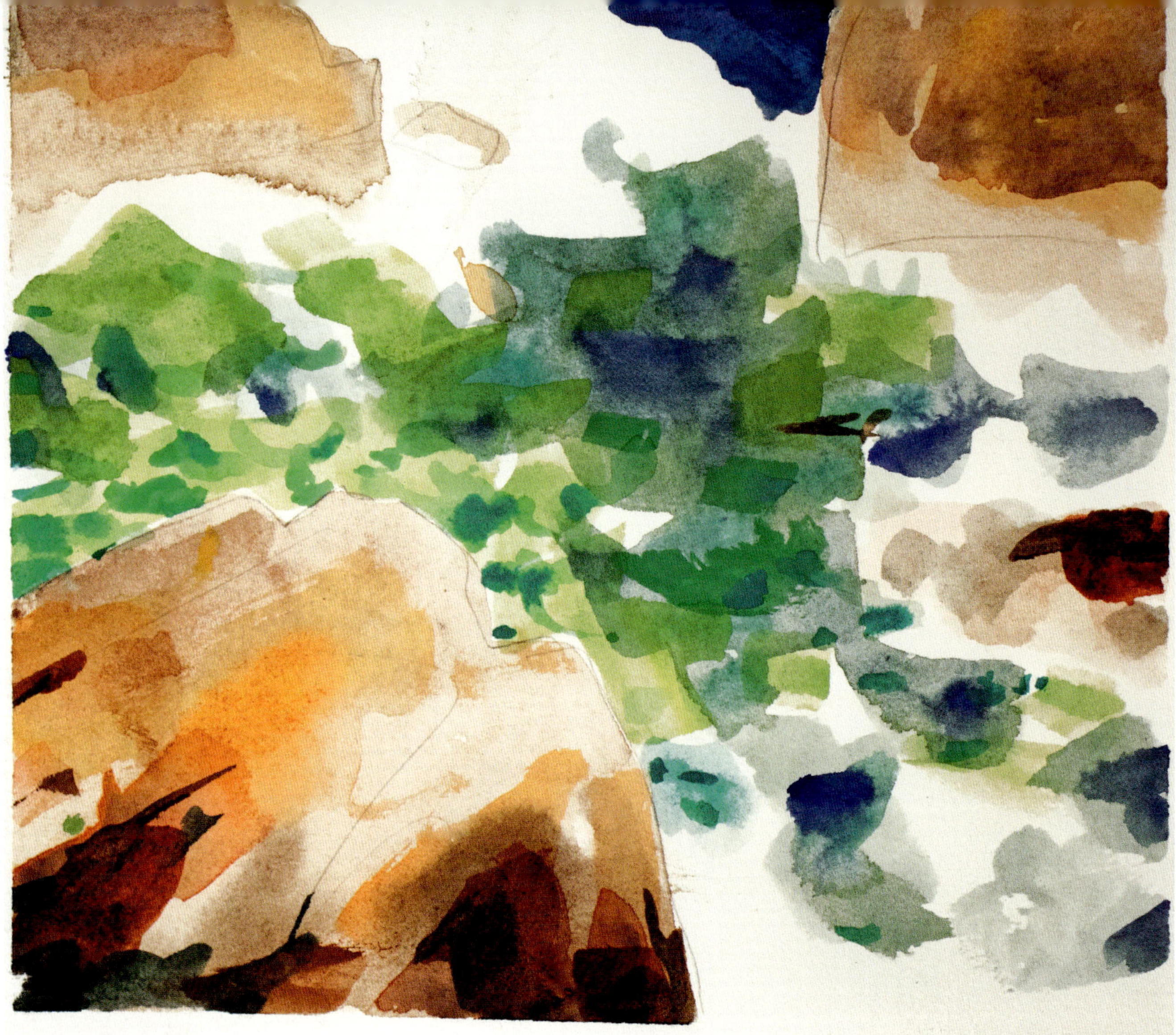

For my color sketch, the palette that I choose will determine the mood of this painting. If I use Payne's gray and indigo rather than bright turquoises, I will end up with a very different painting. Choosing lively blues that hover between warm and cool, such as cobalt and cyan, makes the drama more inviting, so that I could almost feel the spray of the waves.

Step 3. Color. I've decided to paint energetic waves and choose a bright assortment of blues: cobalt, cyan, ultramarine, and cobalt turquoise. To add to the green of the water, and to highlight the rocks, I choose my favorite cadmium yellow light, as well as yellow ochre.

For the rocks, I select burnt umber because it is a reddish brown and a bit of cadmium red. So, in fact, I have a version or two of the three primary colors—red, yellow, and blue—on hand. My palette becomes almost infinite with these colors. I also have a tube of Chinese white paint. This is one of the rare times I include opaque white on my palette. I will use it for the final foamy touches.

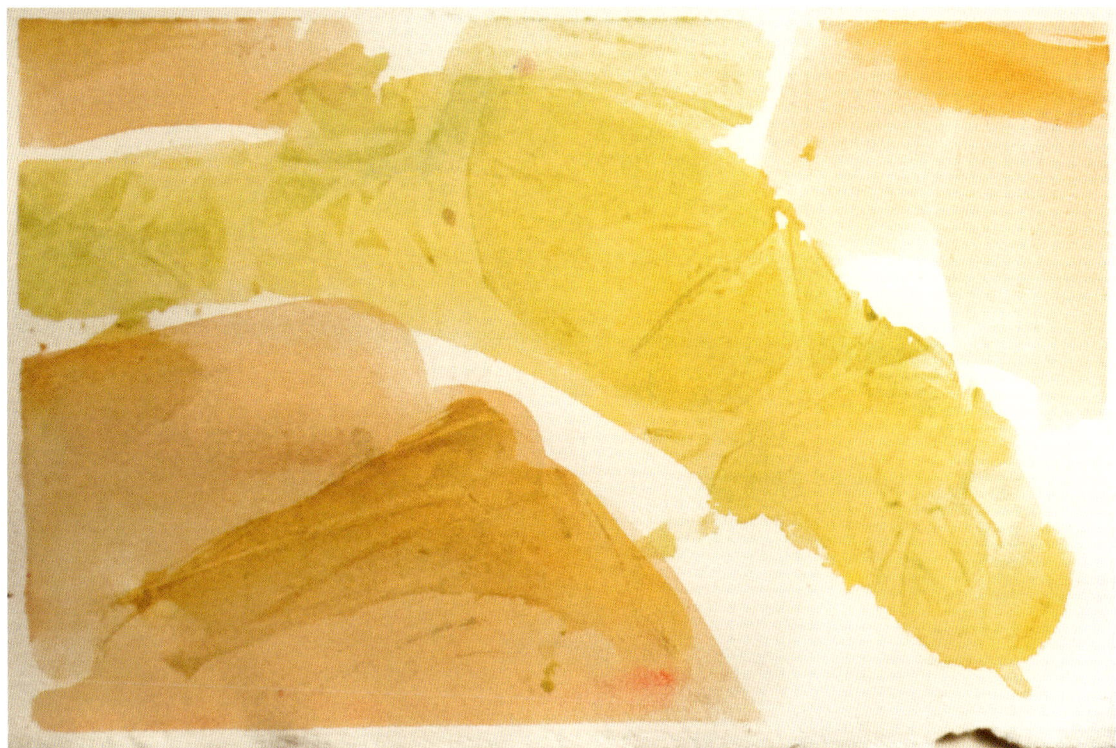

For the studio watercolor painting, I have chosen a warmer palette. For the first wash, I brush in a light layer of yellow ochre and add a bit of red for the rocks. Then I brush in pure cadmium yellow light for the water.

Step 4. Now that I have the design, value, and color figured out, I begin with the studio watercolor painting. I start with the plastic-wrap technique (see pages 74 to 77) to create a different feeling through the texture. I want the patterns created by the plastic wrap to suggest the flow of water.

I start with the water. My first light wash of yellow sets the image in place. I pull off a long strip of plastic wrap and use the one piece to cover the water flowing from top to bottom. (Because my water will be green, I can start with bright yellow and overlay washes of blue to produce organic greens.)

When the paint is dry under the plastic wrap, I lift it. Even with this first wash, I am thinking about how much foam and splash I will want later on. To prepare, I center the wash of color between the rocks and leave bare white paper all around it. I mix some browns and lightly add them where the rocks will be. Again, I use the plastic-wrap technique on the rocks to create short and ragged patterns, different from the long, smooth pattern of the flowing waves. I crinkle up some wrap and press it on the still-wet brown paint.

Note: Using plastic wrap serves two purposes for me. First, I don't know exactly what the results will be when I use it, so it keeps the first steps of a painting looser than if I simply painted in a shape. Second, the technique dries as mottled color, and when I paint over it in watercolor, the color does not even out. This adds layered richness and a free, unstructured pattern to the transparent layers.

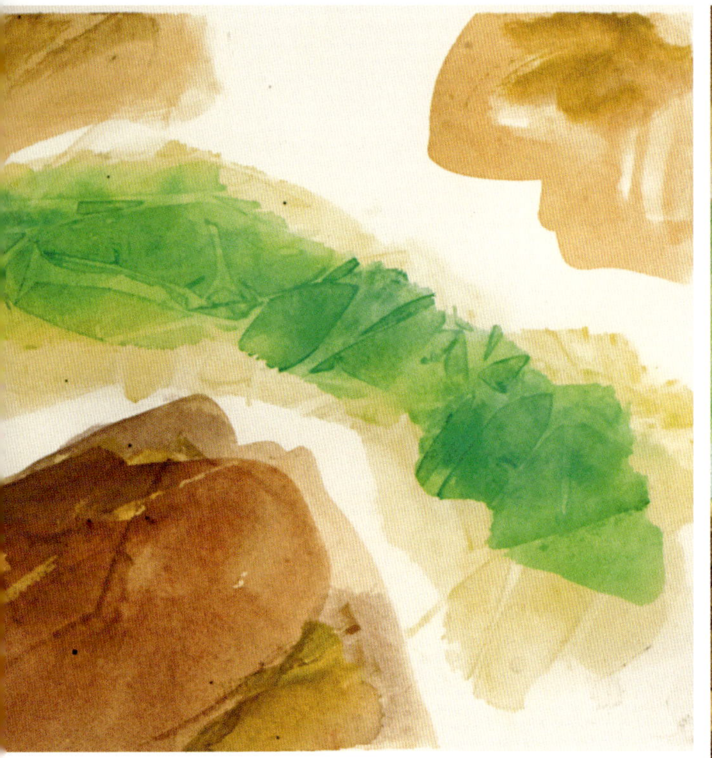

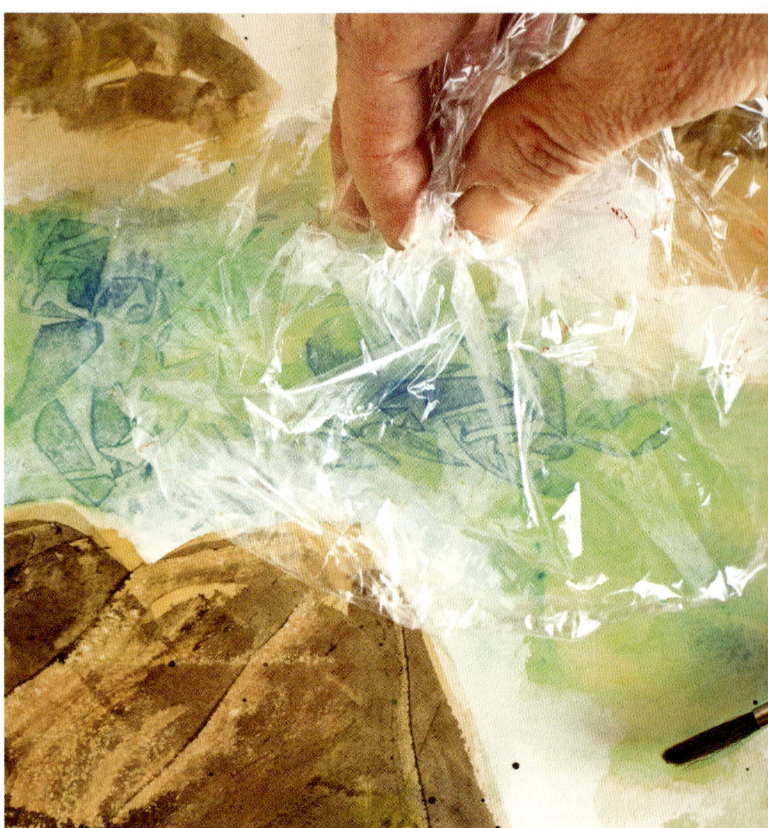

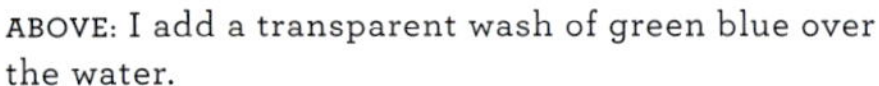

ABOVE: I add a transparent wash of green blue over the water.

RIGHT: Use the plastic wrap to suggest the flow of choppy water.

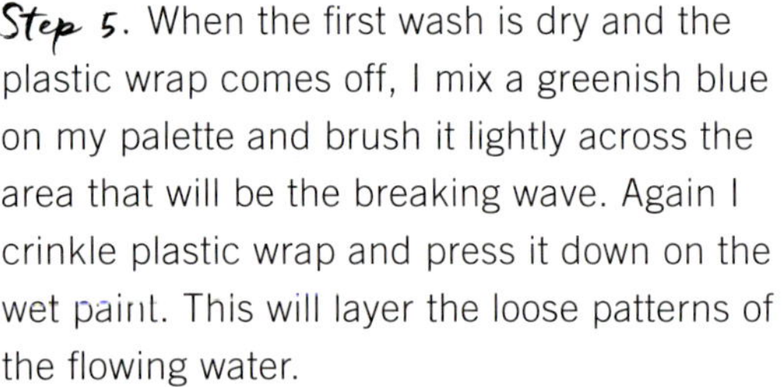

Step 5. When the first wash is dry and the plastic wrap comes off, I mix a greenish blue on my palette and brush it lightly across the area that will be the breaking wave. Again I crinkle plastic wrap and press it down on the wet paint. This will layer the loose patterns of the flowing water.

While the green paint is drying under the plastic wrap, I brush a light coat of burnt umber on the rocks to darken them. While the burnt umber is wet, I texture the rocks by dragging the flat edge of a razor blade or a credit card through the paint to suggest striations in the rock. (See "Special Watercolor Technique: Wax Resist and Scraping for Texture" on pages 118 and 119.)

Step 6. I turn my focus back to the waves, painting in a bit of blue wash through the water. I vary the blues, using green toward the bottom just as the sea turns green when it churns, and cooler ultramarine blue farther away. I'm careful not to cover all of my earlier delicate blue washes or the white areas around the rocks. I want to keep areas of the initial blue wash as fresh as I can.

I'm pleased by the white areas along the edges of the rocks and the water. They already look like they are moving with the wave. I'll turn them into foam later.

I build layers of texture on the rocks and contrast between the surface of the rocks and the water. Though they both start with washes and plastic wrap, I continue to emphasize their differences.

Step 7. I continue to build up texture on the rocks with wax resist. Using wax as a resist in watercolor is a technique that was used by the masters John Singer Sargent and Winslow Homer. The trick is to use it sparingly or it will discolor the paper in time. Draw with it like a crayon in the areas you want to use it. If you bear down too hard and the wax goes on too thick, scrape it off with a razor blade. Then try a color wash over the waxed area and see what happens. (See pages 118 and 119 for more on this technique.)

Now I begin to add the blues.

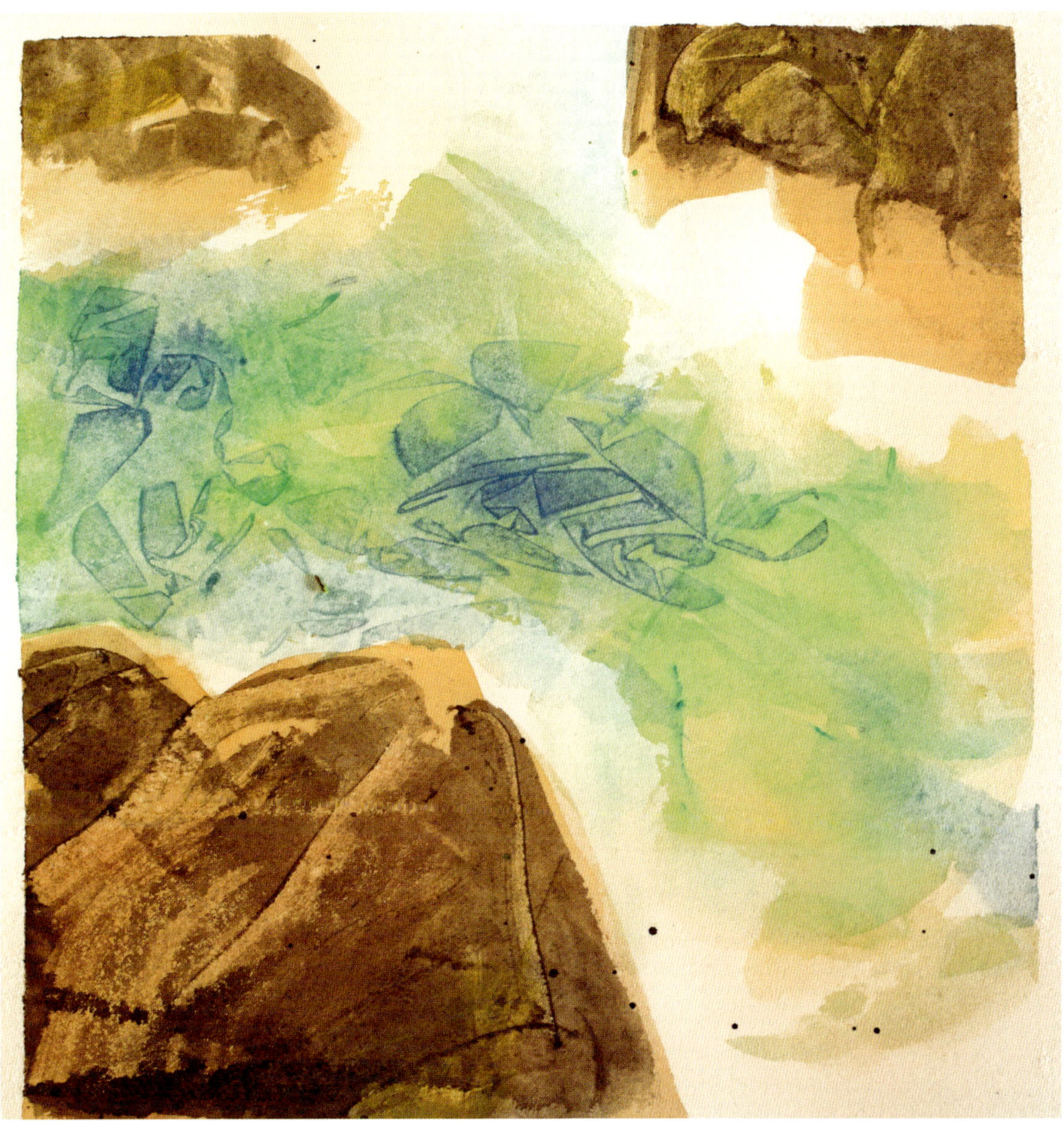

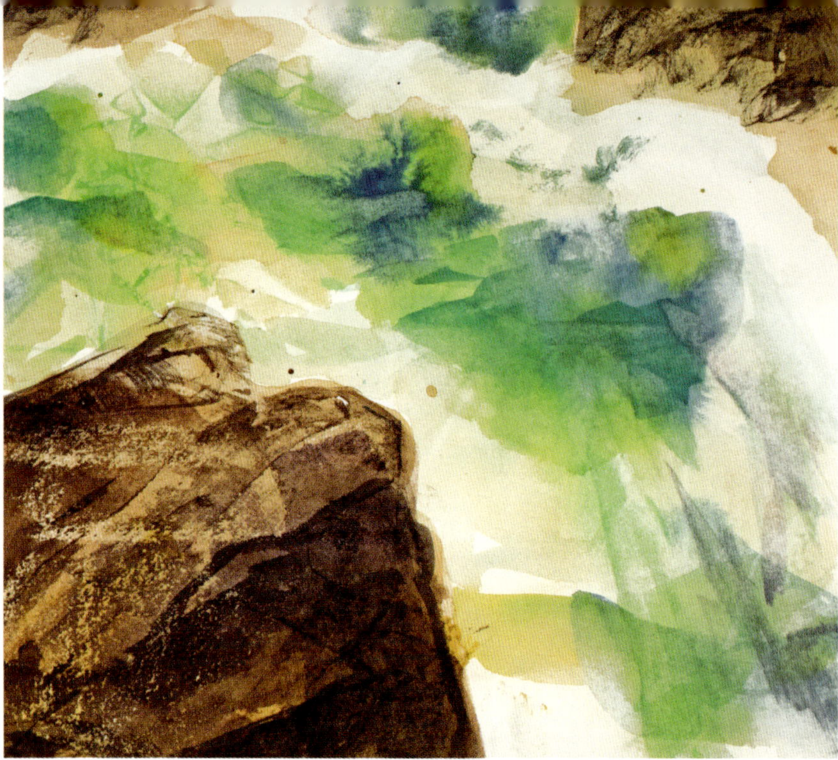

The rocks feel heavier and more solid when I darken the side.

Step 8. I have darkened one side of the rock in the foreground so that it feels weighty. This also gives the rock a three-dimensional look. The dark shadow is simply a stronger mix of the rock colors I've been using. I might add a little ultramarine blue to the burnt umber for a good, dark color.

Step 9. Now I add loose blue brushstrokes to the water. I move my brush like it is the churning water, whispering watery sounds to myself without meaning to. Each brush stroke is clear. The water seems to spill actively and unimpeded from the top to the bottom.

Step 10. The painting is almost done. I take a walk around the studio, thumb through my music collection, and put on an Ella Fitzgerald CD. My dog Lilly gets a biscuit for keeping the studio chair warm. I sit down and ask myself what exactly is going on in the painting? I try to look at it with fresh eyes. What jumps into focus? Are the rocks the most important or is the water dominant? What areas are mushy and uncertain? Are the values balanced? Is there a range from white to dark? Are my colors clean?

Some artists look at their work in mirrors or upside down. Some use a "receding lens" which is the opposite of a magnifying lens. I just take off my glasses. The details disappear and the larger design, values, and color relationships are all I see.

This is a simple painting. It's about rushing, churning water and hard-textured rocks. The water is slightly more interesting than the rocks because of the lovely blue and green colors. I move on to make tiny adjustments.

Step 11. After some thought, I rewet an area of the water that is too bold a blue. Using my #10 round brush, I dab a few drops of clear water on the blue, count to five, and then lift the drop back up with my brush tip. (Using a "thirsty brush" this way is described in detail on pages 38 to 41.)

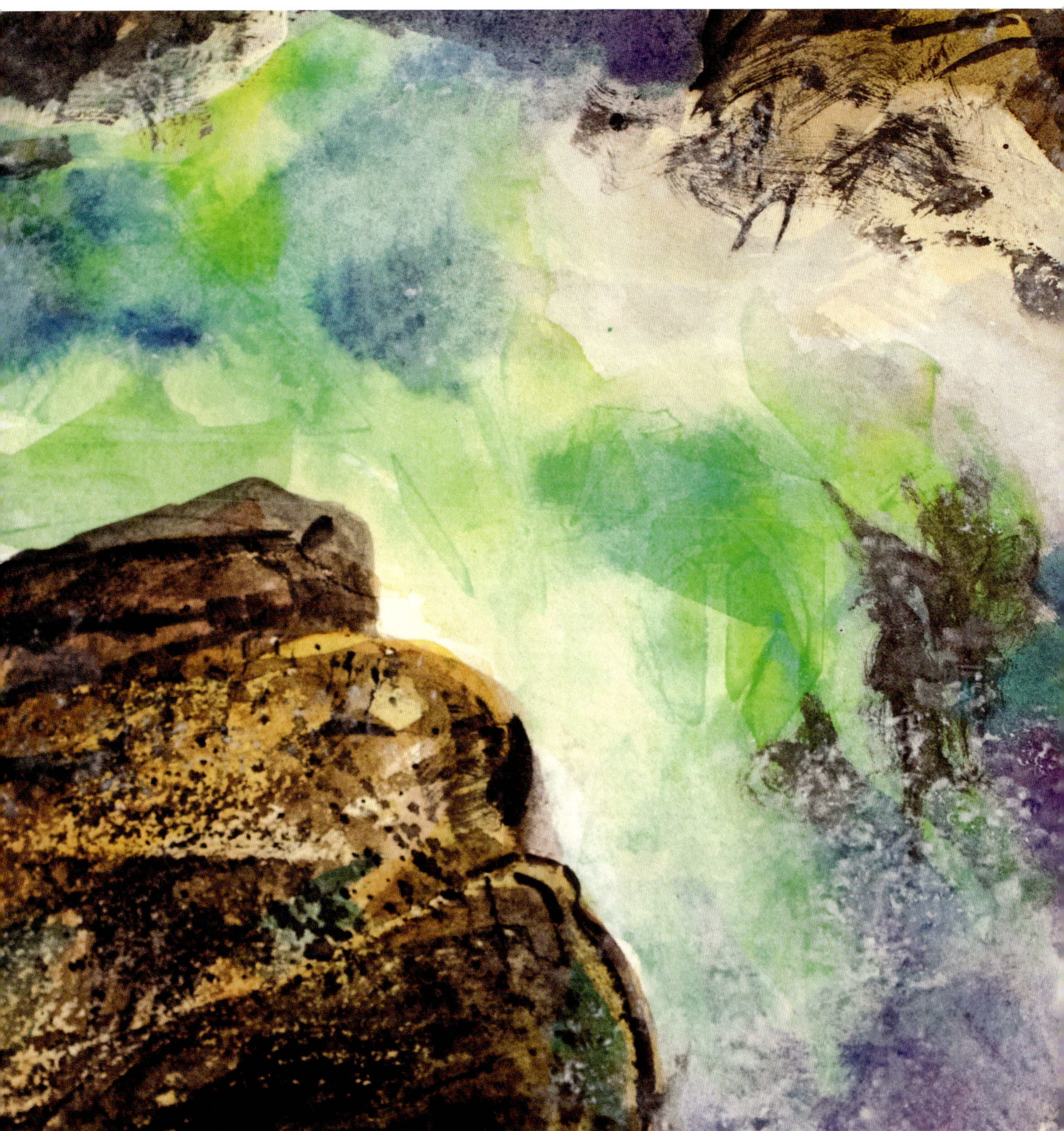

Getting closer to completion

Step 12. I decide that adding a triangle of darker blue along the top center edge will lend more of an ocean-like feel. Using a clean brush, I wet the area with enough clear water to sit on the surface like an oil slick. I put the blue from my palette into the middle of the wet spot. The idea is that the new wash of darker blue will spread, darker in the center of the wet area and lighter along the edges, thereby blending visually into the previous dry layer.

Step 13. I step back to gain a wider perspective on my paintings. The larger the painting, the farther away I walk back. Distance allows me to assess the overall composition, values, and colors and determine whether to make any final adjustments. I use the damp watercolor sponge to blur an edge and a brushstroke that seem too hard.

As a last touch, I dip the old toothbrush into Chinese white paint. It goops on the bristles, which I flick my finger across to spritz a fine spray of white where the rocks meet the water. I like the effect so much, I dip the toothbrush into the blue and brown puddles on my palette and spray more color across the same area. It looks better when the spray is uneven.

I am pleased with the energy of these watercolors. It is time to decide whether to work on a larger watercolor painting for exhibition or move directly into acrylic on canvas. I have resolved several questions about watercolor technique and process. I have simplified my experience into a clear, bright impression of the ocean waves crashing on the shore of New Castle Island.

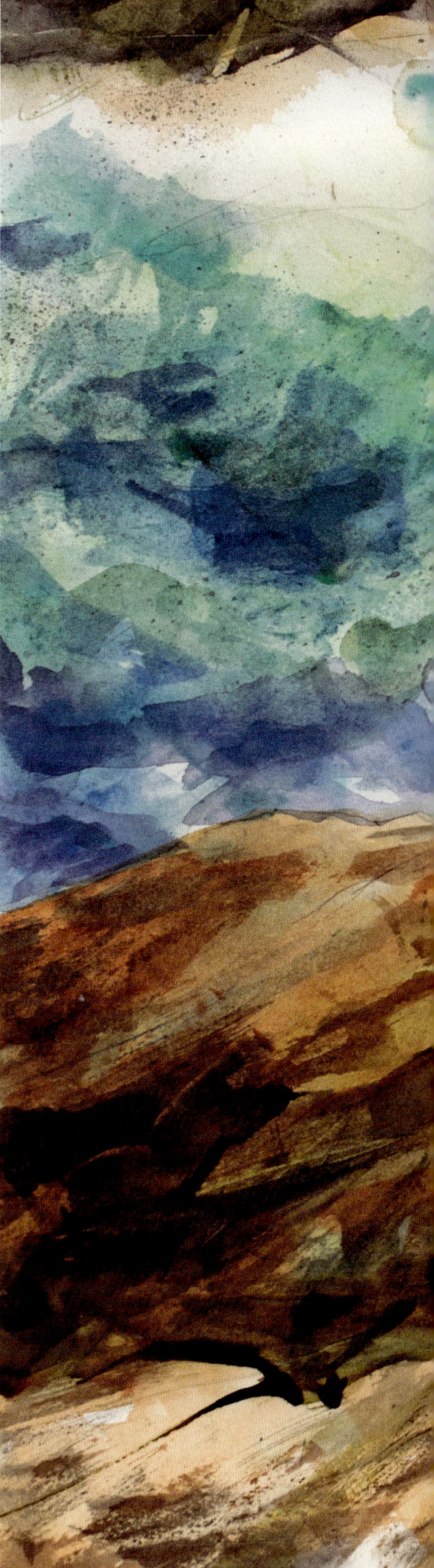

Finished in-studio watercolor of the rocks and sea.
10" x 10" (25.5 x 25.5 cm).

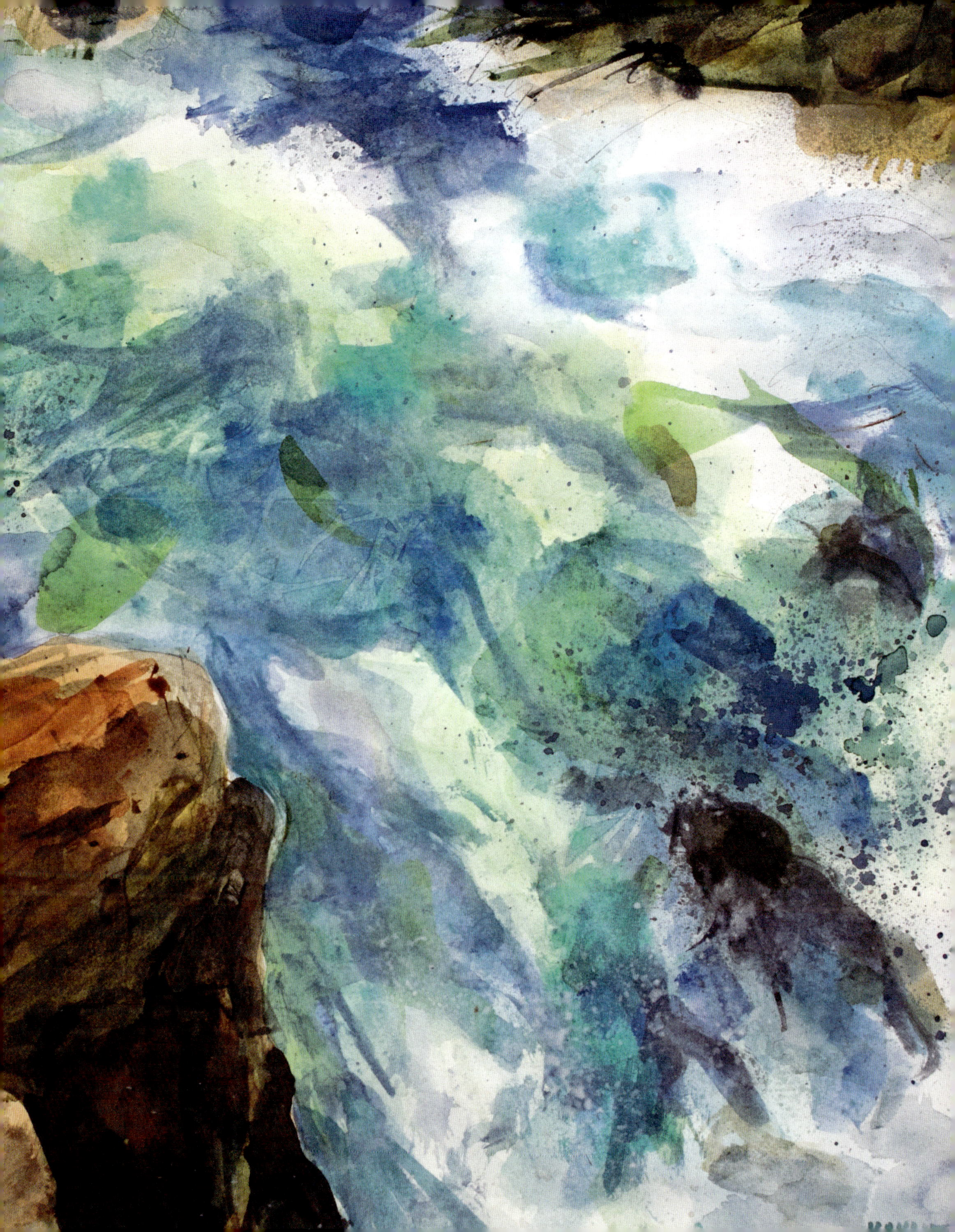

Special Watercolor Technique: Wax Resist and Scraping for Texture

Creating the effect of textures in watercolor invites your imagination. The advantage to using these techniques is that they create detail easily. After you gain experience with them individually, you can use them together so they blend into the watercolor background and no technique shows.

Along with your paints and brushes, you'll need a white wax candle and a single-edge razor blade or an old credit card.

Step 1. On our coast, the gray-brown shoreline rocks consist of multiple layers of rough granite. They have coarse, uneven surfaces and often-distinctive striations of quartz or darker stone running through them.

In setting up my palette, I choose cobalt blue, cadmium yellow light, and turquoise for the water, and burnt umber mixed with a touch of red for the rocks. That gives me all three primary colors.

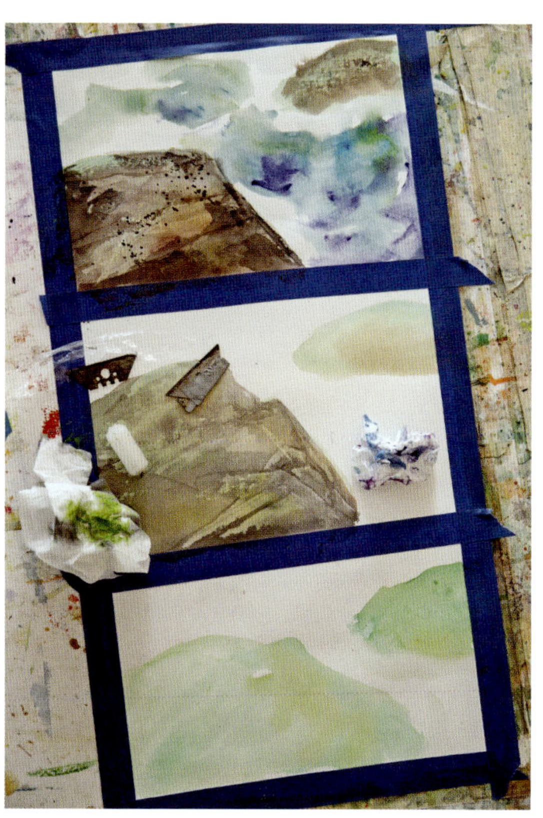

FROM BOTTOM TO TOP: Three steps demonstrating how to create texture using plastic wrap and razor blades. Notice the progression from light and loose toward darker and more defined—classic watercolor "light to dark" approach.

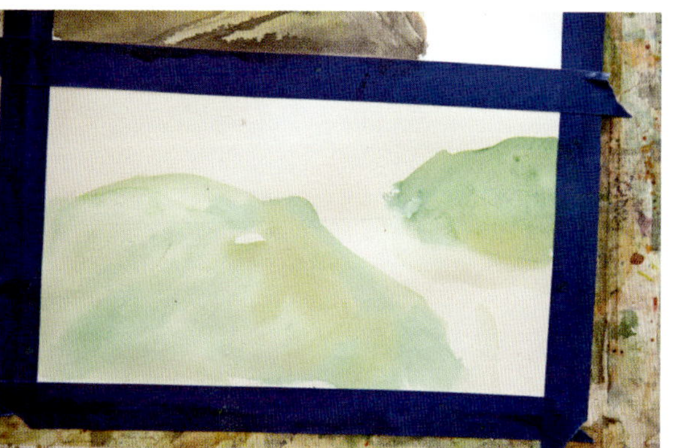

Step 2. I mix an under color for the rocks—in this case a lime green, like the summer seaweed. I block out the shape and position of the rocks and let the color dry.

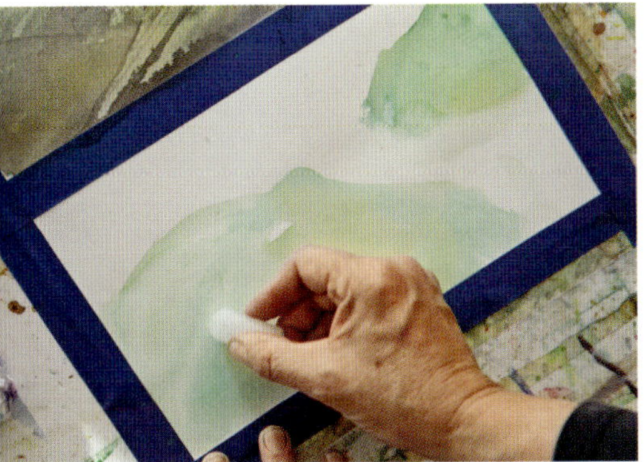

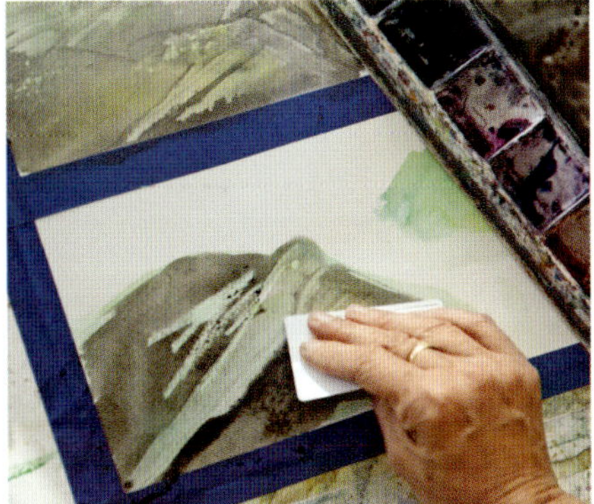

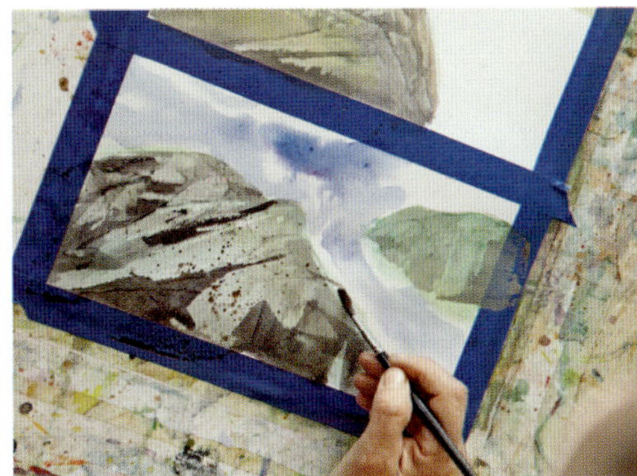

Step 3. Next, I hold the candle sideways and I draw with it, making marks across the rock shapes, following the rough cuts and gouges in the actual rocks. Mixing my colors into a rich brown puddle on my palette, I wash the paint over the rock shapes and the wax.

Step 4. While the paint is wet, I drag the razor blade or the edge of the credit card across the rocks to leave darker lines that suggest the rock is receding from the foreground. As I drag the blade, I hold it at a slight angle, so that it pulls the paint like a squeegee. This leaves the rocks lighter at the top and darker toward the base,as they are in nature.

Step 5. The technique takes practice, but you will become more comfortable with it each time you try it. Here I have let the first scraped layer dry and repeated the process. I've added soft, wet blues to the water and the side of the rocks.

Step 6. Once I have the shape and texture of the rocks as I want them, I let the paint dry. I may go back in and add darker details later. Notice how the scraping allowed the first wash of green to shimmer through the brown texture, in the same way that seaweed clings to actual rocks.

Capturing a Moment

There is a familiar truism that the Impressionists were masters at "capturing a moment" in nature. In a seascape that would certainly be a challenge with each rising wave following another, smacking individual rocks differently and all at the same time, spraying this way and that.

But of course the truism isn't exactly true. The Impressionist painters didn't freeze a moment like a camera still or a Japanese woodcut. They encompassed a moment. They blurred the edges, overlapping many moments into a rich surface.

In impressionism, you can experience the sunlight changing and the water surface shifting. And in painting in this style you share your impressions of the time, not just the moment, that you spent feeling the pounding of the waves, smelling the aging seaweed, and hearing the slap of the water.

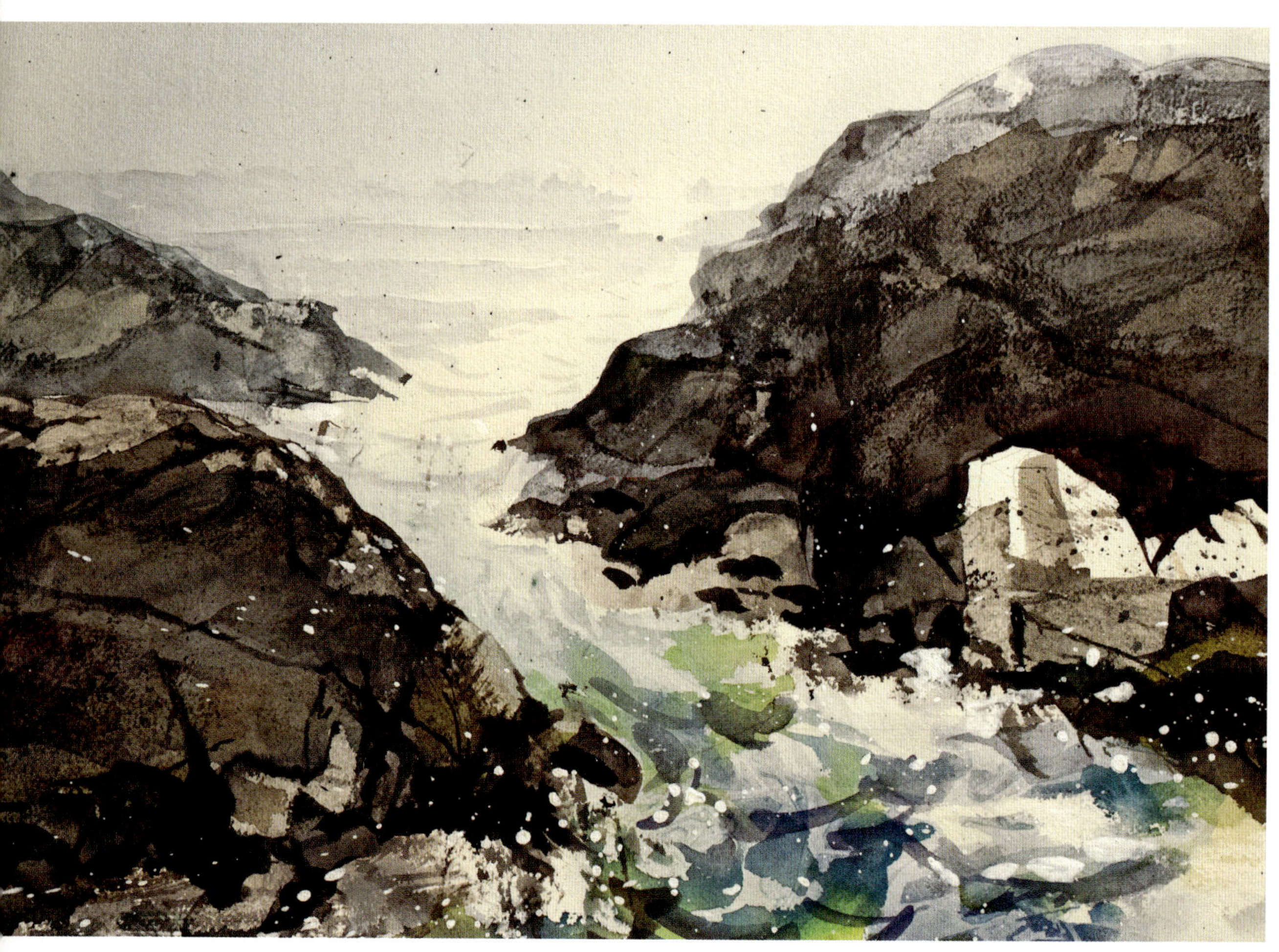

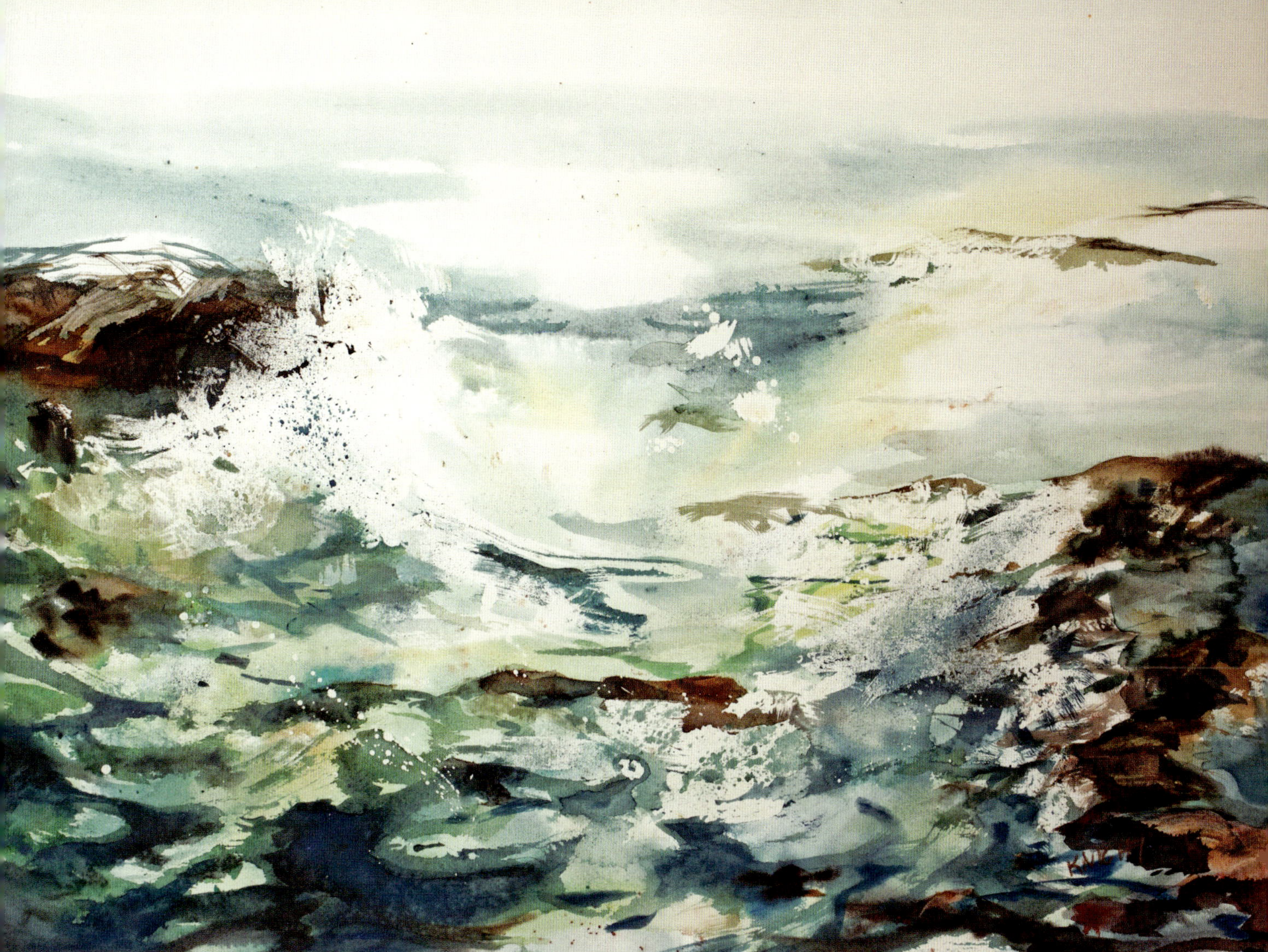

ABOVE: *Ocean Surf.* Watercolor. 22" x 30" (56 x 76 cm).

OPPOSITE: *Wild Island Sea.* Watercolor. 22" x 30" (56 x 76 cm).

Gallery

These paintings show what I like best about working outside along the rocky seashore.

Demonstration: Painting the Rocks and Sea in Acrylic

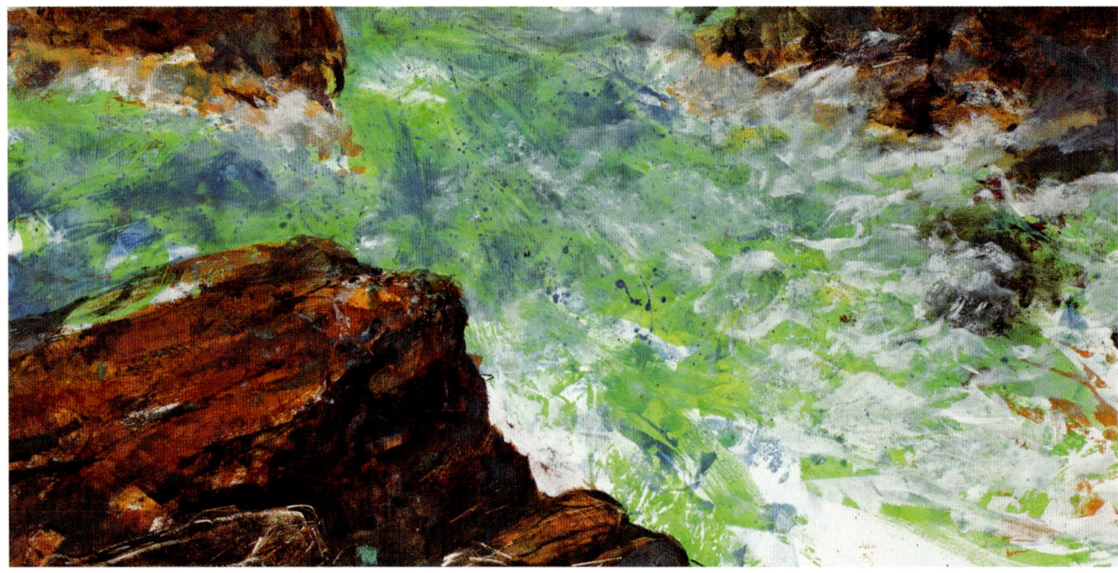

Foaming up

I decide to start a large canvas to see how the nature of the acrylic enhances the impression of the water and rocks. I expect it will have a different feeling from that of watercolor, as the surface textures build up with layers of paint.

I remember hearing that Winslow Homer, one of the greatest American watercolorists, chose to paint the thundering rocky Maine Coast at Prouts Neck using heavy oil paint. He was enamored with the collision of two elemental forces and wanted to express the physical weight of the breaking waves. The thick impasto brushstrokes he wanted would not be possible to attain with watercolor paint.

Getting Ready

In getting my supplies ready for acrylic, I add an old toothbrush to my brushes and a heavy paper card about the size of a credit card for creating texture. I will use this for scraping acrylic paint, the way I did with a razor blade in my watercolor.

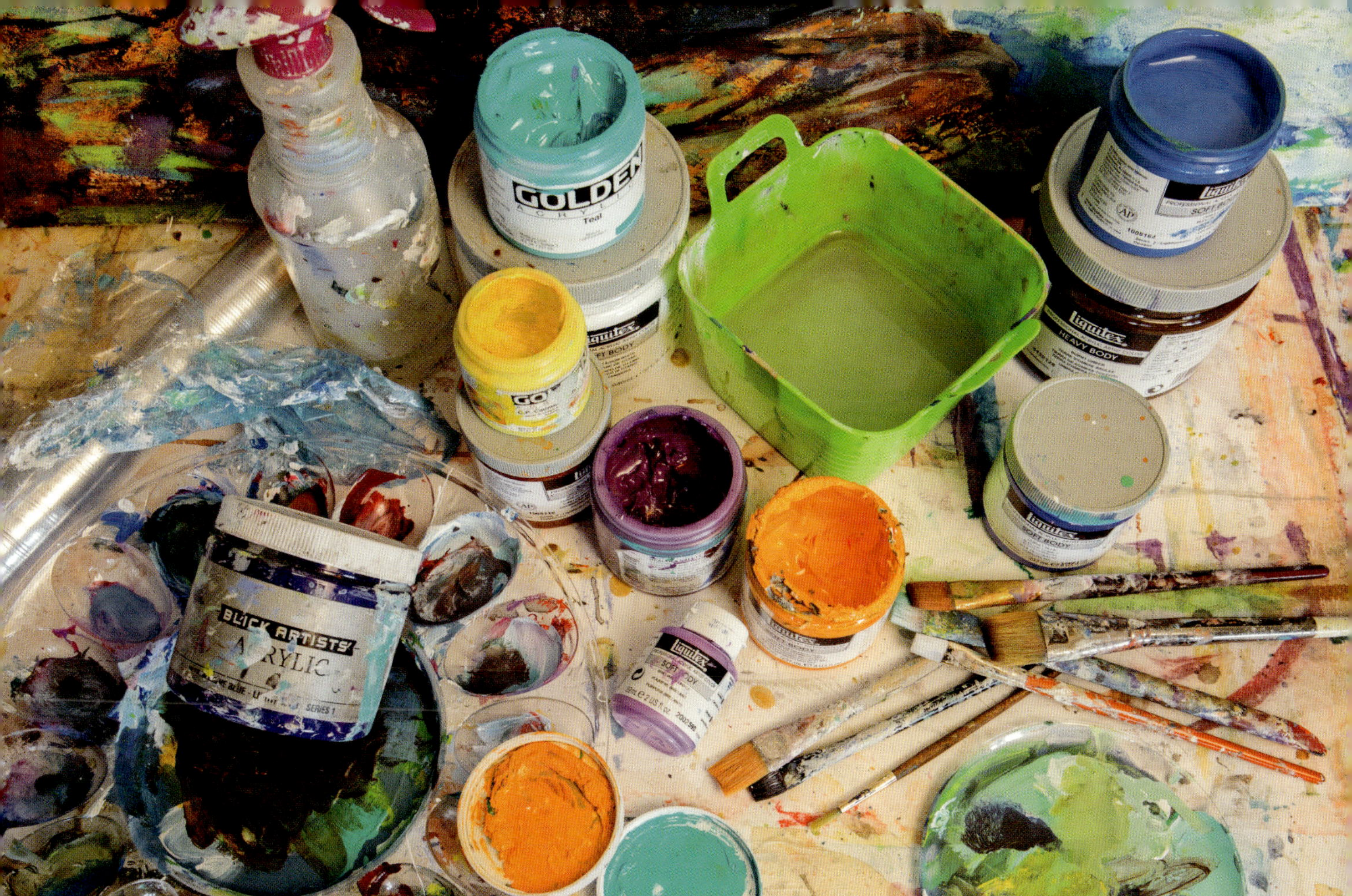

I've collected another old toothbrush for this painting, and have a stack of plastic lids for palettes. I'm equipped with plastic wrap, paper towels, and an old kitchen towel. I rinse out some plastic coffee cans and fill them half way with water and place my jars of paint within easy reach.

I select a 30" x 30" (76 x 76 cm) cotton canvas, already gessoed, and put it on the easel. The assortment of acrylic brushes, ranging from big synthetic Goliath rounds to 1" (2.5 cm) and ½" (1.3 cm) flats to small #1 and #00 rounds, is close at hand.

I will use cadmium yellow light, lemon yellow, titanium white, burnt umber, cobalt blue, cerulean blue, ultramarine blue, and viridian green. I also have a little alizarin crimson, which is a transparent red. This red can turn the greens that I mix on my palette almost black.

NOTE: When my good watercolor brushes become too frayed and tired for use in watercolor, I often add them to my collection of acrylic brushes. Using watercolor brushes on gessoed canvas with the coarser acrylic paint definitely hastens their demise, but it gives them a useful purpose in their old age.

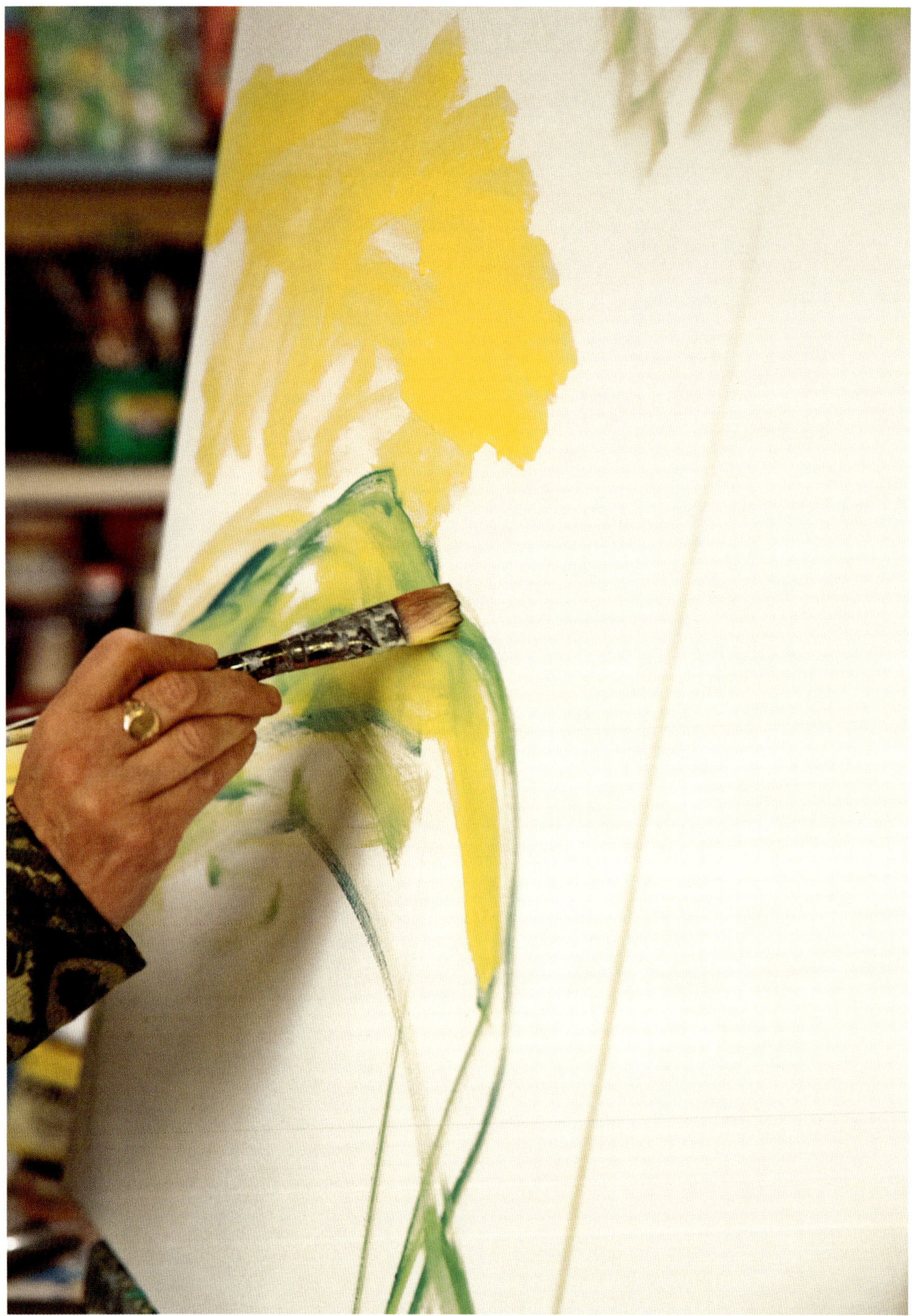

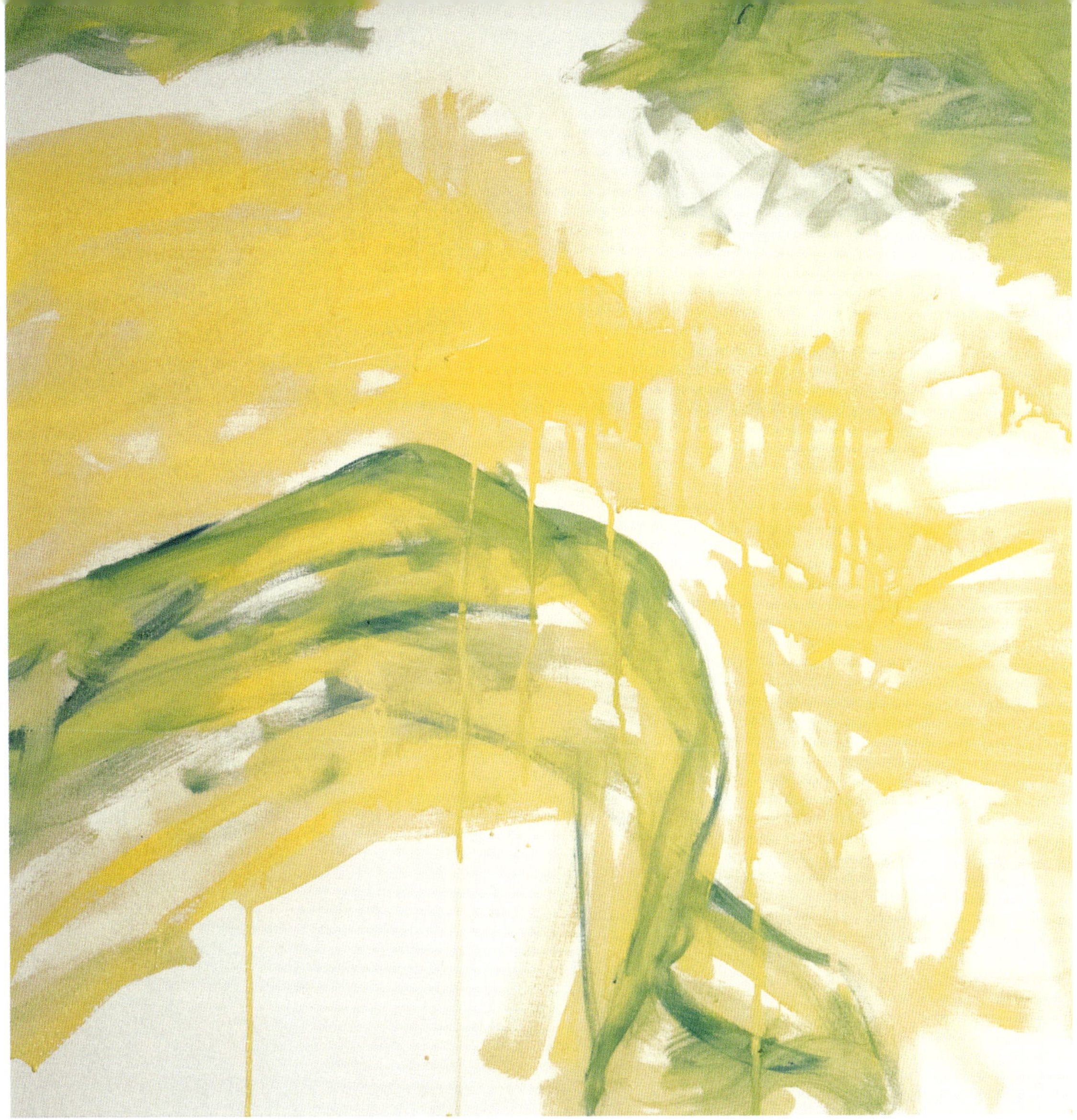

OPPOSITE: I start with bold gestures to establish design.

ABOVE: Next I add light yellow-greens to build up the shapes.

In the Studio

Step 1 I go back and look at my on-site sketches of the rocks and water that I did using watercolor. I am going to paint the same view, making adjustments as I go along. Acrylic has a great flexibility and I can easily change the painting at any time.

I lay in a wash of yellows where the wave will be and brush in browns and blues to establish my rocks. I let them dry. It doesn't matter how thick the paint is at this stage, because I will be building up some very thick impasto textures.

By starting with the light color of yellow, I can concentrate on creating a good design before adding the dramatic values.

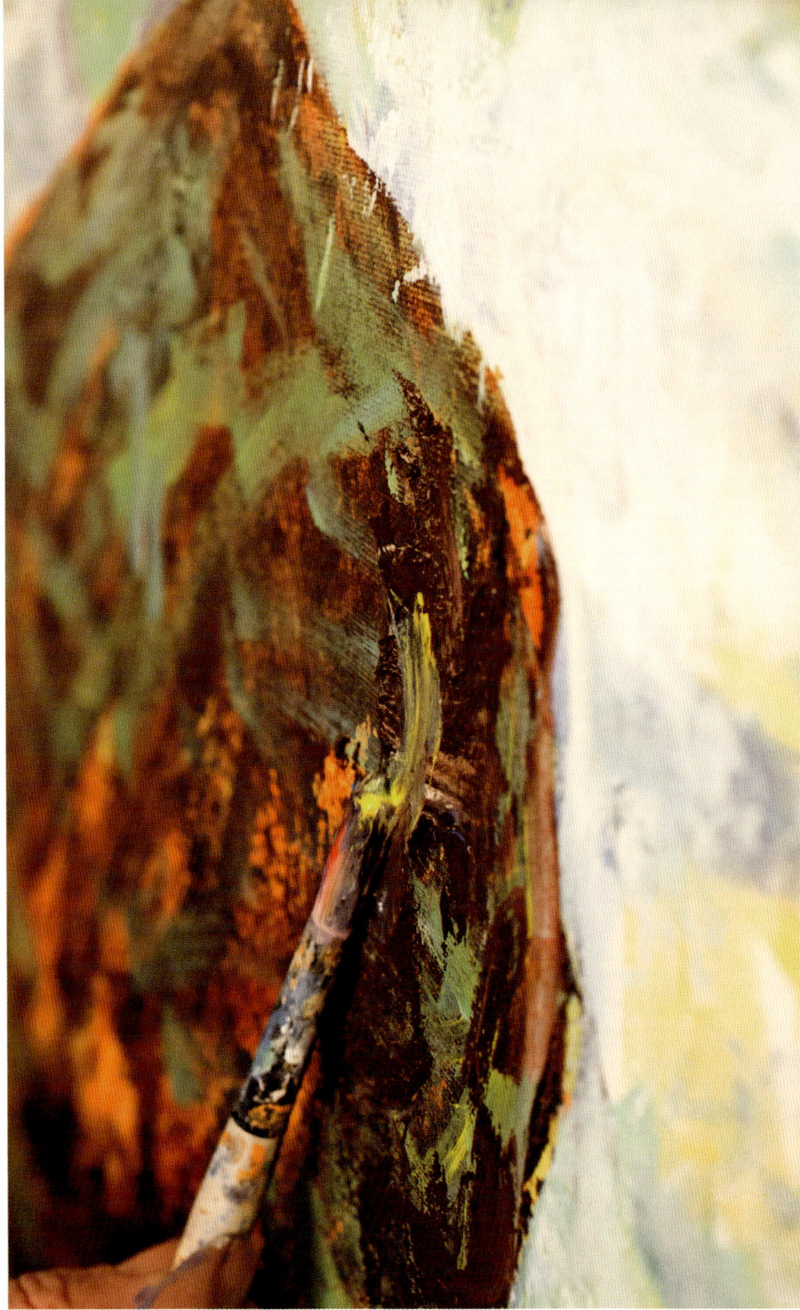

Building up bits of color and active brushwork to create impression of rock textures

Step 2. I begin to build up the color and texture of the rocks, adding layers of different browns. While the brown paint is still fresh and wet, I press some crinkled plastic wrap into it and let it sit for a few minutes. With acrylic it's not necessary to leave the plastic wrap on for a long time. (See the plastic-wrap technique on pages 74 to 77.)

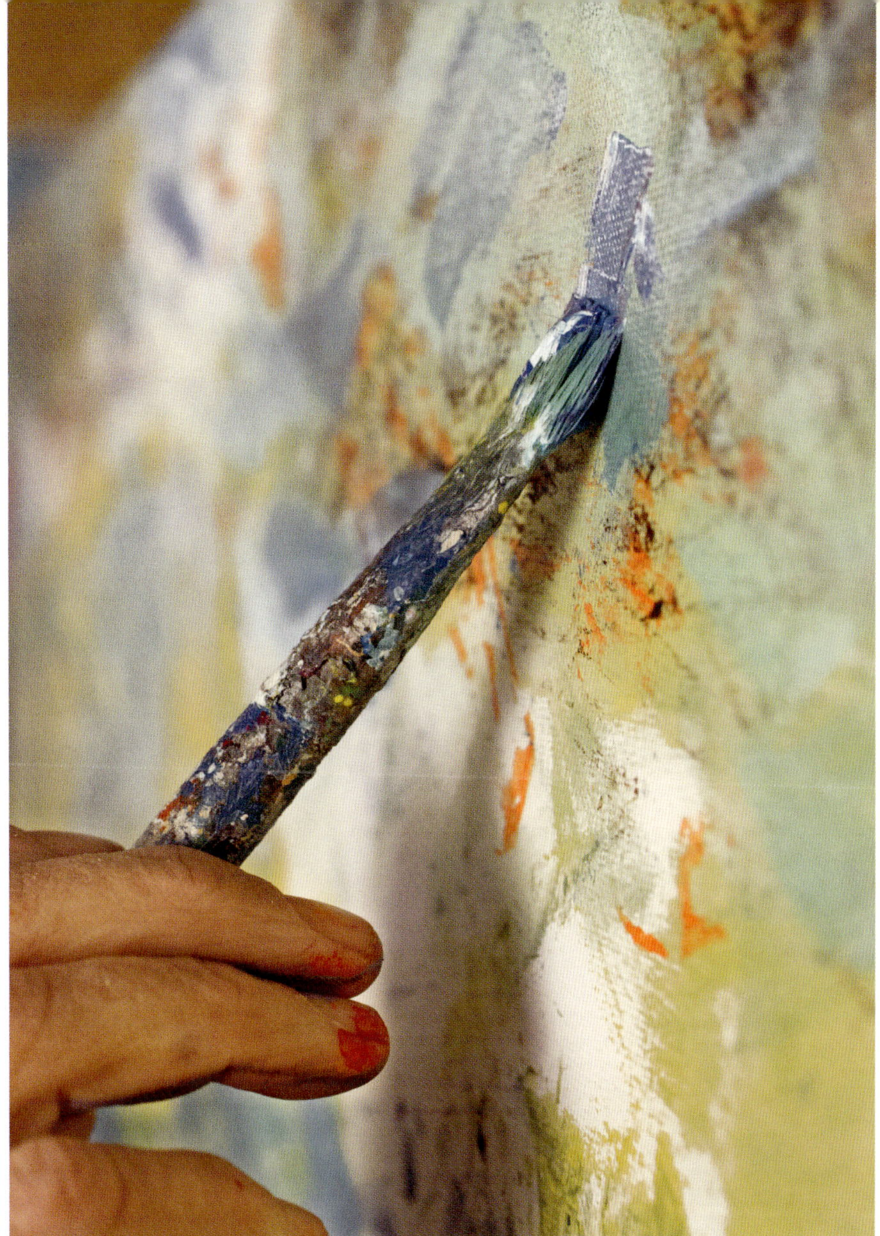

Double loading my paintbrush with various blues

Step 3. While I let the brown paint set up on the rocks, I turn my thoughts back to the water. I want to create the feeling of real movement in the water, so I double load my paintbrush, dipping one corner of the brush into cobalt blue and the other corner into light cerulean blue. When I stroke the paint onto the canvas, I press some crinkled bits of plastic wrap over the thick paint. The colors mix and blend with each other. You can't go wrong with this technique for painting water if you stick to blues and greens.

Step 4. Once the second round of paint has partially dried, I remove the plastic wrap from the rocks and water and prepare to add more texture. Painting back into semi-wet areas is a wet-on-wet technique. I highlight some areas with fresh new color, and blend others.

The acrylic is partially dry on the rocks and still damp on the water. I scrape the rocks with the edge of the card to create an uneven texture. (See the scraping for texture technique on pages 118 and 119.) Then, deciding the pattern left by the plastic wrap on the water is too obvious, I smooth it down with my brush.

Step 5. I build up richer layers of color in the water. To paint the waves on a rocky shore, you need to re-create the movement.

I remember the feeling of being there at the shore, the sound of the waves as they hit the rocks, the hissing as they slip back into the ocean, and the constant motion. Each wave is different, the light sparkles and the foam erupts and dissolves in an instant.

I find that in painting the waves, it helps if I move my hand like the water. I think about the way the waves push out from the back of the painting space toward me, and I make them hit rocks and swirl around them. The beauty of working with acrylic is that you can add those layers of churning movement with color and brushstrokes. And you wait until the end to add the foaming highlights.

RESHAPING

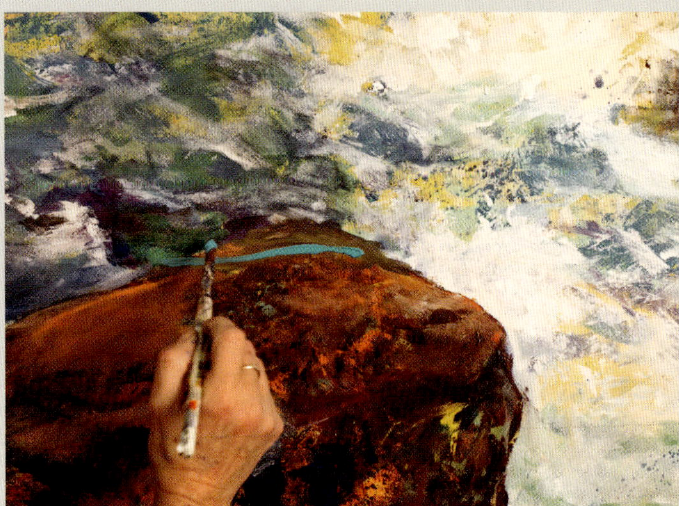

Acrylic allows you to change things once you put them down on canvas. Here I sketch a new line to the edge of the rock.

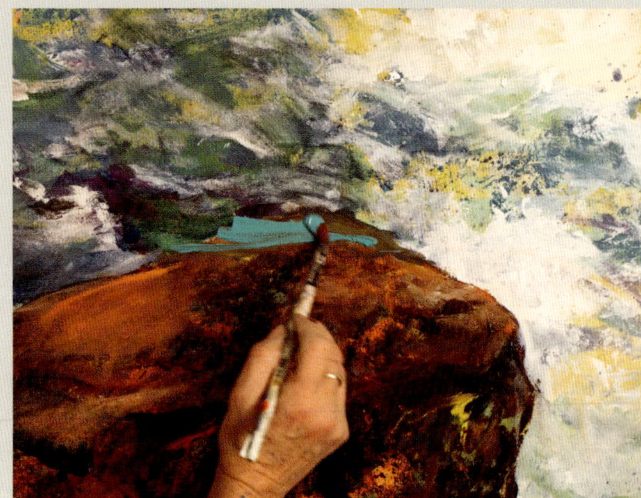

I fill in the area with blue.

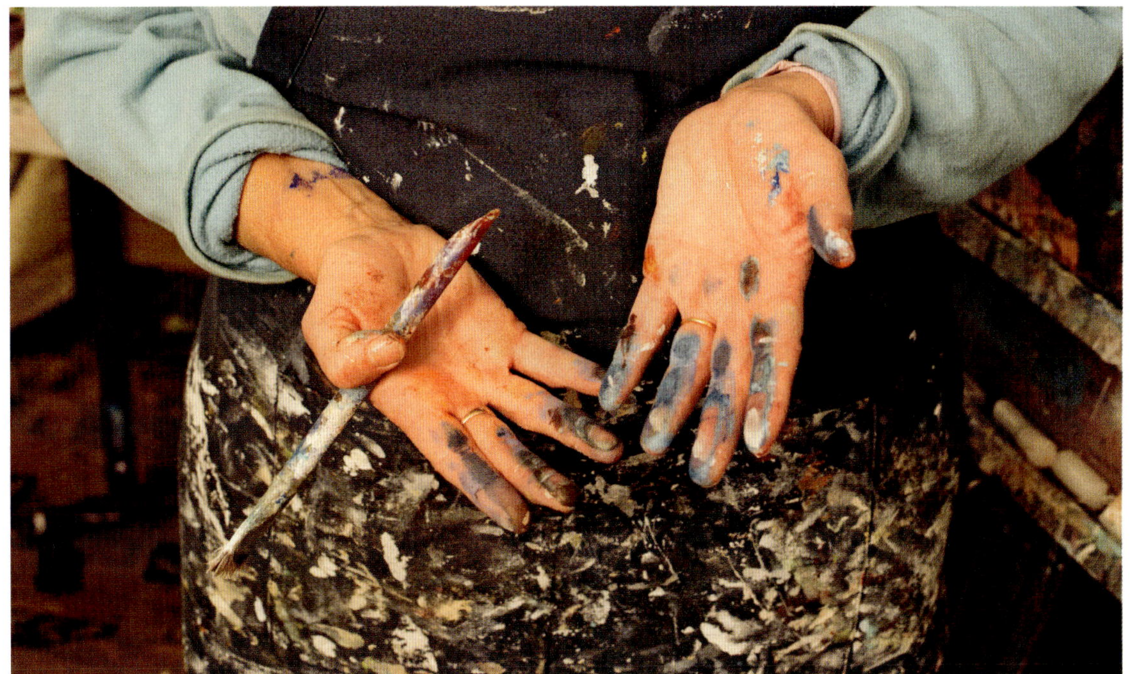

Getting messy is part of the fun.

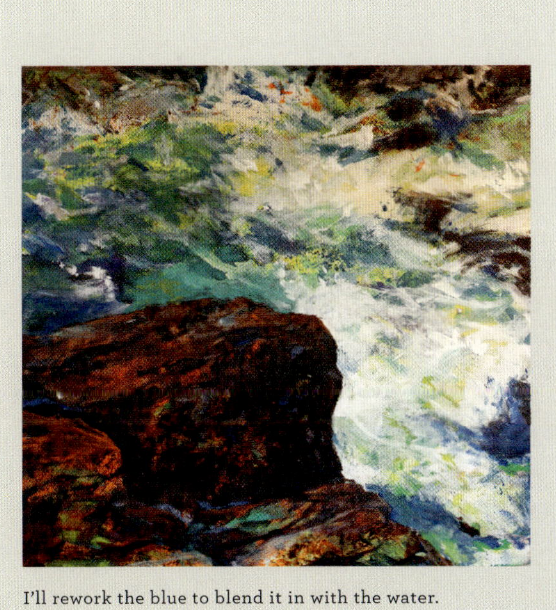

I'll rework the blue to blend it in with the water.

Step 6. Be sure to clean your water and brushes before using white. First I cover the areas I don't want to splatter with scrap paper as a shield. Then, making a puddle of liquid white paint on my palette, I dip the toothbrush into the paint and, while holding it about 3" (7.5 cm) from the area along the base of the rocks, I splatter white. Take your time and have fun. You can splatter white paint anywhere in this demo and it will help create the impression of ocean waves. Try making areas of thicker spray and areas of thinner spray.

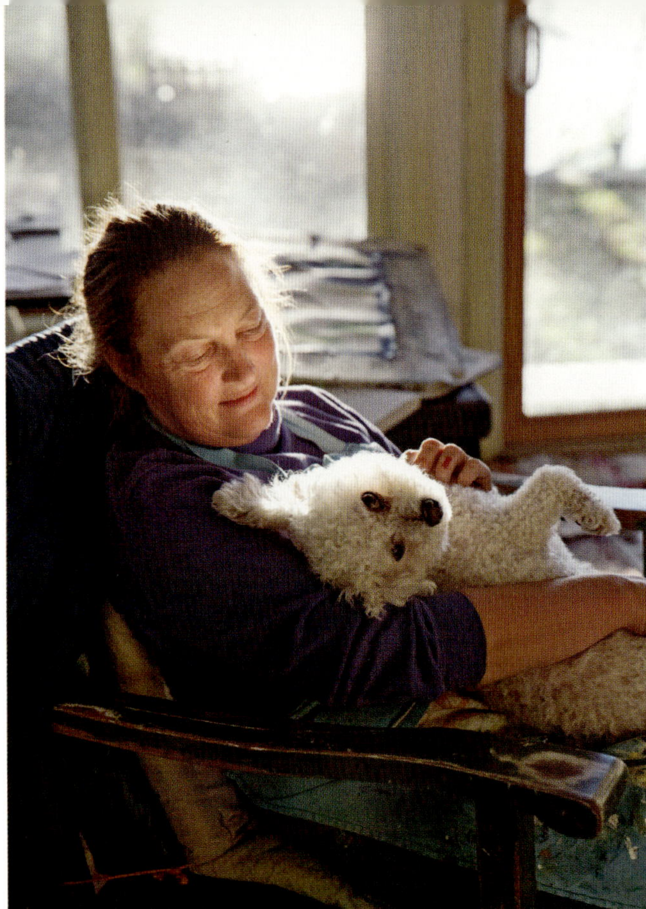

After a day in the studio, little Lily gets a cuddle.

Step 7. Acrylic painting is definitely a more physical activity than the gentle watercolors. Sinking down into the studio chair is a big relief. I remember the exhilaration of standing on the rocks while the ocean rumbled around me. Every time a wave crashed I felt both small and vulnerable and brave and wild. I felt like running back home and yet mesmerized and unable to turn away.

As I sit looking at the painting on the easel, I look to see if there are any traces of those conflicting heightened impressions. The brightness of the paint color is joyfully unrestrained. The gestural brushwork and heavy texture is weighty and yet seething with energy. The image is simplified, balanced, but not boring. There are wonderful surprises of color in the rocks. The water flows through the image in infinite, transparent layers.

Step 8. Everything looks good. I feel like dozing for a moment, but then I see a little something that should really be changed and jump up to do it. Just as with the watercolor, the final step is adding details wherever you want to draw your audience's attention.

I use a small round brush and add gray-black squiggles to the front rock. I use a little rock color to suggest a glimpse of a rock deep under the froth of the breaking wave. It adds more transparency to the water. Yes that's exactly the impression of the ocean and rocks I felt that morning I rode my bike out to New Castle Island's ocean edge.

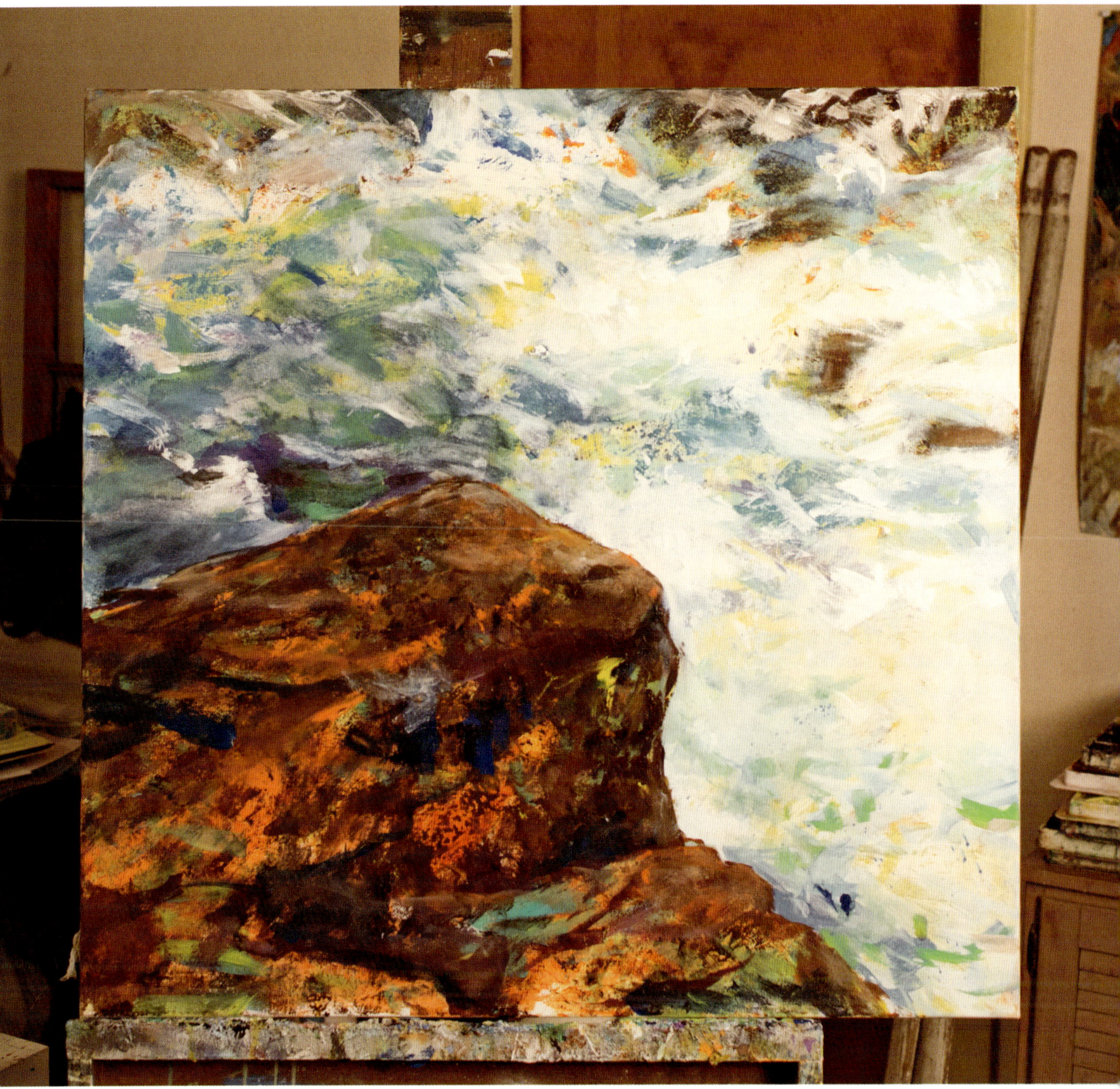

Almost finished acrylic on canvas, 36" x 36" (91.5 x 91.5 cm).

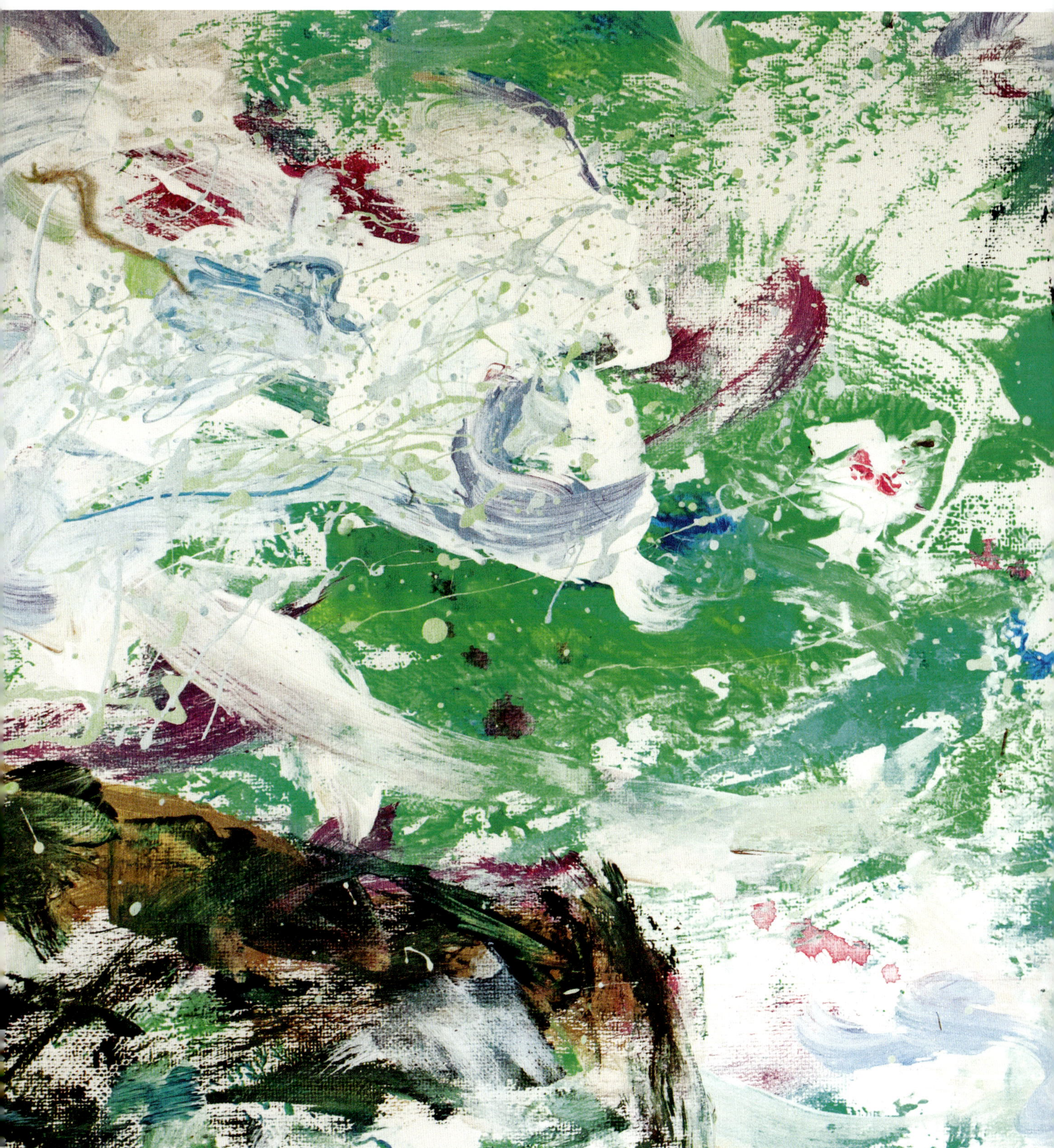

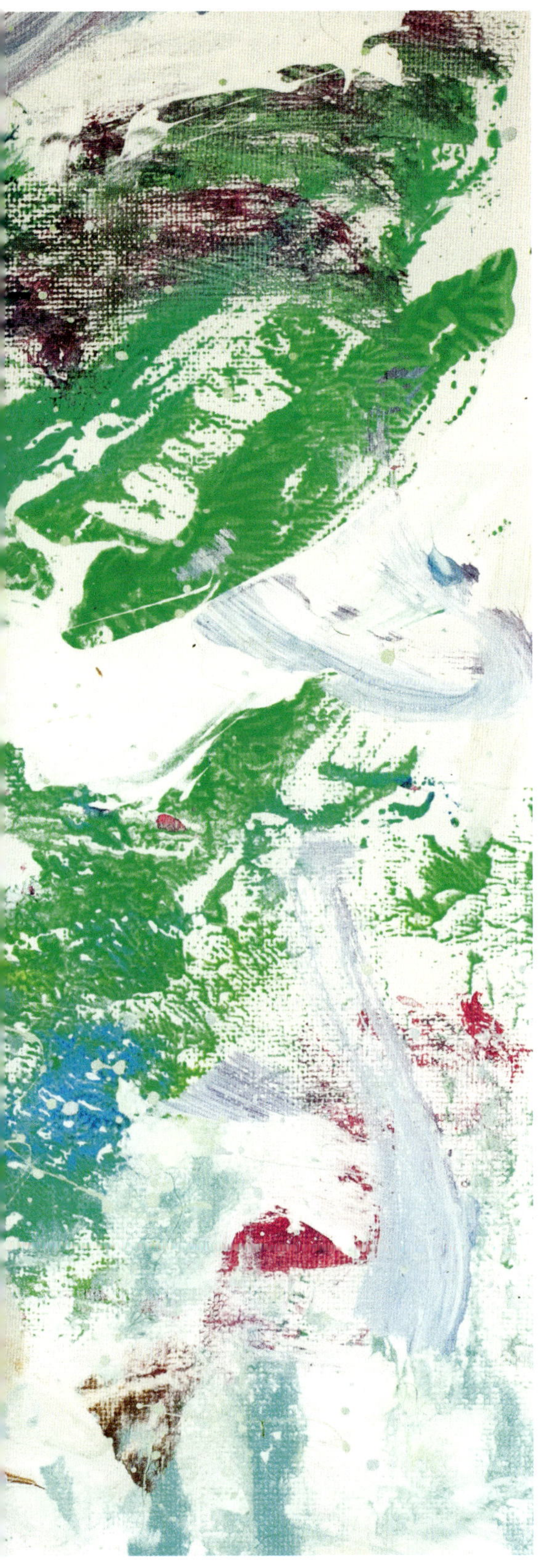

Gallery

Here is another view of the ocean painted in acrylic.

Surf Explosion. Acrylic on prepared paper.
22" x 30" (56 x 76 cm).

Conclusion

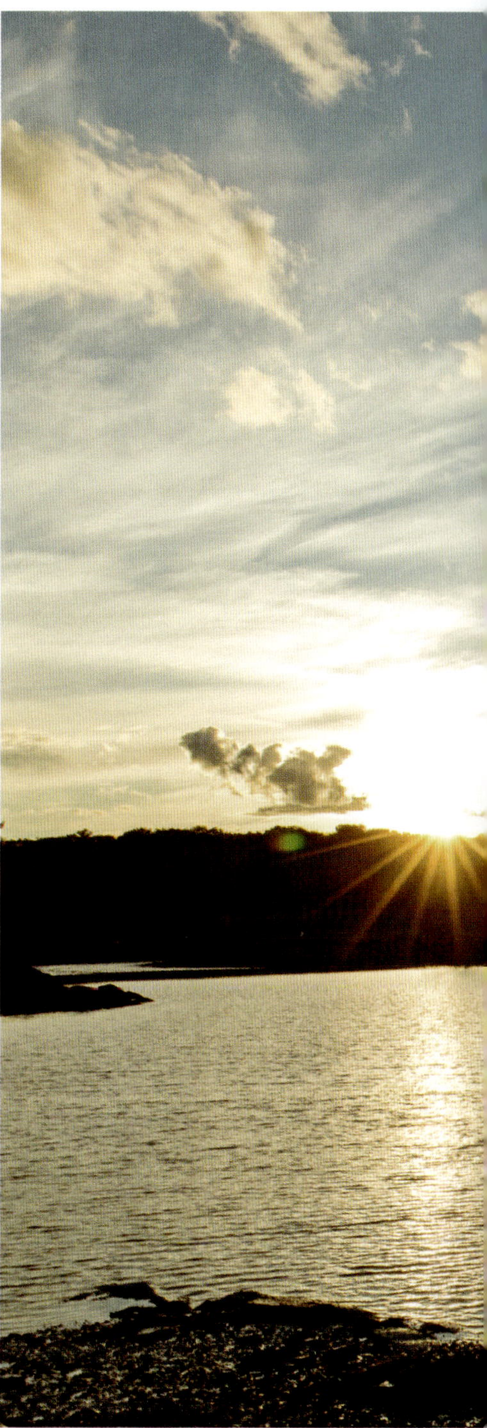

A friend of mine who loves to read biographies once told me that Renoir said if painting wasn't fun, he wouldn't do it. A lot us feel that way. That doesn't mean it has to be easy or obvious or come out the same every time. In fact, that's what we *don't* want. It's fun to paint. It's work, but it's fun.

The artistic necessity of lingering in the garden to listen to the bees after everyone else has gone in for tea, or walking farther out on a breakwater than you ought to just to feel the ocean's spray is a rich way of living. Setting up your palette and paper and containers of water and assorted brushes is a glorious prelude to the manifestation of creating something.

Losing yourself in making a brushstroke and watching as it thickens and thins, drips and stutters, or as colors mix and squabble and merge, is a level of sensual awareness that's difficult to beat.

The painting won't always turn out great. The process is an attempt to make whatever you have put down better. It will get better. I think I have exhausted practically every wrong turn and missed so many shots that I just automatically improve.

If every time you make art you celebrate the experience of seeing and creating, the end result becomes a step on the way to becoming better. With that in mind, I hope the demonstrations in this book encourage you to paint—and, like Renoir, to have fun with it.

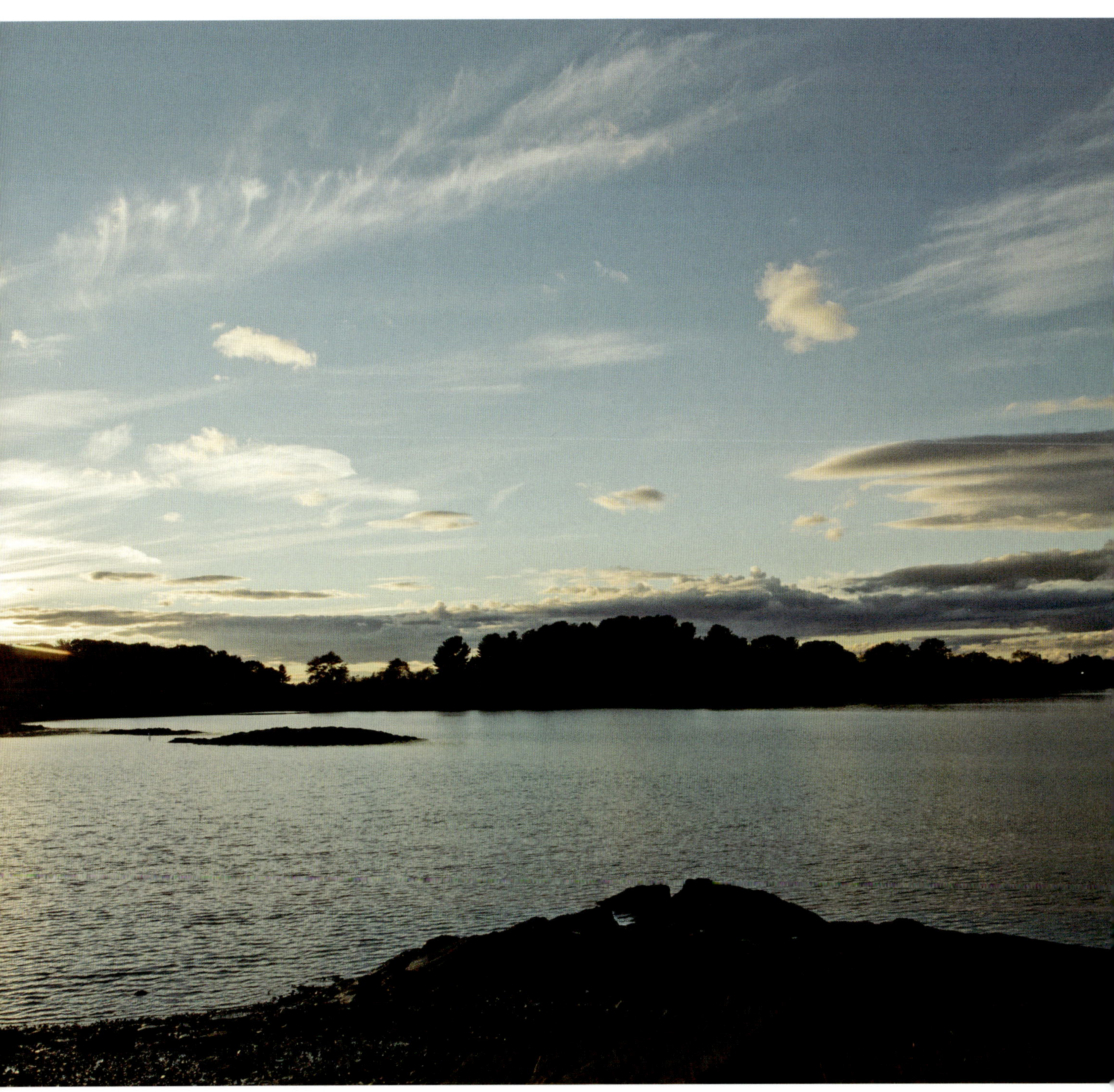

A peaceful ending to an island day

Resources

If I have a few moments over coffee, I peruse the catalogues for the following companies and compare prices, but they are very competitively priced and the deliveries are fast. I recommend them all. The service departments at Dick Blick and Cheap Joe's are outstanding. There is always a knowledgeable person—live—on the phone, who usually knows the packing and the delivery guys by name. It feels real.

CHEAP JOE'S ART STUFF
374 Industrial Park Drive
Boone, NC 28607
888.583.2312
cheapjoes.com

Cheap Joe's is especially good for watercolor products and extra watercolor tips. It now offers Daniel Smith Watercolors (gorgeous) as well as its own brand (American Journey), which is good and dependable. It offers an important directory of watercolor workshops and helps keep the watercolor community connected.

DICK BLICK ART MATERIALS
P.O. Box 1769
Galesburg, IL 61402-1267
800.828.4548
dickblick.com

I tend to use Dick Blick Art Supplies a lot, and it has never let me down. It provides a wide range of materials for a lot of arts education programs: studio fundamentals, paints, brushes, canvases, its own brand of paper, and inventive student art project ideas. These often inspire new ideas for me and may lead to trying a series of monoprints or gold leafing, keeping the creative fires hot.

JERRY'S ARTARAMA
6104 Maddry Oaks Court
Raleigh, NC 27616-9997
800.827.8478
jerrysartarama.com

Jerry's is a great all-around art supply store with specials and active online deals. It is competitive and presents new items not offered by other companies. Just recently, it came out with a new panel product by Da Vinci that I am experimenting with in the studio as I write these pages! Fun, fun, fun!

Special Brands I Love

AMPERSAND—ARTIST PANELS

I was purchasing my panels from this Texas company when it was very small and now it actually has more than three folks on the payroll! It's earned every bit of the success it's achieved. Staff are always available for questions, special orders, and just plain encouragement. Plus, Ampersand products are the absolute best I have found.

DA VINCI has just came out with a panel with a built-in wood rim called a liquid art panel. Every time Da Vinci presents something new, it's like an electric charge of inspiration!

GOLDEN ARTIST COLORS—ACRYLIC PAINTS AND MEDIUMS

This company has a great acrylic product line and fantastic technical department. It also has inventive new products with a geeky newsletter. It's recently introduced a watercolor paint line called "QoR." The staff are always so gracious when I call with questions. It feels like I am a part of something bigger and grander when I chat with them.

LIQUITEX—ACRYLIC PAINTS AND MEDIUMS

This company's acrylic products are my old faithfuls—smooth, steady, and always there. Liquitex is expanding its range of acrylic products from mediums to acrylic pens and spray paints. It emphasizes the compatibility of its materials.

WATERCOLOR BRANDS I USE THE MOST

- Daniel Smith
- MaimeriBlu
- Sennelier
- Winsor & Newton
- Holbein
- M. Graham
- QoR

WATERCOLOR PAPER

Arches is my rock-steady paper. I prefer 140 lb (300 g/m^2) bright white hot press paper, which I purchase in pads, blocks, and rolls.

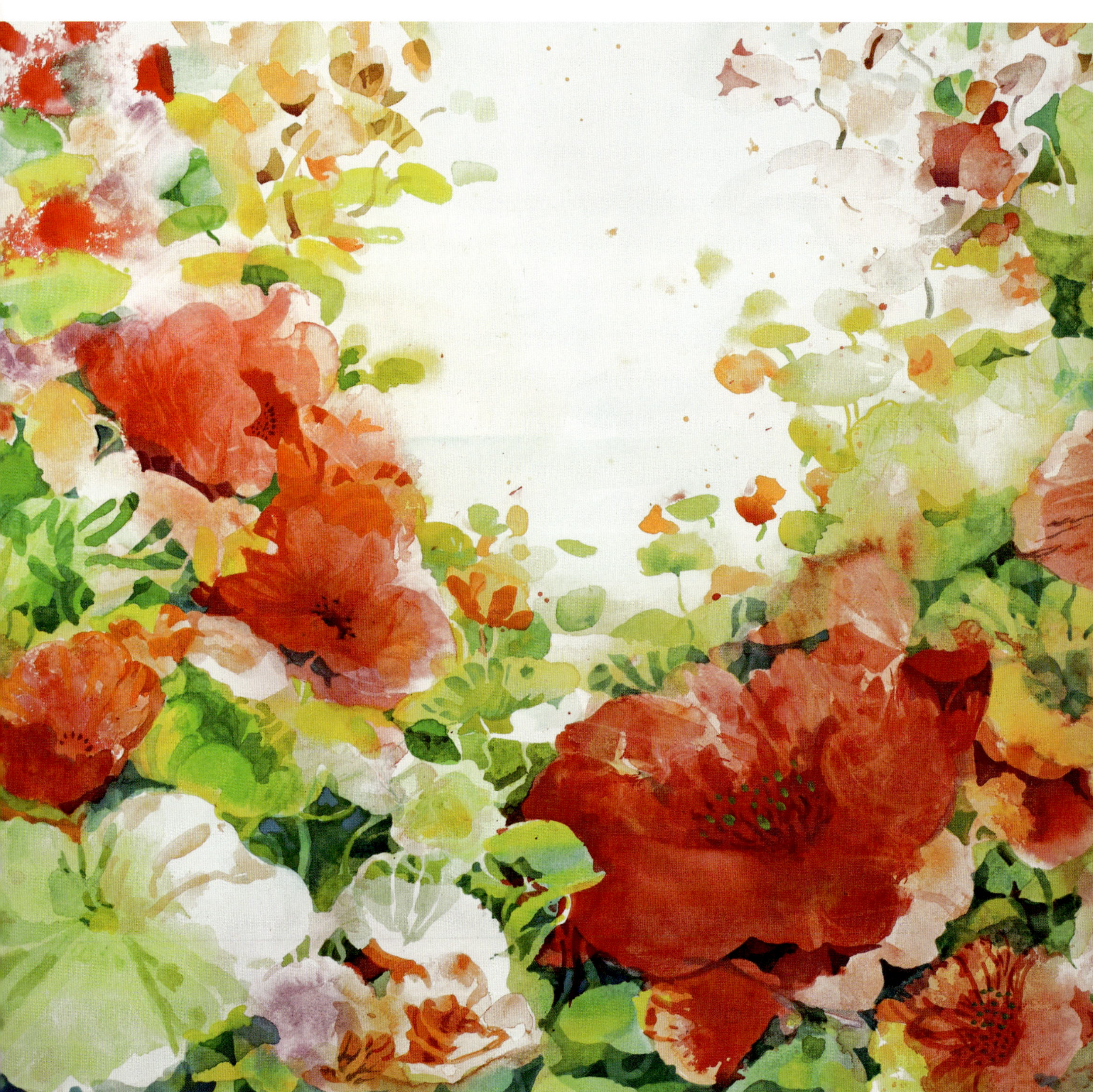

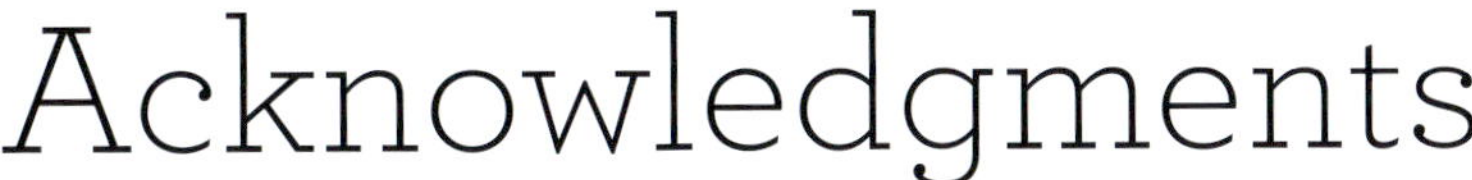

Acknowledgments

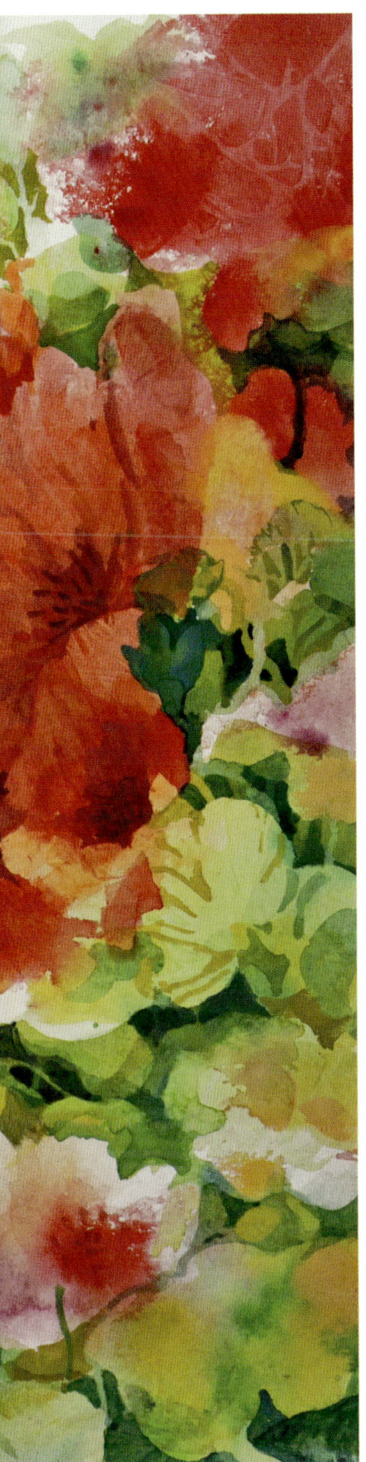

I was thrilled to be able to write this book and I'm grateful to everyone who picks it up, thumbs through it, and finds a picture or a page that causes them to pause and read more closely. Thank you. Perhaps the reason I even thought I could write a book like this is the encouragement of my husband and daughters, who stick with me through every artistic up and down.

When my editor, Judith Cressy, called me about beginning this book, I could hardly believe it. I so appreciate her guidance and patience throughout the process. Her good humor and keen eye made the experience a fun one. She made it happen. I was also fortunate to have Regina Grenier as my art editor; I admire the energy and artistic sensibility she brings to her projects.

One of the most important participants in this book has been my close friend, internationally known photographer Karen Hill. We have been friends since attending Pratt Institute in the eighties. She has documented my life with astounding photographs. I am so grateful that she took time to help me make this book more than just a "how to" project. Thanks to Karen, it's an inspirational photographic document of my creative lifestyle.

I would also like to acknowledge the support and encouragement of all my students. I love teaching because of them. I have a special group, the Merrimack River Painters, who have helped me develop and verbalize my ideas with a clarity I could not have achieved on my own. I am so grateful for every student, of every experience level, who crosses my path and renews my faith in our desire to create.

Thanks to everyone. This has been great!

Great Island Beauty. Watercolor. 22" x 33" (56 x 84 cm).

About the Artist

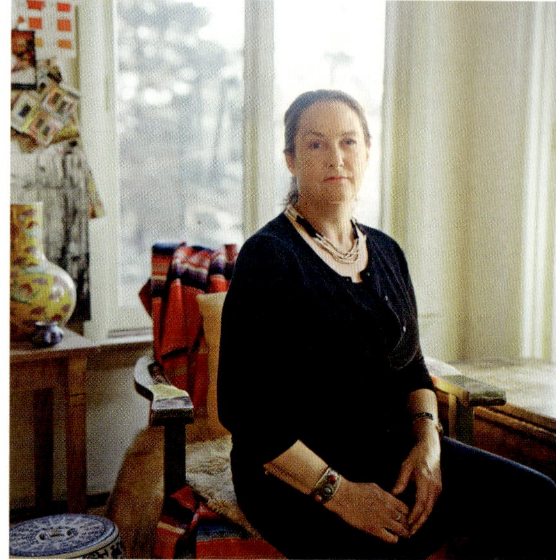

Photo credit: Karen Hill

Dustan Knight is a professional artist, educator, and art writer. She earned her MFA from Pratt Institute in New York and her MA in Art History from Boston University. She was a recipient of a New Hampshire State Fellowship for the Arts, a MacDowell Colony residency, and a Cummington Artist Colony residency. Dustan is represented by galleries across the United States, including Art Three in Manchester, New Hampshire, the Ogunquit Art Association in Maine, and Alpers Fine Art in Andover, Massachusetts. Corporate collections include Macy's, Oracle, and Coveris. (DustanKnight.com)

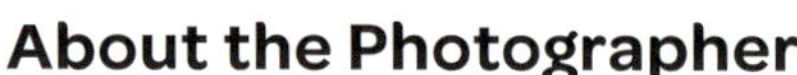

About the Photographer

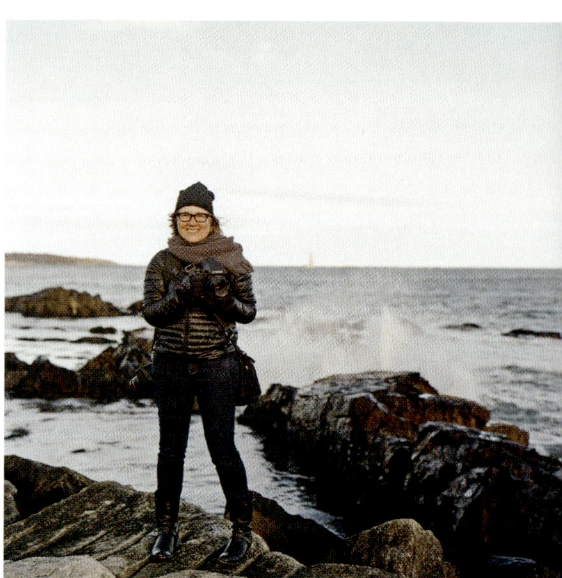

Photo credit: Dustan Knight

Karen Hill is a fine art and wedding photographer and the director, with her husband Frank, of Karen Hill Photography in New York City. She graduated with a BFA from Pratt Institute and an MFA from the Yale School of Art, both in photography, and has been shooting ever since. Her work has been seen in publications and online wedding sites, such as *Martha Stewart Weddings*, the *Knot*, and *Top Knots*, *Style Me Pretty*, *Snippet and Ink*, *Carats + Cake*, *Once Wed*, and *Junebug*. (KarenHill.com)

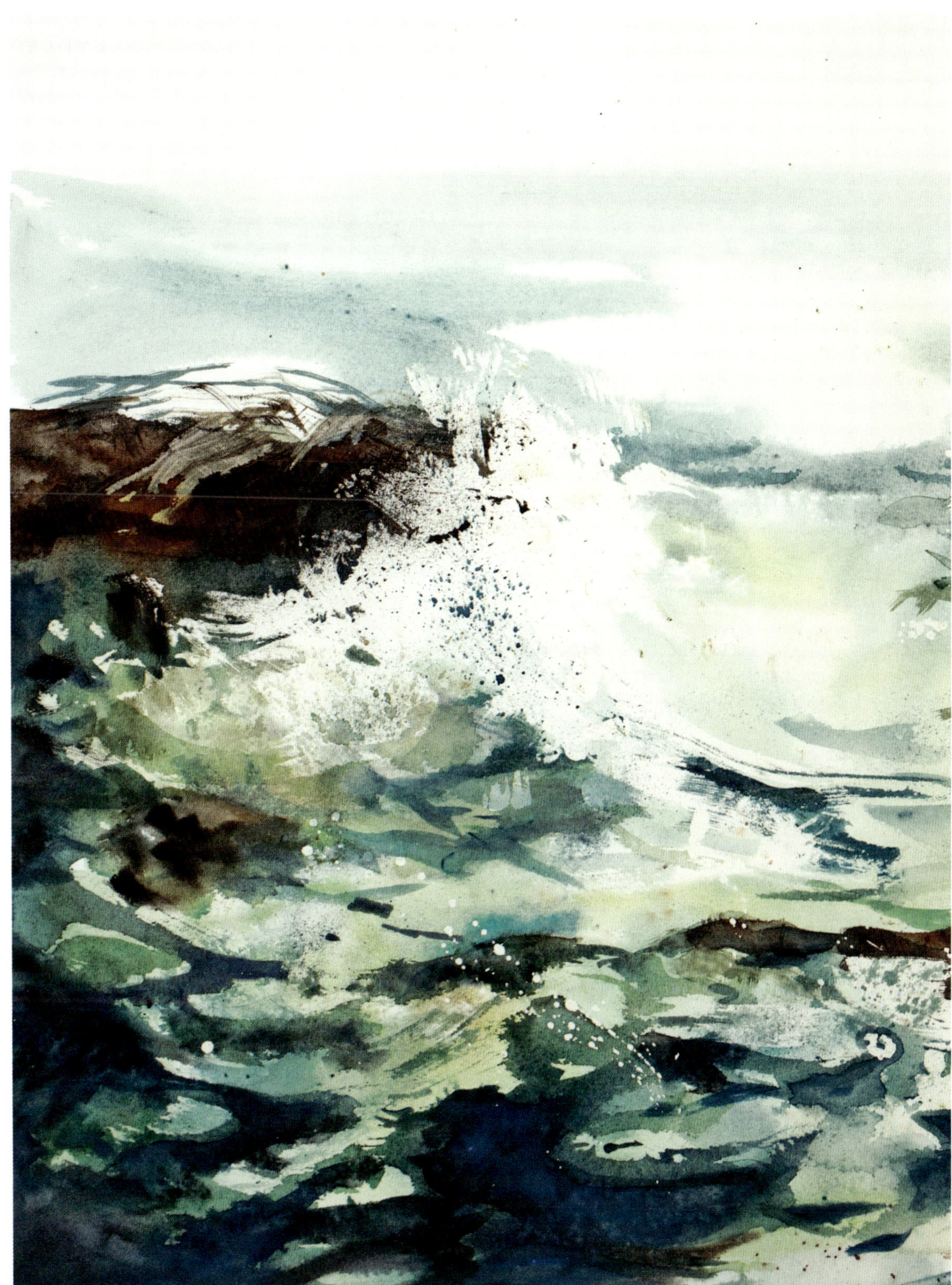

Index

Italicized page numbers indicate an illustration, photo, or its caption.

acrylic painting
  canvases for, 15, 136–137
  Demonstrations, 44–51, 82–91, 122–131
  Galleries, 92–95, 132–133
  paints for, 18–19, 136–137
Ampersand (company), 137
Arches watercolor paper, *15*, 60

Berry Brook (Knight), *23*
Big, Bold and Beautiful (Knight), *83*
brushes, 16–17, 123

canvases, for acrylic painting, 15, 136–137
Cheap Joe's Art Stuff, *18*, 136
cold press paper, 15
color schemes, 33
color sketching. *See* watercolor sketching
cotton duck canvas, 15

Dancing Garden (Knight), *52*
Daniel Smith watercolor paint, *18*, 137
Da Vinci (brand), 137
Day Lilies (Knight), *56*
Demonstrations
  in acrylic, 44–51, 82–91, 122–131
  in watercolor, 24–37, 58–73, 100–119
design sketching, 32, 63, 108
Dick Blick Art Materials, 136
Duck Island, Isles of Shoals (Hassam), *13*

Early Island Morning (Knight), *96*
Early Spring Morning (Knight), *42*

flowers, painting
  about, 53–57
  in acrylic, 82–91
  acrylic gallery of, 92–95
  in watercolor, 58–73
  watercolor gallery of, 78–81

Galleries
  acrylic, 92–95, 132–133
  watercolor, 42–43, 78–81, 120–121
garden flowers. *See* flowers, painting
Geraniums (Knight), *92*
Golden acrylic paint, *18*, *85*, 137
Golden Melody (Knight), *81*
Great Island Beauty (Knight), *138*

hands, as tools, 49
Hassam, Childe, *13*
Holbein watercolor paint, *18*, 137
Homer, Winslow, 12–13, 98, 122
hot press paper, 15, 137

Impression of Nasturtiums (Knight), *61*
Impressions of Nasturtiums (Knight), *78*
indoor studio work. *See* studio work, indoor
Island Trails (Knight), *42*

Jerry's Artarama, 136
Joyful Garden (Knight), *57*

L'Allée des Alyscamps (van Gogh), *11*
linen canvas, 15
Liquitex acrylic paint, *18*, *85*, 137
"listening" to your painting, 90, 114, 116, 130

MaimeriBlu watercolor paint, *18*, 137
materials and tools, 14–19, 136–137
M. Graham watercolor paint, *18*, 137
Monet, Claude, *10–11*
Moonlight on Peonies (Knight), *79*
Morning Chop (Knight), *6*, *99*
Morning Garden in June (Knight), *80*
Morning Woods (Knight), *37*

Nasturtium Impression (Knight), *55*
Nasturtiums #5 (Knight), *94*

Ocean Fog Along the Road (Knight), *22*
Ocean Surf (Knight), *121*

paints, 18–19, 136–137
paper, watercolor, 14–15, 136–137
pencil sketching, 26–27, 32, 58–59, 102–103, 108
photography, 22, 25, 58, 101
plastic wrap technique, 70–72, 74–77, 86–89, 111–112, 126
Poplars on the Epte (Monet), *10–11*

QoR watercolor paint, 137
Queen Anne's Lace Evening (Knight), *93*

Rebecca's Flower (Knight), *9*
The Red Canoe (Homer), *12*
rocks and sea, painting
  about, 97–99
  in acrylic, 122–131
  acrylic gallery of, 132–133
  in watercolor, 100–119
  watercolor gallery of, 120–121
rough press paper, 15

Sennelier watercolor paint, *18*, 137
site selection, 25, 54, 58, 100
sketching
  design, 32, 63, 108
  pencil, 26–27, 32, 58–59, 102–103, 108
  value, 32, 64, 109
  watercolor, 28–29, 60, 104, 110
Snowy Woods (Knight), *43, 141*
studio work, indoor
  acrylic, 46–51
  watercolor, 30–37, 62–73, 107–119
Surf Explosion (Knight), *132*

Tango Tulip (Knight), 2
  Techniques, Special Watercolor
  plastic wrap, 70–72, 74–77, 111–112
  thirsty brush, 34–35, 38–41, *42–43*, 114
  wax resist and scraping for texture, 112–113, 118–119
texture technique, 112–113, 118–119, 128
thirsty brush technique, 34–35, 38–41, *42–43*, 114
tools and materials, 14–19, 136–137
On the Trellis (Knight), *55*
Tulip Tango #2 (Knight), *95*
Turner watercolor paint, *18*

value sketching, 32, 64, 109
van Gogh, Vincent, *11*

watercolor painting
  Demonstrations, 24–37, 58–73, 100–119
  Galleries, 42–43, 78–81, 120–121
  paint for, 18–19, 136–137
  paper for, 26–27, 32
  techniques, 38–41, 66, 74–77, 118–119
watercolor sketching, 28–29, 60, 104, 110
wax resist and scraping for texture technique, 112–113, 118–119, 128
Wild Island Sea (Knight), *120*
Winsor & Newton watercolor paint, *18*, 19, 137
Woodland Road (Knight), *20, 51*
woods, painting the
  about, 21–22
  in acrylic, 44–51
  in watercolor, 24–41
watercolor gallery of, 42–43

Also Available

Brave Intuitive Painting: Let Go, Be Bold, Unfold.

ISBN: 978-1-59253-768-6

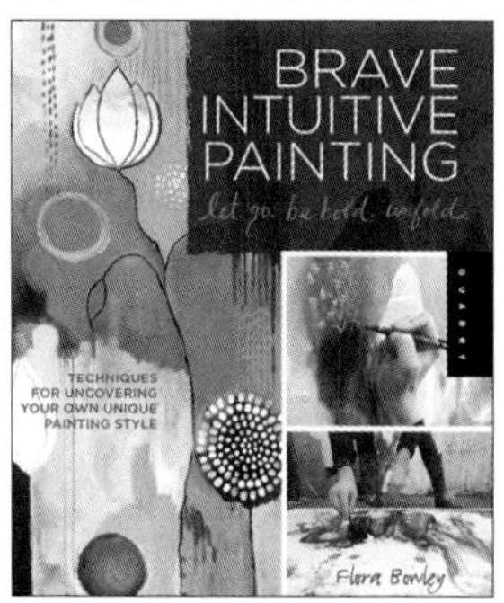

Paint Lab: 52 Exercises Inspired by Artists, Materials, Time, Place, and Method

ISBN: 978-1-59253-782-2

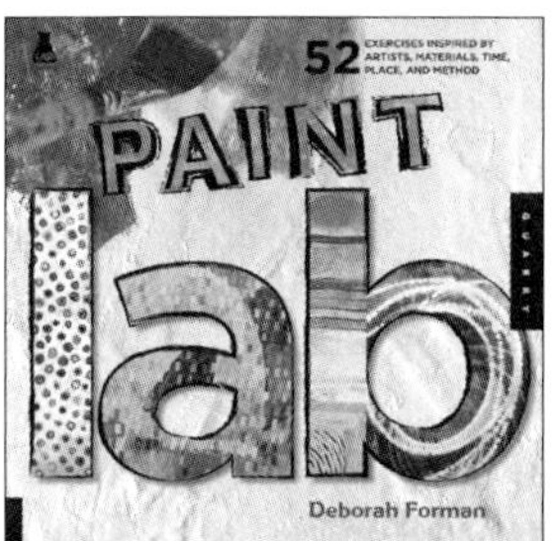

One Watercolor a Day: A 6-Week Course Exploring Creativity Using Watercolor, Pattern, and Design

ISBN: 978-1-59253-857-7

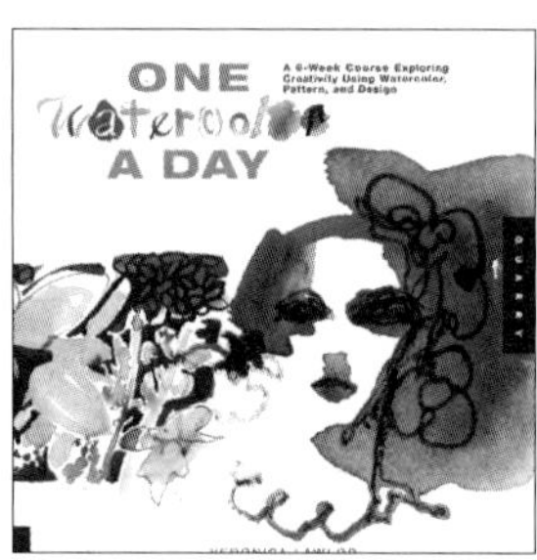

Water Paper Paint: Exploring Creativity with Watercolor and Mixed Media

ISBN: 978-1-59253-655-9

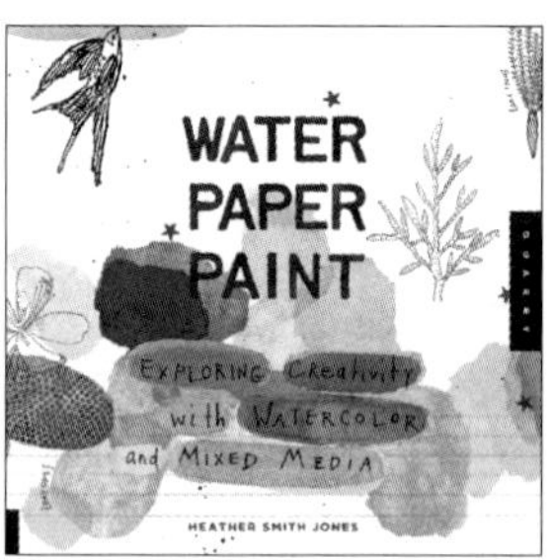